Jim Britt's

Cracking the Rich Code^8

Inspiring Stories, Insights and Strategies from Entrepreneurs Around the World

STAY IN TOUCH WITH JIM AND KEVIN

www.JimBritt.com

www.JimBrittCoaching.com

www.CrackingTheRichCode.com

www.KevinHarringtom.tv

For daily strategies and insights from top entrepreneurs, join us at

THE RICH CODE CLUB COMMUNITY

FREE

www.RichCodeCommunity.com

Co-authors from Around the World

Jim Britt

Kevin Harrington

Susan Welton

Gina St George

Jessica Brothers

Teon Singletary

Greg Andruk

Nanci Lublin-Good

Bonnie Kowaliuk

Adam Ringham

P. Nathan Thornberry

Manny Lopez

Jess Stewart

Mega R. Mease

Ken Steven

Donna Connor

Heidi Glunz

Lou Vickery

Dr. Stephen J. Kosmyna

Monique Elliott

Nicole Weyer

PY Nicole Chang

Seonad Cook

Karen Floyd

DEDICATION

Entrepreneurs will change the world. They always have and they always will.

To the entrepreneurial spirit that lives within each of us.

God Bless America and the World!

Foreword by Kevin Harrington

You probably know me as one of the "Sharks" on the hit TV show Shark Tank, where I was an investor in many entrepreneurial ventures.

But my life and business wasn't always like that. I used to be your regular, everyday

guy patching cracked driveways to make money. I had hopes and dreams just like most, yet I worked around people who didn't support my dreams. But you know what? I not only found a way out, but I found a way to my dreams... and so can you.

Now, I wake up every morning excited about my day, and I surround with only the people I want in my life; entrepreneurs who really want something more than just getting by paycheck to paycheck.

Today we hear stories -- mostly from the mainstream media -- everyday about how bad things are, businesses are closing and jobs being lost, interest rates are on the rise, how the gap between rich and poor is growing and how you'll never make it on your own.

But here's what I know for sure. Entrepreneurs are going to change the world. We always have and we always will.

Forget the 1% vs the 99%. 100% of us entrepreneurs need answers. We need solutions. We need something more than what we're being told by those who don't have a clue. We need to start saying Yes! to opportunity and No! to all the noise.

The fact is that it's a new world and a new economy. The "proven" methods of doing business and investing that produced successful results, even two years ago, simply may not work anymore.

If you want to succeed (or even survive) in our new world, you need an entirely new set of skills and information.

You need to "reposition" yourself…often.

You need to revamp how you do business…often.

You need to change how you handle and invest your money…often.

Like any other situation, if you know WHAT to do and WHEN to do it, you'll not only be "safe"... you could easily skyrocket financially.

If you have the right knowledge for today, the right opportunities for today, the right strategies for today and most of all the right character and mindset for today, you can win — and you can win big!

What I've discovered in my over three-decade career as an entrepreneur, is that success in the face of financial adversity boils down to 3 things:

The right knowledge at the right time.

The right opportunities at the right time.

The right you... ALL the time.

The bottom line is this: you can no longer afford to rely on anyone else to navigate your financial future. You have to rely on your "self." The question is... do you have a "self" you can rely on? Unfortunately, when it comes to entrepreneurship and money, many people don't. They don't have the financial education, the mental toughness, the knowledge and the skills to build wealth... especially in an ever-changing marketplace. You need to get RE-educated. You need to REINVENT yourself for success in the new economy. You need to learn new strategies in the areas of business and career, finance and real estate that create wealth or at least financial freedom in today's new world. But that's not all...

Skills and strategies and all that profound new knowledge won't do you one bit of good if you don't have the CHARACTER, the HABITS and the MENTALITY it takes to get rich. If you have internal barriers, your road to success will be slow and full of pain and struggle. It's like driving with one foot on the gas and one foot on the brake and always wondering why you aren't getting anywhere. Your mind is working against you instead of for you.

I have seen business owners come to me with their business ready to go under — and have the next year be their best financial year ever. I've see others that had a business that should skyrocket, yet fail because they didn't have the mental toughness to go the distance. I have seen people stuck in dead-end, dreary jobs break out of their rut, get involved in a brand-new passion, and become wildly successful.

No matter what you do for a living...regardless of your education, level of business experience or current financial status...If you have a burning desire for financial change then you won't want to miss this rare opportunity to learn from the entrepreneurs within this book.

It will provide you with some of the same success strategies that Jim Britt and I have used personally and shared with tens of thousands of people who've had tremendous financial success...people just like you, who wanted to get out of the rat race and enjoy financial freedom.

In addition, you'll learn what others have done, mistakes they made and how you can avoid them. You'll discover strategies that could make your business into a major market leader. I always say, "Just one good idea can change everything."

Success is predictable if you know what determines it. This book offers some valuable tips, knowledge, insights, skill sets, that will challenge you to leap beyond your current comfort level. If you want to strengthen your life, your business and your effectiveness overall, you'll discover a great friend in this book. You'll probably want to recommend it to all your entrepreneurial friends.

Although I haven't followed Jim Britt's career over the last 40 years, but I do know that he is recognized as one of the top thought leaders in the world, helping millions of people create prosperous lives. He has authored 13 books and multiple programs showing people how to understand their hidden abilities to do more, become more and enjoy more in every area of life. I also want to recognize Joel Sauceda, our online business partner. He is the brains behind the many online PR, Marketing, Branding and Lead Generation strategies each entrepreneur coauthor and reader of the book will benefit from.

The principles, concepts and ideas within this book are sometimes simple, but can be profound to a person who is ready for that perfect message at the right time and is willing to take action to change. Maybe for one it's a chapter on leadership or mindset. For the next, it's a chapter on raising capital, or securing a business loan. Each chapter is like opening a surprise empowering gift.

The conclusion to me is an exciting one. You, me and every other human being are shaping our brains and bodies by our attitude, the decisions we make, the intentions we hold and the actions we take daily. Why is it exciting? Because we are in control of all these things and we can change as long as we have the intention, willingness and commitment to look inside, take charge of our lives and make the changes.

I want to congratulate Jim Britt for making this publication series available and for allowing me to write the foreword, a chapter in each book and be involved with the entrepreneurs within this book and series. I honor Jim and the coauthors within this book and the series for the lives they are changing.

As you enter these pages, do so slowly and with an open mind. Savor the wisdom you discover here, and then with interest and curiosity discover what rings true for you, and then take action toward the life you want.

So many people settle for less in life, but I can tell you from my experience that it doesn't have to be that way.

Be prepared…because your life and business, is about to change!

Jim Britt & Kevin Harrington

As co-creators of this book series Jim Britt and Kevin Harrington have devoted their lives to helping others to live a more prosperous, fulfilled and happy life. Over the years they have influenced millions of lives through their coaching, mentoring, business strategies and leading by example. They are committed to never ending self-improvement and an inspiration to all they touch. They are both a true example that all things are possible. If you get a chance to work with Kevin and Jim or becoming a coauthor in a future Cracking the Rich Code book, jump at the chance!

Table of Contents

Contents

Jim Britt

Jim Britt is an award-winning author of 15 best-selling books and seven #1 International best-sellers. Some of his many titles include Rings of Truth, Do This. Get Rich-For Entrepreneurs, Unleashing Your Authentic Power, The Power of Letting Go, Cracking the Rich Code and The Entrepreneur.

He is an internationally recognized business and life strategist who is highly sought after as a keynote speaker, both online and live, for all audiences.

As an entrepreneur Jim has launched 28 successful business ventures. He has served as a success strategist to over 300 corporations worldwide and was recently named as one of the world's top 50 speakers and top 20 success coaches. He was presented with the "Best of the Best" award out of the top 100 contributors of all time to the Direct Selling industry.

For over four decades Jim has presented seminars throughout the world sharing his success strategies and life enhancing realizations with over 5,000 audiences, totaling almost 2,000,000 people from all walks of life.

Early in his speaking career he was Business partners with the late Jim Rohn for eight years, where Tony Robbins worked under Jim's direction for his first few years in the speaking business.

One of Jim's latest programs "Cracking the Rich Code" focuses on the subconscious programs influencing one's relationship with money and their financial success.
www.CrackingTheRichCode.com

Think Like Superman

By Jim Britt

"Waking up to your true greatness in life requires letting go of who you imagine yourself to be."

--- Jim Britt

FACT: Becoming a millionaire is easier than it has ever been.

Many people have the notion that it's an impossible task to become a millionaire. Some say, "It's pure luck." Others say, "You have to be born into a rich family." For others, "You'll have to win the Lotto." And for many they say, "Your parents have to help you out a lot." That's the language of the poor.

A single mother with five children says, "I want to believe in what you're saying. However, I'm 45 years old and work long hours at two dead-end jobs. I barely earn enough to get by. What should I do?"

Another man said, "Well, if you work for the government, you cannot expect to become a millionaire. After all, you're on a fixed salary and there's little time for anything else. By the time you get home, you've got to play with the kids, eat dinner, and fall asleep watching TV."

Everyone has a story as to why they could never become a millionaire. But for every story, excuse really, there are other stories OR PEOPLE with worse circumstances, that have become rich.

The truth is that all of us can become as wealthy as we decide to be, and that's a mindset. None of us is excluded from wealth. If you have the desire to receive money, whatever the amount, you have all of the rights to do so like everyone else. There is no limit to how much you can earn for yourself. The only limitations are what you place on yourself.

Money is like the sun. It does not discriminate. It doesn't say, "I will not give light and warmth to this flower, tree, or person because I don't like them." Like the sun, money is abundantly available to all of us who truly believe that it is for us. No one is excluded.

There are, however, some major differences between rich and poor people. Here are some tips for becoming rich.

Change Your Thinking

You have to see the bigger picture. There are opportunities everywhere! The problem is that most people see just trees, when they should be looking at the entire forest. By doing so you will see that there are opportunities everywhere. The possibilities are endless.

You'll also have to go through plenty of <u>self-discovery</u> before you earn your first million. Knowing the truth about yourself isn't always the easiest task. Sometimes, you'll find that you are your biggest enemy—at least some days.

Learn from Millionaires

Most people are surrounded by what I like to call their, "default friends." These friends are acquaintances that we see at the gym, school, work, local happy hour, and other places. We naturally befriend these people because we are all in the same boat financially. However, in most cases, these people aren't millionaires and cannot help you become one either. In fact, if you tell them you are going to become a millionaire, some may even tell you that it's impossible and discourage you from even trying. They'll tell you that you're living in a fantasy world and why you'll never be able to make it happen. Instead, learn from millionaires. Let go of these relationships that pull you down when it comes to your money desires. It's okay to have friends that aren't millionaires. However, only take input from those that have accomplished what you want to accomplish. Hang out with those that will encourage and help you get to the next level. Don't give your raw diamonds to a brick layer to be cut.

Indulge in Wealth

To become wealthy, you must learn about wealth. This means that you'll have to put yourself in situations that you've never been in before.

ON OCCASION, DO SOME OF THESE:

Fly first class and see how it makes you feel.

Eat out at the finest restaurant and don't look at the price.

Take a limo instead of a cab or Uber. Watch how you feel.

Reserve a suite in a first-class hotel.

If you are used to drinking a $20 bottle of wine, go for the $100 and see how it tastes. It does taste different.

All I am saying is, try some of the things that wealthy people do and see how it makes you feel.

Believe it is Possible

If you believe that it is possible to become a millionaire, you can make it happen. However, if you've excluded yourself from this possibility and think and believe that it's for other people, you'll never become a millionaire.

Also, be sure to bless rich people when you can. Haters of money aren't likely to receive any of it either.

Read books that have been written by millionaires. By gaining a well-rounded education about earning large sums of money and staying inspired, you'll be able to learn the wealth secrets of the rich. I just saw a video on LinkedIn with my friend Kevin Harrington from the TV show Shark Tank. He said that one of his new companies just had a million-dollar day on Amazon.

Enlarge Your Service

Your material wealth is the sum of your total contribution to society. Your daily mantra should be, *'How do I deliver more value to more people in less time?'* Then, you'll know that you can always increase your quality and quantity of service. Enlarging your service is also about going the extra mile. When it comes to helping others, you must give it everything you have. You just plant the seeds and nature will take care of the rest.

Seize ALL Opportunities That Make Sense

You cannot say "No" to opportunities and expect to become a millionaire. You must seize every opportunity that has your name on it. It may just be an opportunity to connect with an influential person for no reason. Sometimes the monetary reward will not come immediately, but if you keep planting seeds, eventually you'll grow a fruitful crop. Money is the harvest of the service you provide and sometimes the connections you have. The more seeds you plant, the greater the harvest.

Have an Unstoppable Mindset

Want to know some of what my first mentor shared with me that took me from a broke factory worker, high school dropout, to millionaire?

First, he said, you have to start thinking like a wealthy, unstoppable person. You have to have a wealth mindset. He said that wealthy people think differently. He said, "I want you to start thinking like Superman!" Sounds crazy, right? Well, it's not. It's powerful and here's why. How you think will change your life.

Wealthy people think differently. They really do. And anyone can learn to think like the wealthy.

I'm not talking about positive thinking, Law of Attraction, or motivation. Let's get real. None of that stuff works anyway. Otherwise, we would all be rich and happy already. I'm talking about thinking based in quantum physics science. Once you understand and apply it, it will change your life. You will become unstoppable!

If there was any person, fictional or real, whose qualities you could instantly possess, who would that person be? Think about it. Personally, I would say that Superman is the perfect person. Now, you are probably thinking I have lost it right? Just stick with me here. I think you will like what you are about to hear.

Superman is a fictional superhero widely considered to be one of the most famous and popular action hero and an American cultural icon. I remember watching Superman every Saturday morning when I was a kid. I couldn't get enough. He was my hero!

Let's look at Superman's traits:

Superman is indestructible.

He is a man of steel.

He can stop a locomotive in its tracks.

Bullets bounce off him.

He is faster than a speeding bullet.

No one can bring him down.

He can leap tall buildings in a single bound. Great powers to have in this day-and-age, wouldn't you say? What else would you need?

Now, for all you females, don't worry, we have not left you out. There is also a female version of Superman, named Superwoman. She has the same powers as Superman.

Now, this is where it gets interesting. Let's first look at the qualities that Superman possesses that you want to make your own. And to make it simple, I will refer to Superman for the rest of this message, and you can replace with Superwoman if you are female.

Again:

Superman is powerful and fearless.

Superman is virtually indestructible—except for kryptonite of course.

Superman can stop bullets.

Superman has supernatural powers. He can see through walls.

Superman can stop a speeding locomotive.

Superman can stop a bullet.

Superman jumps into immediate action when troubles arise.

Superman can crash through barriers.

Superman can even change clothes in a phone booth in seconds. Not too many of those around anymore. You'll have to duck behind a building to change.

So, you're thinking right now, *'Ok, I know that Superman has incredible supernatural powers, how can that help me? What good will it do me to think I am Superman, a fictional character?'*

Here is where science comes in. This is the part where you will be amazed when you learn about the supernatural powers that you already possess! NO, REALLY!

Your brain makes certain chemicals called neuro peptides. These are literally the molecules of emotion, like love, fear, joy, passion, and so on. These molecules of emotion are not only contained in your brain they actually circulate throughout your cellular structure. They send out a signal, a frequency much like a radio station sending out a signal. For example, you tune to 92.5 and you get jazz. Tune to 99.6 and you get rock. And if you are just one decimal off, you get static. The difference is that your signal goes both ways. You are a sender and a receiver.

You put out a signal, a mindset, of confidence about your financial success and people, circumstances, and opportunities show up to support your success. When you put out a signal of doubt and uncertainty and you receive support for your doubt and uncertainty. You've been around someone that you didn't trust, or you felt less than positive just being in their presence, right? You have also been around people that inspire you. That's what I'm talking about. You are projecting a frequency, looking to resonate with the frequency you are transmitting.

Anyway, the amazing part about these cells of emotion is that they are intelligent. They are thinking cells. These cells are constantly eavesdropping on the conversation that you are having with yourself. That's right. They are listening to you! And others are listening to your cells as well. Others feel what you feel when they are around you.

Your unconscious mind, your cells, are listening in, waiting to adjust your behavior based on what they hear from you, their master. So just imagine what would happen if you started to think like Superman…or like a millionaire.

Here are some of the thoughts you might have during the day:

"The challenges I face day today are easily overcome, after all I am Superman."

"I am indestructible."

"I have incredible strength."

"Nothing can stop me.....NOTHING."

"I have supernatural powers and can overcome anything."

"I can accomplish anything I want when I put my mind to it."

"I can break through any barrier."

"I can and I will do whatever it takes to accomplish my goal."

"I fear nothing."

The trillions of thinking cells in your body and brain listen, and they create exactly what you tell them to create. Their mission is to complete the picture of the you they see and hear when you talk to them. They must obey. It's their job!

Since you are Superman, you cannot fail. Why? Your thinking cells are now sending out the right signal, because you told them to. They are making you stronger, more successful, everyday! You have the ability to fight off all negativity, doubt, fear, and worry—nothing can stop you!

Superman has total confidence. So, your cells of emotion relating to confidence will now create more neuro peptide chemicals to promote feelings of power and confidence that others will feel in your presence.

Superman is fearless. So, your cells of emotion relating to fear will now create more neuro peptide chemicals to create feelings of courage. You are unstoppable!

And here's the key. Others will respond to you in the same way that you are talking to yourself.

If you are confident, others will have confidence in you.

You have thousands of thoughts every day. Make sure your thoughts are leading you in the direction you want to go. Make sure you are telling your cells a success story, and not a 'woe is me' story.

Most have been conditioned to think that creating wealth is difficult, or that it's only for the lucky few. What do you believe? It doesn't cost you any more to think like Superman; and it's much more inspiring!

Mediocrity cannot be an option if you decide to be wealthy and think like Superman.

Your decision, and communication with your cells, creates a mindset; that mindset influences how you show up.

None of that old type of thinking matters anymore...after all, you are Superman, and you can accomplish anything.

If you want wealth, you have to stretch yourself. You have to do the things that unsuccessful people are not willing to do. You have to say "yes" to opportunity, then figure out how to get the job done.

Maybe you are uncomfortable selling and asking for money. If that's the case, then learn sales and learn to ask for money every day until you feel comfortable asking for it. You will never have money if you don't learn to ask for it.

I've learned a lot in the past 40+ years as an entrepreneur. I've learned that in order to have more, you have to become more. I've also learned that if you are comfortable, you are not growing. I learned that I couldn't go from a nervous rookie speaker with minimal self-confidence to hosting TV shows and speaking in front of 5,000 people overnight. I simply wasn't ready. I grew into that, one speaking engagement at a time. Every time I finished a speaking engagement, I would ask myself, "How did I do, and how could I do it better?" I still do that today.

And I've learned from the hundreds of thousands of people I've trained, coached, and mentored that none of us can do something we don't believe is possible. It's not going to happen if you're not ready to step out of your comfort zone and stretch yourself.

This has led me to understand the single most important principle of wealth-building, that has meant the difference between poverty and riches for people since humans first traded for pelts.

Are you ready?

Come in just a little closer. Listen up!

Every income level requires a different you, a different mindset! If you think that $10,000 a month is a lot of money, then $100,000 a month will be completely out of reach. If you believe that having $5,000 in the bank would make you rich, then $50,000 won't miraculously appear. You will never earn more money than you believe is "a lot" of money.

What you do as a business is only a small part of becoming rich. In fact, there are thousands, if not tens of thousands, of ways to make money—and lots of it. What I've learned over the years is that, by focusing on who you want to become instead of what you need to do, you're going to multiply your chances of getting rich a hundred-fold.

Ask anyone who's found a way to make a large sum of money legally, and he or she will tell you that it's not hard once you crack the code. And cracking the code starts with you and your mindset. The "code" to which I refer isn't a secret rite or ancient scroll. It's not even a secret. It's a certain way of thinking and believing in which you've trained your mind to see money-making ideas.

That's where you see a need in the marketplace, and you jump on the idea quickly. It might involve creating a new product; or, it may just be teaching others a special technique you've learned. It may even require raising capital to start a company or to market a product or idea on social media.

Don't Hold Back. You Have to Take Action to Change.

Start right now to imagine yourself as already having wealth. How would your life be? How would your day unfold? Start to own your wealth mindset now! The subconscious mind is unable to differentiate between actual fact and mere visualization. So, by imagining that you already have it, you're encouraging your subconscious mind to seek the ways and means to transform your imaginary feelings into the real thing.

Find yourself some mentors. Nobody has all the answers. Surround yourself with people that will support, inspire, and provide you with answers that keep you moving in the right direction. If you truly want to attain wealth, have a thriving business, or reach the top of your game in any endeavor, having a qualified mentor is essential.

Okay, lets come in for a landing ...

It is absolutely essential to have a crystal-clear picture of what you want to accomplish before you begin. If you want to attain wealth, you must learn to operate without fear and with a sharply defined mental image of the outcome you want to attain. This comes from thinking like a wealthy person, (like Superman) making decisions like a wealthy person and being fearless (like Superman) when it comes to stepping out of your comfort zone. Look at the end result as something you're already prepared to do, you just haven't done it yet.

Think about this. Your success is something that you have been preventing; it's not something you have to struggle to make happen. The key is to not let fear, doubt, other people, or mind chatter push your success away. You'll find that the solutions taking you toward your goals will come to you in the most unexpected and sudden ways. You don't need the *perfect* plan first. What you need is a perfectly clear decision about your success, the right mindset, the right mentoring, and the ideal way to get you there will materialize.

The greatest transfer of wealth in the history of the human race is happening right now. Are you positioned to get your share?

Remember, in order to get a different result, you must do something different. In order to do something different you must know something different to do. And in order to know something different, you have to first suspect that your present methods need improving.

THEN, YOU HAVE TO BE WILLING TO DO SOMETHING ABOUT IT.

***

For more information on Jim's work:

www.JimBritt.com

http://JimBrittCoaching.com

www.facebook.com/jimbrittonline

www.linkedin.com/in/jim-britt

For free audio series www.RichCode1.com and www.RichCode2.com

To find out how to crack the rich code and change your subconscious programming regarding your relationship with money: www.CrackingTheRichCode.com

Kevin Harrington

Kevin Harrington is an original shark from the hit TV show *Shark Tank* and a successful entrepreneur for more than forty years. He's the co-founding board member of the Entrepreneurs' Organization and co-founder of the Electronic Retailing Association. He also invented the infomercial. He helped make "But wait... There's more!" part of our cultural history. He's one of the pioneers behind the *As Seen on TV* brand, has heard more than 50,000 pitches, and launched more than 500 products generating more than $5 Billion in global sales. Twenty of his companies have generated more than $100 million in revenue each. He's also the founder of the *Secrets of Closing the Sale Master Class* inspired by the Master of sales—Zig Ziglar. He's the author of several bestselling books including *Act Now: How I Turn Ideas into Million Dollar Products, Key Person of Influence,* and *Put a Shark in Your Tank.*

Becoming A KPI

By Kevin Harrington

The Key Person of Influence (KPI) in any given industry is the leader. It is the leader of the business world, the leader of automobile dealerships, the leader of selling hats—you name it. In other words, being the KPI means being the go-to person. The crazy thing? Anyone can be a Key Person of Influence. Any entrepreneur can be a KPI, a doctor, a salesperson, anyone. Just follow five steps and you will be well on your way. What comes with being a Key Person of Influence is value, ideally a massive amount of money, and being the leader in your field. The KPI is the person who comes up in conversations when it relates to a certain product, business, company, industry, or field. This is the person others seek out, the go-to person. Being the Key Person of Influence is how I got on *Shark Tank*.

Here's the story: I got a phone call from Mark Burnett's company. Mark Burnett is a television producer. He produced shows like *Survivor* and *The Voice*. His office called to set up an appointment. Mark was starting up a new show and wanted me to go out to Los Angeles to talk business. I was curious as to how Mark Burnett's company found me, and why they reached out for my services. They told me it was because I was a Key Person of Influence. I was all over the internet as a result of everything I was doing. It was 2008, and I had been in the business for 25 years. I had created huge brands. I helped build Tony Little. I helped build Jack Lalanne. I helped build Food Saver. We did the NuWave Oven. We worked with people like George Foreman and countless others. The problem was, everybody knew the brands, which was good for business, but did nothing for my personal brand. Consumers knew about the Food Saver, they knew about Tony Little, and they knew about Jack Lalanne, but not everyone knew I was the guy behind all of these people. Nobody knew me.

At that point, I made a conscious effort to build my brand. I wanted to become the go-to person so I could get the hot products and the phone calls. I helped build Tony Little's business, but everyone called him; they weren't calling me. What's wrong with that picture? Well, for one, I invested millions and millions of dollars of my own capital into Tony Little, and then he got all the phone calls. Shame on me for doing that, right? So, I decided to build my brand, and that's when I came out with my book, *Key Person of Influence*. I promoted myself by doing radio talk shows, TV shows, trade journals, speeches, etc. This is how I got on *Shark Tank*.

If I hadn't met Daniel Priestley, my book could have become *How To Become The Go-To Guy* because that's what I was looking to do, but Daniel very eloquently created this five-step system called the "Key Person of Influence." Realizing we were on to something, we co-authored and launched *Key Person of Influence*. Let's look now at the necessary steps to become a KPI.

Obtaining Customers

In 1984, I started a business of obtaining customers on TV. One evening, I was watching the Discovery Channel and suddenly the channel went dark for about six hours. I then called the cable company just in case there was a problem. They told me there wasn't a problem, that the Discovery Channel was an 18-hour network. That's when the light bulb went off. This was downtime. They put no value on those six down hours. Instead of showing something during this time, bars were put up on the screen. I started thinking about what I could put in place of that downtime, to sell something, obtain customers, and make money. I'm like the Rembrandt TV guy. I created and invented the whole concept of going to TV stations and buying huge blocks of remnant downtime. In all these years of me doing this, no one has challenged the idea that I was the person who did it, created it, and invented 30-minute infomercial blocks.

I was buying big blocks of time. Why? Because I wanted to obtain customers. How do you obtain customers? A lot of ways, but you ultimately have to get some form of media. How does it start? There are two metrics you have to look at when obtaining customers. What does it cost to obtain the customer? That is called the Cost Per Order (CPO). What is your Average Lifetime Revenue Value (ALRV), or Average Order Value (AOV)? The cost to obtain the customer obviously has to be less than the cost you are going to receive in income from the customer. The bottom line in obtaining customers: you have to set up a system. You have to set up testing. You have to set up as many sources for obtaining customers as possible. Even though I was in the TV business, I didn't just get customers through TV. Customers came through TV, radio, the internet, retail stores, international distribution, home shopping channels, etc. The first step is to make a laundry list of every possible resource for attracting these customers.

Today, some people who are into the digital space are basically just getting customers on the internet. Some of the areas I mentioned above have become very expensive. It's tougher to make money on TV. While we started on TV, the cost to get customers has become too high; so we now have made the switch to digital. When you talk about internet, there's many different ways to obtain customers, from Google AdWords to Facebook ads to social media, etc. You can also attain customers with public relations and influencers. You have to decide what works best with your product. The bottom line is a lot of people do not realize they have to be sophisticated, from a business analysis standpoint, to set up a business. You need a marketing plan to obtain customers.

First, focus on two numbers: your Customer Acquisition Cost (CAT) and Average Order Value (AOV). Those numbers have to work. Customer service is crucial in the business world as well. A business can't have bad customer service and retain customers This is especially true in this day-and-age.

Raising Capital

I had a 50-million-dollar-a-year business, making $5 million a year in profit. Feeling confident, I met with seven banks to get some financing. I thought it was going to be easy because I had a very profitable business. Unfortunately, bank after bank after bank turned me down. I had great credit and all of that. The only asset I had was the business. Part of the problem was I didn't know how to approach the banks. I was a young entrepreneur in my twenties. I had no real credibility in the banking world; I was walking in and just showing my numbers from the year before.

So, what did I do to get the capital? Well, I ran into a mentor who was a former bank president, and he said, "Kevin, you went about it all wrong. I come from the banking business, and if you walked into my office and said, 'I need 5 million bucks,' I would have told you to turn around and get the hell out of my office. What do you have to do? You have to sell them on the future. What you did last year is well and good, but they are giving you money because they know that you are still going to be in business three years from now repaying their loans. You need projections. You need your forward business plan. You need your five-year master plan. You need to talk the talk and walk the walk, otherwise they aren't even interested."

I hired my mentor as a consultant to the company. I brought him in on the ground floor as part of my dream team. To make a long story short, we went back to re-pitch some of the same banks. We didn't get 5 million dollars, but we got a 3-million-dollar line of credit. It was all in how we talked to the banks. We had the same business, but it was all in the presentation. It's all in how you talk and how prepared you are. Raising capital is mental. It's in the pitch. It's in the relationships you build, etc.

One of the biggest challenges with any business is having enough capital to do the things you want to do. You have to have a successful business plan if you want to raise money. Here are the elements of a successful business plan.

(1) You need an executive summary (one page summarizing the whole plan). You need an industry overview, defining the problem you are solving and an overview of the market.

(2) You need a description of your product or the service. How does it serve as a solution?

(3) You need a competitive analysis. What/who is your competition?

(4) You need a sales and marketing plan.

(5) You need to identify your target customer and proof for your concept.

(6) What is your method of operations?

(7) Who's on your management team, your board of advisers, your dream team?

(8) What are your financial projections?

(9) You need to outline your risk analysis and appendix.

If you are going to raise capital, you don't just talk to an investor. I get people all the time that come to me saying they have an idea, and boom… it's on a napkin. They tell me that they just need $100K for 10 percent. I ask if they can send me their business plan. They then ask me what I mean when I say, 'business plan.' If they don't have one, that means I am going to end up giving them 100K and never see it again.

One of the most important parts of raising capital is coming up with a reasonable ask, and then explaining how the proceeds will be used. Many entrepreneurs don't understand this. For example, a guy came on *Shark Tank* saying he needed 150K for 10 percent of his company. I asked what he was going to use the 150K for?

His response was essentially this, "Well, I am going to use the money as a down payment for a piece of real estate where we are going to build a building, then launch the business."

"Okay, so you are going to build the building and then equip the building with furniture. Where is that money going to come from?" I asked. He said once he got the real estate, then they would figure out that batch of money at that time. I told him, "$150K dollars doesn't get you in business. $150K dollars gets you a piece of land. How are you going to build the business, generate revenue, and pay me back?" This guy told me he thought I would have more money for him after that. I said, "Well, no. You are not going to get the first batch of money based on the answers you are giving me."

Instead, he should have said he was going to lease a small office and start generating massive amounts of revenue with the money I gave them. Then, pay me back all of my money, plus a huge return on my investment, and then build it into a global business. That's what I wanted to hear. I want to know that people have a successful business plan, a successful marketing plan, and then I will talk about how to go about raising the capital, how to call on investors, and what the sweet spots are for the investors.

The bottom line on raising capital is, you can't just go build yourself a huge global business without thinking about how you're going to finance it. In the old days, I thought if I built a successful business, money was going to be easy. It's not, unless you know how to do it. There's an art to raising capital. Part of it involves making sure you are prepared and know how to pitch your business properly.

The Perfect Pitch

While the actual product or service you are trying to sell is a critical part of the process, it is just as important to sell the customer on yourself, your services, and your business. Even though I have made thousands upon thousands of pitches, have spoken to thousands of people, and have seen a great amount of success, I still pitch myself and my businesses. No matter who you are, or what you do, you have to be ready to drop the perfect pitch. It doesn't matter if you are going to make this perfect pitch in front of a crowd of thousands, or a crowd of one. To help with the concept of a perfect pitch, I have created a 10-step system.

Before you can start perfecting the perfect pitch, you have to ask yourself a couple of questions. What are you pitching? In other words, what product, business, or service are you trying to sell? Next, what do you want to get out of this pitch? More customers? More sales? Nonetheless, these questions are for you to answer, and you need to answer them before devising your perfect pitch. The perfect pitch can be broken down into these 10 steps:

(1) The **Tease** is your hook; the period of time when you plant the seed. This is when you reveal a problem. You have to explain to your customers why you are giving the pitch. You also have to use showmanship, which sets the pace for the rest of the pitch. If your showmanship skills are demonstrated in the Tease portion of your pitch, then you will have your audience (or your customer) hooked from the very beginning.

(2) Next up is **Please**. In this part of the perfect pitch, you are telling your customer how your product or service can solve the problem you mapped out in the first step. Ideally, your product or service will solve this stated problem in the most efficient, elegant, and cost-effective way. You have to relay to your customer that your solution is the best solution, and it will solve the problem better than anything (or anyone) else. It is important to also show off your features and benefits, and to display the magical transformation that will take place.

(3) The third step to the perfect pitch is **Demonstration/Multi-functionality**. First, you have to ask yourself if you can demonstrate your product, your service and your value. This is the key to any successful pitch, and it brings multi-functionality to the forefront. It shows it off. Think of this step as an added value. Ideally, your service or product is multifunctional. If you can show this off to your customer, then you just brought bonus points to the table.

(4) But Wait There's More! is the fourth step, and it's not just for infomercials on TV. This is the step where you give more value to your product or service by showing and adding more to the pitch—maybe added bonus items or "buy 2 get 1 free if you act now" incentives. At this point, your customer should already be biting, but now is the time to really win them over. So, show them what else you have to offer.

(5) Testimonials are the fifth step to creating the perfect pitch. You are now using someone else to do the pitching. In other words, who says so besides you? This is the proof behind your business, product, or service. Testimonials can include consumers (actual users of the product or service), professionals (leaders in your industry), editorial (articles, experts, press, journals, trade publications, magazines, newspapers), etc. Testimonials can also feature celebrities. Celebrity testimonials can be very powerful for the simple fact that people love celebrities. Then there are documented testimonials, which can include clinical studies, labs tests, and science. Once again, this is one of the most important areas for creating the perfect pitch.

(6) Another important step is **Research and Competitive Analysis**. For this step, you should be asking yourself if you have done your research. If so, then this is the portion of the perfect pitch when you show off all of that information. This can include information on the industry, market and competitors. It can also be facts, figures, and statistics. This research should show off the fact that you, your company, and your product/service is unique.

(7) The seventh step is **Your Team.** In this step, you are bringing the credibility of your team and putting it right there on the metaphorical table. Who makes up your team? It could be advisers, management, directors, and strategic partners. Your team will help scale, open connections, add on the knowledge factor, and so much more.

(8) Why? is the eighth step. Why are you pitching? How will the person in front of you help? This step will change based on who you are actually pitching to. For example, if you are looking for funds, then this is a big section, and you need to incorporate many talking points.

(9) The ninth step is **Marketing Plan.** You have done your pitch and given out all your information. Now, how will you make everything happen? For instance, you need to know your marketing and distribution plan. As is the case throughout your entire pitch, it is essential that you show confidence. Sell whoever you are pitching on your product or service, and yourself as well. People invest in people all the time.

(10) The 10th and final step is **Seize**. You laid everything out, now ask! What are you trying to accomplish? Ask it! Being the final step, this is the time to present the final call to action.

Remember, each pitch will be different. Some pitches last for over an hour and others last only a few seconds or minutes. It just depends on how much time you are given or how much time you need. That is why you need to craft your pitches accordingly. Practice, practice, and more practice.

***

To contact Kevin:

www.KevinHarrington.tv

Jess Stewart

 Hi, I'm Jess, a Strategic Business Guide dedicated to helping leaders achieve operational excellence and live better lives. It is my mission to equip leaders to scale their businesses, make more money, and enjoy the climb along the way. I am dedicated to climbing right along with you, providing maps, helping to set your compass and getting the right people in the right boots so your company can deliver results, grow with confidence, and reach the pinnacle.

Raised by a Marine Corps pilot on a cattle operation, I learned the keys to running an entrepreneurial company from the ground up. Grit, hard work, and getting things done the right way infused in me a work ethic that I live and breathe to this day.

After moving to a small town with my husband, Murt, a lack of available jobs pushed me to start a medical billing software company from my kitchen table, with two young children underfoot—though I knew nothing about medical billing. To call life during this time a 'cluster-f***' would be an understatement. Fifteen years, two national locations, and one international division later, I sold that company at an exceptional price point—an achievement which let my family and me move to a ranch west of Fort Worth called, "The Empty Wineglass."

This oasis allows me to treat clients to an engaging, transformative experience under the peaceful Texas sky. Join us! Workshops, team retreats and mastery groups are available to truly elevate professional development in your organization.

View from the Top:

Guiding you Through the Cluster-F*** of Strategy & Management

By: Jess Stewart

I'm going to go out on a limb and guess that you aren't 100% where you want to be in your career. You have probably sat through one too many dead-end meetings, where your leadership team came up with a whole lot of nothing in terms of solutions to your productivity, revenue, or expansion problems. Maybe you have found yourself wondering why this team (that you hand-picked, by the way) is failing to level up given the collective potential they possess. Is it you? Are you failing to develop them properly? Is it your strategy? Does it not provide a clear enough roadmap onward and upward? Perhaps you are running so fast on the hamster wheel of your workload that you don't have the time or energy to ask yourself these deeper questions. Who am I kidding? You have time. You and I both know you aren't sleeping. Regardless, you are miserable. Am I right? Of course, I am. Do you want to know how I know? Because I have been there. I have lived that life. I have worked around the clock and lost sleep and watched my health deteriorate all in the name of growing my enterprise.

I know exactly who you are. You are someone who sets big goals. Someone who appreciates a challenge. Someone who doesn't stop and rarely slows down. Someone who laughs in the face of limits. You, my friend, are motivated, strategic, and a little obsessed. Those closest to you may describe you as performance-driven or competitive—whether you are competing with others or against yourself is irrelevant. You simultaneously have a one-track mind and an inability to focus on any one thing for too long. You have probably been accused of being relentless, impulsive, and "a little much" by friends, family, and colleagues. You might not always rub people the right way, but they know they can count on you to follow through, get things done, and carry your team across the finish line of success. Sound familiar? Yeah, I know who you are. Because that's who I am too.

I was raised in a home where grit was the foundation of everything we did. My father instilled in me a desire to innovate and strive for excellence. He taught me to fight, to be bold, and to be brave. He taught me that there was no problem too big to solve. This was crucial because surviving as an Executive/Entrepreneur is not for the faint of heart. I don't mean to offend, but if you aren't willing to get off your ass and get your hands dirty, you'll never earn anything worth having. Being successful and the commander of your ship does not equate to laying around getting drunk on a beach and expecting everything to fall in line. You have a responsibility to lead, to think of the *bigger* picture, to consider everything no one else on your team has thought of, and to evaluate the potential of every step your organization takes in any direction at any given time.

My father taught me that failure is never an option. If I ever came to him saying that I wanted to quit, he would tell me to adapt, rethink, and pivot instead. He would tell me to go back to the drawing board and find another way. Becoming an effective leader is what equips you to surround yourself with a capable, efficient, and relentless team who is willing to go to war with you to find another way—an A-Team who won't stop. Period.

When there is a 150-foot concrete wall towering above you, you can't shortcut your way through. The only options are to go around or go over. That's when having an intelligent, innate, relentless drive to fight becomes necessary. That's when effectively developing your leadership team becomes a priority. That's when executing your strategic plan at its max capacity becomes crucial. Both professionally and personally, being a business leader is hard as f***. You know that. I know that. But what you might not know is how to get off the hamster wheel. What you might not know is that there is a better way—getting over the wall is possible—but you must be willing to climb. You must acknowledge your teams' weaknesses and harness their strengths.

My dad was an amazing problem solver—taught me everything I know—but even when something was not working the way he wanted it to, he refused to ask for help. That ultimately resulted in a greater weight being placed on his own shoulders. Things could have been different had he been willing to accept a little help. Stay with me. I told you that to tell you this: being in a position of leadership doesn't alleviate you from experiencing some real obstacles. You will be thrown some serious curveballs. There's not a way around that. *However*, there are ways to 1) minimize the number of curveballs coming at you, and 2) to adequately prepare so that your team is ready to hit them out of the park when they do come. To help you get clear on how you might be in your own damn way, I have created this fun little evaluation for you. Every 'No' answer earns you 1 point. Every 'Yes' answer earns you 2 points. Be honest. Because I will be able to tell if you aren't being honest, and I will call you out.

1. Your Executive/Leadership team is 100% aligned with your vision and the path to achieve it. If asked, each member would be able to clearly articulate it in simple terms and numbers.
2. You have a 3-year plan, a 1-year plan, and 90-day goals.
3. Your meetings are on the same day, at the same time, each week and are 80% focused on solving issues versus reporting out.
4. When asked about accountability and timelines, the "survey" would (for the most part) say, strong, consistent, reliable.
5. You and your leadership team understand the levers that impact all key financial metrics across the income statement, balance sheet, and cash flow.
6. Your company makes enough profit to fuel the strategy exactly the way you want it to.
7. Your Executive/Leadership team works seamlessly together. Conflict is healthy and encouraged, issues are resolved, and you are unified in your strategy and execution.

If you scored a 10 or below, keep reading! If you scored an 11 or higher, you are an anomaly, and I would like to have you committed for scientific investigation and testing.

The goal of this chapter is to help you identify and combat the strategic roadblocks that may be destructive to the health and viability of your organization. Trust me. I have been there, and it was rough. A royal cluster you-know-what. But it doesn't have to be. Success is not an accident. Your commitment and drive have gotten you where you are and have allowed you to develop your team—but commitment alone isn't enough. I have busted my ass through it, so you don't have to. You aren't alone. Do you hear me? I know what it feels like. I have your back. And I will see you through. The 7 points that follow are legitimate game-changers—only a few of the many I could share. I'm confident I would have grown my company three times as fast had I known these strategies sooner. You have no excuse.

1.   What is working/not working?

How powerful would it be to have a quick "temperature check" on your organization? It is a daunting task when you think about asking yourself what is really working and not working in your organization. But what if I told you that these answers are just a quick meeting away? And you don't need to do this alone?

What if you could peel back the curtain and look inside your organization frequently and see what is really going on? It takes courage and an open mind, but you can do it!

Here you go: In your next leadership team meeting ask 2 simple yet powerful questions:

  a.   What is working in the organization
  b.   What is not working in the organization

Now, first and foremost, you must be intentional about establishing an environment that welcomes suggestions and encourages collaboration amongst your team. If that last statement makes you break out in hives because you have no idea how to do that…call me. Your team needs to feel supported when your intention is to solicit feedback.

If your team is healthy, then what comes out of these 2 questions can be game changers—inspiring the team to discuss further and gain clarity. The point of this exercise is to identify where you have kinks in the chain, in order to then build a solution-focused plan.

I'm not claiming that this is rocket science, but the fact of the matter is, you will never get the important answers until you ask the important questions. This is not something you need to conquer alone. Your day-to-day team knows the answers. The power in this exercise comes from a collaborative, honest discussion. Have fun with it, lean in, and fix the issues—use the resulting insights to make critical decisions and build a better organization.

2. Meeting Cadence

This is probably the last thing you are considering when it comes to calendaring productive, effective, intentional meetings, but I swear, if I would have embraced this concept earlier in the game, I could have saved myself countless headaches. Rule #1: (you're seriously going to love me for this one) <u>No internal meetings on Fridays. Period.</u> No exceptions. You're welcome. Leaving Friday open is useful for a wide variety of reasons. For me, the value came from being able to catch my breath and have dedicated 'head down' time to catch up on whatever had been backburnered (for whatever reason) and to strategize for the coming week. Feeling like I was starting a new week ahead, instead of already behind, was a small but powerful adjustment to my personal and professional well-being. It created desperately needed white space and breathing room. Trust me, you can't really wrap your head around how much you need it, until you have it.

Another crucial piece to the meeting puzzle is to establish a Daily Stand-Up Meeting. Verne Harnish suggests that every day (except Fridays!), for no more than 15 minutes, you should gather your leadership team together to evaluate the following questions:

a. What happened yesterday?

b. What is happening today?

c. Where do you need support?

The advantages of regularly scheduled touchpoints such as these cannot be stated enough. It will help eliminate unnecessary interruptions throughout the day, allow bonding time as a team, and will smoke out issues early on, eliminating the opportunity for trouble to fly under the radar for weeks or months. Billionaire Richard Branson said, "Communication is the most important skill any leader can possess." Cowboy up. Don't shy away from digging in and getting dirty. It's part of the fun.

3. Here Lies [Your Company]

I am now going to ask you to write your company's obituary. "What the hell are you talking about?" you may be asking. Allow me to explain. I want you to imagine shuttering your organization. It's dead. Donezo. No hope of resurrection. If you were to close your doors today and call it quits, what would you say in the obituary? What went wrong? Who came to the funeral? Who didn't? Why? What were our biggest accomplishments? What lessons did we learn and what kind of legacy did we leave behind?

Spend some time as a team discussing. Listen for patterns around vision, core purpose, and strategy. Then, reverse-engineer the solution. A simple but incredibly impactful exercise.

4. Celebrate!

In my experience, corporations do not take enough opportunities to celebrate their wins. A continual spirit of improvement cannot be maintained if you and your team are unable to acknowledge and show gratitude for all that went (and is going) right. Gratitude is an important aspect of influential leadership. Nobody wants to go to battle for a Debbie Downer who only criticizes and critiques every breath the organization takes. Let your hair down! There is always enough time to honor and encourage a job well done. Harness the energy in the exercise, you are what you think!

5. Channel Your Inner Peter Drucker

For those who don't know, Peter Drucker is best known as the founder of modern management. When it comes to corporate success, Drucker is most often attributed to the bold statement that, "Culture eats strategy for breakfast." I had to learn the hard way how ridiculously true this statement is. Your internal strategy doesn't stand a snowball's chance in hell if your culture is spewing toxic waste. Culture is what is happening when you aren't looking. Do you know how your people are treating others? Are your customers being well cared for? Is your operation bumpy or glitchy? Are you constantly playing whack–a–mole? You're exhausted, rung out… but here's the kicker, you are what you tolerate!

More likely than not, you are focused on the numbers and internal strategy, assuming the rest (people/culture) will fall into place on their own. What you tell people to do and what they actually do need to be aligned; and until they are, your culture will continue to eat your strategy for breakfast. Culture. Is. Everything. Align your culture around strategy and be amazed by what happens.

6. Don't Ever Let a Good Crisis Go to Waste

Even the best laid plans go astray—there are simply too many things that are out of our control. Lucky for you, failure is one of the greatest teachers there is. As spoken by the incredible Winston Churchill, "Don't ever allow a good crisis to go to waste." So what if it all went to hell? Dry your tears and have a post-mortem meeting about it. Gather your A-Team and do these 4 things:

d. Analyze what happened.
e. Compare it to what should have happened.
f. Identify the delta between the two and plan for the next round.
g. Turn that frown upside down (or make lemonade out of lemons) – failure is something they don't teach in school. Take what you have learned in this exercise and USE it! Congratulations, you now have a great competitive edge above others!

Effective leadership and professional development are two things you never stop learning. Remember: CSI – a continual state of improvement.

7. Success is Not an Accident

Soccer legend Pele said, "**Success** is no accident. It is hard work, perseverance, learning, studying, sacrifice and most of all, love of what you are doing or learning to do." I've said it before; you have worked hard to be sitting in that cozy corner office. That wasn't an accident. It wasn't luck. It was grit, diligence, and ambition, and it took a whole hell of a lot of courage. Do yourself a favor and surround yourself with people who know what it takes to be at the top. Find a guide, a mentor/advisor, a group— somewhere you can relax, lean in, and ask for help. Find your safe place. Being a leader can be lonely and hard. Find a guide, a teammate, that will push you to the next level because they love you and your success is their success.

I've been in the trenches. I started my company at my kitchen table in a dinky mobile home with two young kids underfoot. Equipped with legitimately zero experience in a new industry, I had a massive mountain before me. To say that I had a rough go of it is the understatement of a lifetime, but what it taught me was invaluable. I learned to build a company from scratch and to assemble an exceptional leadership team. Within 15 years, my kitchen table career exploded into 2 national locations and 1 international division. I sold for a price that now allows me to enjoy the fruit of my backbreaking labor. I made it to the top, and guys, the view is amazing!!! I have struggled. I have succeeded. And now I want to be significant. I want to help others avoid the avoidable and achieve the same experience of bliss and fulfillment I have found. I know who you are, friend. You are a gift, and you have great things to share with a waiting world. I can help you and your team harness the strengths of your own strategy, drawing out what's rock solid and stabilizing what is weak, to execute the potential of your organization with excellence. It can be achieved. I'm proof that it can. Just know that I know how to help. Please understand that you don't have to suffer on your road to success. There is another way.

You need a guide to point out where all the landmines are hidden— a long-term support system to help your team get on track and maintain its trajectory. Together we can. I'm not going anywhere.

Ready to reach the mountaintop? You'll need an experienced guide, a supported strategy, refined tools, and the A-Team. I'm ready when you are!

***

To contact Jess:

Website: www.jess-stewart.com

Linktree: linktr.ee/jess_stewartllc

Jess Stewart is devoted to sharing what she's learned. She brings world-class tools and long-term resources to help leadership teams run better businesses and live better lives. She is a respected Strategic Business Guide/Leadership Team Coach and Speaker, offering executive-level leadership development workshops and programs, mastery groups, and online learning academy opportunities.

Referenced Resources

Lencioni, Patrick. 2004. *Death by Meeting: A Leadership Fable…About Solving the Most Painful Problem in Business.* Jossey-Bass.

Lee Yohn, Denise. Write Your Brand's Obituary, Harvard Business Review. January 28, 2014. Write Your Brand's Obituary (hbr.org)

Gina St. George

In following advice to "become employable", Gina St. George studied Chemical Engineering and subsequently earned an MBA in Finance. The education served her well for 17 years in the chemical industry, and also gave her the skills she uses now as a small business and private equity consultant – business process, systems, financial analysis & management.

During her corporate career, she was a road warrior, managing operations and working on mergers & acquisitions. After working and traveling too much and subsequently getting divorced, she wanted to find a way to enjoy life before it passed her by. She knew there was a way to thrive in business and have a great life at the same time. She was told she was crazy when she exited her "great career".

Joining two small businesses, she discovered that many small businesses don't have good systems and structure, and that small business owners are often overworked. She decided to become her first small business client. After doing the hard work to define processes and systemize, she exited daily operations of one business and sold the other to a multi-national corporation using her M&A skills.

Today, Gina enables small business owners and lawyers operating small and solo law practices to create a growing, thriving business that can be sold for maximum value – or kept and enjoyed by its owner.

Trust the Process: With Resolve & Confidence We're Not Going Anywhere.

By Gina St. George

Sometimes the application for the lessons our parents give us show up much later in life. My father gave me a lesson when I was 10 years old that become very useful to me over 40 years later.

My family enjoyed going to the amusement park near our home, and I was excited to be able to ride the big rides along with my older brothers. That summer, I was finally big enough to ride The Demon, the best roller coaster in the park. The Demon had big drops, upside down turns, and barrel loops. I was so excited that I was finally going to be able to ride, and I was so proud that I could stand next to the measuring stick to prove that I was tall enough. My dad was with us and, after waiting in line for over an hour, we were able to board the train. We agreed I'd ride with him, and my two older brothers would ride together in the row of the train directly behind us.

We climbed into our seats, pulled down our harnesses and the train left the station to start its slow climb up the first hill, which led the first big downhill drop. During the slow climb, I realized that my harness was not locked. Back then I hadn't seen the many cell phone videos of people being thrown off amusement park rides like ragdolls, but I still knew that being loose in my seat was not a good situation. I alerted my father to the problem by showing him that I could pull my harness all the way up. I was really glad that it was my dad sitting to my immediate left, instead of one of my adolescent brothers.

He was secured into his own seat by his harness, which was properly locked, so he had to do what he could with his limited ability to move. Looking back with my adult insight, I know that his anxiety on a scale of one to ten was eleven or twelve, but his poker face showed no fear. I saw only the quiet resolve of a father who did the kind of thing that dads do. He reached his right leg over to my side of the car so I could wrap my legs around it, and he reached his right arm across my harness, tucking his hand under my right thigh. While I hugged my harness as tightly as I could, he leaned his elbow into it to keep it against me. Before we reached the top of the hill to begin the descent, he looked at me with perfect calmness and told me, "You're not going anywhere." With that assurance, I was perfectly confident that I'd be fine.

For the next 3 to 4 minutes, I rode that rollercoaster with my dad holding me in my seat with one arm. It's not an overstatement to say he saved my life that day. However, beyond saving my life, he taught me something really important: How you show up will affect how others feel and perform in a situation.

Show up with fear and those around you will worry.

Show up with anger and those around you will throw fits about things being unfair.

But instead…

Show up with resolve and confidence, and people will feel that everything will work out and that they can ride the ride, even if it isn't exactly how they thought it was going to go.

Have you ever slept next to someone who snores? I can certainly attest to the fact that it keeps you awake at night. But I can also tell you that when you sleep next to someone with sleep apnea, it disturbs your sleep even more. When the person you love most in this world stops breathing, then snorts and sputters to start breathing again, you stay awake listening to make sure they are still breathing. Doing that will cause a sleepless night or two.

This was my life with Andy for several years while I begged him to go see an ear, nose, and throat specialist to be evaluated for the solution to the problem. He finally did, not because I'd pestered him, but because a friend told him how much better his life would be if he fixed his problem. When he started sleeping with a CPAP, I finally enjoyed both peace of mind and glorious silence.

At the beginning of 2020, we had been business and life partners for twelve years. Over those years, in any given 24-hour period we probably spent 22 hours together - living, eating, sleeping, working, traveling, planning, scheming, and loving almost every minute of it. I had joined his 14-year-old business in 2009 because I was ready for a big change, and he needed someone with my skills. The drastic career change also gave me a reason to move to Florida from Colorado so that we could be together every day instead of once every three to four weeks.

My formal education is in chemical engineering. After many years in the chemical industry and an MBA, I had come to prefer working on business processes instead of chemical processes, and I'd become good at it. Andy had two sister businesses: a litigation support business and a document shredding business. We frequently joked that one business created paper and the other one destroyed paper.

Working with Andy gave me the opportunity to bring my corporate skills to a small business, and apply the principles of business process, business systems, procedures and people training I had come to know. It also gave me the opportunity to escape the grind, overwork, and burnout that I had allowed to destroy my life and marriage as a road warrior corporate employee. The mahogany desk and travel on the corporate jet were amazingly easy to give up because I was going to be in control of my life – or so I thought.

What I learned is that business owners often don't have good systems and structure, and independent business owners are often overworked. I quickly became my first client. After putting in some long days and hard work, we finally established A-Z processes and procedures, installed better systems, trained the staff, and finally brought in managers to replace ourselves. The work was worth it.

In 2015, we sold the shredding business to a multinational company. That was a very happy day for us. Selling the company gave us more freedom and cash, but the most important thing that it gave us was the credibility of having built, grown, and improved a business, and having built a loyal collection of repeat customers that gave us an asset to sell. Both of us added the title of consultant and we launched our training and consulting business, selling other small business owners on the promise that you can have a thriving business and a great life at the same time. Andy was really great at marketing, sales, building loyal relationships, and getting repeat business and referrals. I was good at the nuts and bolts of process and systems, for both operations and marketing. Together, we were a pretty good team, and we enjoyed being a team.

It isn't a secret that 2020 was a bad year for many small businesses. Ours was no different. The courts were closed, our customers stayed home, and new litigation slowed to a crawl. Our revenue took a dive. We'd never before been thankful for crime, but it gave us the ability to stay open since supporting the judicial system made us essential, and we still had work to do.

We made use of the slow time, rebuilding our website, planning new offers, reducing our expenses, and spending time at home eating healthy home cooked meals. We took lots of walks together and both of us lost weight. The most important thing that we did during that time was to lay the groundwork to launch a whole new business. Andy and I partnered with an attorney, and the three of us leveraged our understanding of law firms. We created a training program and agency to help small law firms systemize their practices to build both a thriving practice and a great life. Together, we became the "Marketer, the Strategist, and the Executioner".

We built our programs, our offers, our delivery systems, our marketing, and our sales funnel. From the very beginning we did it by defining our business processes, implementing our systems, and training the people we brought on to help us. We practiced what we preached to our clients, who were also defining their processes, implementing their systems, and training their staff.

Things were looking up in the summer of 2021. The courts reopened in June and July in the counties we served, and in August we sold the building that housed our business. We began moving to a new location that would cut our fixed costs in half.

That same summer, Andy developed a chest infection and a persistent cough and discovered that the CPAP that he'd been using was the subject of a class action lawsuit because it caused that very problem, among others. He took a course of doxycycline to get it cleared up. At the end of August, the infection had returned. He didn't feel well, and he would have fits of coughing. I took him to urgent care to get him another prescription for the infection, and we hoped that this time it would clear up for good. On Labor Day, after taking care of him all weekend, I climbed into bed next to him and said something like, "Tomorrow is another day. You'll feel better after getting some sleep." I turned off the lights and drifted off.

At 3:45 AM, I woke to an eerily silent room. The silence gave me an unsettled feeling, so I turned on the light. Andy looked exactly like he always did when he was sleeping – except that he was really still and really pale. After shaking his shoulder and getting no response, what I did next would have awakened anyone. Kneeling next to him, I shook him hard with both hands and screamed his name. The next 14 minutes were a blur while I yelled frantically at the 911 dispatcher, who calmly gave me instructions while EMS was on the way. They arrived and stayed very briefly – only long enough to determine that Andy had died in his sleep and too much time had passed to revive him.

It was 3:59 AM, but I began making phone calls to family. At 7:00 AM, I called the company general manager to tell her we wouldn't be in today, and that Andy would never be in the office again. I asked her to call a staff meeting so everyone could be told that the company's founder had died.

I had already been an officer of the company for 12 years, and now I was the only one in charge. Knowing I had to face our staff and make sure that they felt that everything was going to be alright, this was when my father's lesson came to me. Despite the fact that my head was spinning, I clearly knew I had to tell them "We're not going anywhere." With a poker face, I let them to know that I was alright, and they could count on me.

Within hours of my first call to the general manager at her home, I got a call from her asking what to do about the fact that some customers had already heard about Andy's passing, and they were calling and asking questions. With total resolve and confidence, I told her to tell everyone that nothing was going to change. We will still provide our customers with the same great service we always have. Our staff is well-trained and can handle everything. All of the various legal groups we sponsor, and support would get the same support as always. And I made sure she was clear that when anyone asked about our future, the answer was "We're not going anywhere." I told her to pre-empt further questions by sending an email blast to our customers, both to honor Andy's memory and to assure our customers that we were still there for them. I even went a step further and asked the executive director of the Bar Association, who owned a much bigger email list than mine, to send out an email blast. I wrote a social media post, then asked him to share it to his audience. I knew that the news was sad and tragic, but communicating it openly gave us the opportunity to assure everyone with the continuous refrain, "We're not going anywhere."

When I walked into the office for the first time, I entered to find the organized chaos of both an ongoing operation and being partially moved to our new location from the building that we'd just sold 3 weeks earlier. But even in the chaos, everything was working – and it was working with the company's founder gone and with me distracted by grief. Everyone was following the processes and using the systems, and every one of them was busily doing their job. Correctly. Perfectly. Still on track. Still moving forward. Without interruption to the business. Everything worked as it should, even in the face of great sadness, and even during the major disruption of moving to a new location.

I personally spent most of the first 30 days alternating between being in a fog and being very busy handling things that needed to be done. It took me over a month to get back to work, and much longer to function at full productivity due to all of the distractions associated with moving, dealing with probate, and generally figuring out life again.

At the time of this writing, just over six months have passed following Andy's death. To this point, we've lost no staff and we've lost no customers through this major disruption. How that's possible is simple. We created processes to follow for all of things we do. We installed systems that support the processes. We trained the staff to follow the processes and use the systems. I'm sorry to have had it tested and proven by such a tragic event, but we can confidently say that the procedures, the systems, and the training of our people all worked together perfectly.

Our law firm consulting business is another incredible story too. We had been in revenue for only six months at the time of his sudden departure. However, even though the effort was really new, I resolved to never quit. The best way to honor him is to continue the work we began and to continue to pursue the goals we had.

The results we had in the first thirty days were an amazing testament to setting up systems from the very beginning instead of waiting to have too much volume to handle before addressing the need. These results occurred while I did almost no work during that thirty-day period:

For the monthly Practice Management Challenge we ran, we had built a sales funnel that was functioning so well that people continued to sign up. Since we operated that challenge as a three-coach group, each with our own strengths, it was going to be difficult to run the challenge in the immediate month because some things would need to be re-configured for two coaches instead of three. Additionally, I wasn't going to be available to help, which would leave only one of us. My remaining business partner, Matt, made the decision to cancel the current month and push all of the current participants to the next month. Our staff made a flurry of phone calls, and all of the participants were fine with the delay.

When the new month began and it was time to run the challenge again, I showed up to find that my marketing staff had reset all of the membership pages, the new month's challenge Facebook group, and the email follow-up sequences, and the sales funnel pages. The processes that had been set up and the training that was provided to my marketing manager paid off. I left the process to work, and it worked during a period of my total disengagement from the business. When the challenge began, I did nothing except to show up on the first day and introduce myself to the attendee group. For the next ten days, the automations did their job, dripping the content to the attendees and I was available to review homework, give feedback, and answer questions for one hour per day. It ran like we never skipped a beat.

But it's even better.

Because we'd created a reputation in the legal community that we serve, I continued to get consultation requests from new prospects. The sales process that moves people from the Practice Management Challenge to the done-for-you agency consultation continued working without being touched. I did put a hold on new clients, but later built a process for serving agency clients. New staff is currently being added to that effort right now. If there were another disruption that caused me a period of distraction, our agency clients would not be affected.

Finally, we followed a process called the Content Multiplier Formula, which I learned from Peng Joon. With that process, we had a batch of pre-recorded content for social media and our blog. Because this material was already done and available, our social media manager was able to keep working. Anyone scrolling through our social media content would have no idea that I had done almost no work in over a month.

I knew this was all possible. It's what I teach. It's what I help my clients achieve. Even knowing how well processes, systems, automation, and delegation can serve a business, even I was amazed by the results. Most new businesses would not survive two thirds of the operating partners being suddenly unavailable for work. Because of the work we did, we are still in business and not in any danger whatsoever of failing. It took a little regrouping to figure out a new path forward, but we did it and we carry on.

So many years later, it was wonderful to be able to share Dad's comforting words. With resolve, we told ourselves, our staff, and our clients, "We're not going anywhere."

www.BusinessResultsSystems.com

www.LevelUpLawyer.com

www.GinaStGeorge.com

https://www.linkedin.com/in/gina-st-george/ my personal page

https://www.facebook.com/ginastgeorge my personal page

https://www.facebook.com/BusinessDragonSlayer my business page

Heidi Glunz

Heidi Glunz is the CFO of Brain Squared Solutions and the managing partner of Science2Wellbeing. Heidi dedicated herself to the coaching and training profession to help leaders develop the skills and awareness they need to succeed.

After obtaining her Professional Coach Certification from the International Coaching Federation, Heidi joined the executive team, and became a sought-after leadership development coach and instructor for Brain Squared Solutions. She is also a leadership coach and instructor for the University of California at Davis Extension.

Heidi is a certified values coach and the instructor for the Values2Wellbeing Coach Certification Program. She believes understanding our values is the key to long-lasting behavioral change and fulfillment.

Heidi is also a Project Management Professional, with over 15 years of leadership experience. As a project manager for engineering firms such as Idaho National Laboratory and NuScale Power, she was responsible for $40 million projects, leading teams of over 500 people. She learned that great leadership is the key to successful project execution, and that successful project execution includes team engagement and job satisfaction at all levels. She is passionate about helping leaders understand, and effectively communicate their mission, vision, and values to those they lead so they may achieve *unachievable* milestones.

Heidi holds a master's degree in Nuclear Engineering, and a bachelor's degree in Chemical Engineering, both from the University of Utah.

Your Values are Your Business

Values Drive Behaviors

By Heidi Glunz

If you give me a copy of your debit/credit card statements, I could tell you with relative accuracy what values drive your behaviors. Don't believe me? Consider this – money is merely a tool, used to make an exchange of value easier. Instead of trading vegetables for chickens in the town square, we assign a monetary value to the items, and we trade that monetary value for the things we need and want. Ultimately, each of us must decide what is *valuable* and worth spending our money on. If that is true, then if we reviewed your detailed spending habits, a pattern of driving values would start to emerge.

The same can be said for how you spend your time. If you tracked your time for a day or two – not just thinking back about how you thought you spent your time, but thoroughly documenting in real time everything you did that day – you would see patterns of behaviors. Behaviors driven by a set of underlying values.

Our values drive ALL our behaviors.

Let's test this statement. Pause here and really consider the toothpaste you buy. Seems trivial, doesn't it?

Below is a list of questions for you to think about. I encourage you to go deeper than surface level in your answers. Go all the way back to a belief you hold if you can.

- Do you just buy whatever you find, or do you have a specific toothpaste you must buy?
- What is it about that toothpaste that makes you buy it? The flavor? The benefits? The packaging? The advertisements?
- What makes those characteristics so important to you?
- What beliefs do you hold about those characteristics?

- If you could assign a one-word description to those beliefs, i.e., a value, what would it be?
  - Note: The word you choose is completely up to you. Your definition, your understanding of the nuance, depth and meaning of the word is what matters. There is no full and complete list of values. When asked if a word is a value, my answer is always yes – if it is a value to you.

Without giving free advertising to my preferred brand, here are my answers. I absolutely must buy toothpaste for sensitive teeth that is also whitening, and repairs enamel. The taste doesn't really matter to me, but the technology matters a great deal.

I have sensitive teeth, so it is important to me that my toothpaste reliefs the pain from hot and cold foods. At a deeper level, it is not just about the pain. I like to be able to fully participate in meals with other people. I find it embarrassing and unfulfilling if I can't eat the same as others because of my teeth. I believe that belonging and shared experiences with others is important to my happiness. The value behind my desire to belong is community.

The toothpaste must be whitening because I do not want yellow teeth – or more directly I do not want to be judged for having yellow or unhealthy-looking teeth (my belief). Appearance as a value is coming up for me but tied to appearance is also confidence. I feel more confident when I look the way I want to look.

Lastly, it must repair enamel. Long story short, I used to brush my teeth too hard, and I have damaged enamel. I want to do what I can to repair the damage because studies show how important your oral health is to your overall health. I want to stay healthy because I always want to be able to take care of myself. I don't want to burden others with my needs in the future. I must be self-reliant. This goes directly to my responsibility value.

Whew! I pulled a lot of self-awareness out my toothpaste, and I could have kept going. If values and beliefs have this much influence over what toothpaste we buy, imagine the insights we can find by looking at our spending habits and how we spend your time.

Each transaction and each activity could represent numerous beliefs and values we hold.

Take another moment here to reflect on what you learned about yourself from the toothpaste you buy. Did you uncovered a belief and/or a value, you did <u>not</u> realize was impacting your decisions?

Two Sets of Values

In her book, *Be You: The Science of Becoming the Self You Were Born to Be,* Dr. Senka Holzer presents a theory that we have two sets of values:

- Core Values that are innated to who we are, our "psychological DNA" and our internal intrinsic motivators.
  - Who you can't help but be.
  - Make time disappear.
  - YOUR secret to a happy life.
- Acquired Values that we collect from external sources, such as family, friends, society, and the organizations we join.
  - Who you **"should"** be.
  - The carrot and the stick.
  - What others tell you is the secret to a happy life.

She also states that these two sets of values can differ in their ability to bring us long-lasting fulfillment.

When we act from our core values, we feel fulfilled long after the act or achievement occurred. Our expected fulfillment, even years later, aligns with the reality of how we actually feel. That does not mean acting in alignment with our core values is easy or even pleasant at the time. You may have to muster the courage, conviction, energy and will to act from your core values – but it will be worth it.

When we act out of our acquired values, we might feel fulfilled at first, but the satisfaction does not last. Often, we don't even feel as happy as we expected at the time of achievement, let alone years later. The reality does not live up to the hype. However, acting from an acquired value can feel pleasant or easy at the time. Going with the flow is easier than fighting up stream. You may even get rewarded for being a team player or joining in the fun. You might feel good at first, but when the dopamine in your brain wears off, you feel empty.

No Bad Values

All values are rooted in true principles.

Acquired values are not good or bad. But they can serve us, or they can hold us back. When the true principle represented by an acquired value gets twisted, distorted, or taken to an extreme with obsessive qualities, then that acquired value is not serving us. Those acquired values prevent us from finding fulfillment and happiness.

It is important to remember, the people we acquire values from are only trying to help us grow or prevent us from suffering by sharing messages about what is true for them. We all want to help each other find the shortcut to fulfillment. We all share our values with others every day. How we internalize the messages we receive is up to us.

The Implied Third Category

There is also a third category: values that are part core and part acquired. Human psychology is never strictly black and white. This is the gray area.

We are born with a set of programming – our core values – but we are not capable of understanding these values until we learn language and higher thinking skills. As we are learning, our environment is also teaching us values. We internalize messages and beliefs that get mixed in with our original programming. These messages may be internalized as a new acquired value. Or we might internalize a belief that adds to or alters our original core value. These additions and adaptations can create synergies with our core values, increasing their effectiveness; or they might work against our core values, diminishing our fulfillment.

As an example of core values, acquired values, and everything in between, let's look back at the values I associated with my toothpaste.

Community – As much as I hated team projects in school, this is a core value of mine. I naturally seek out people with whom I can share ideas. I am an extrovert, energized by being with people. I find being a solopreneur difficult because I crave having someone to look at my work and give me feedback. That part of this value is core to me.

However, I used the word *embarrassing* in my description. It sounds like there is a "should" around this value – I *should* be able to fit in without accommodations. Do I really feel that way? I would not think less of anyone else for avoiding cold foods or waiting for food to cool. Why do I view myself differently? The *should* component and the negative connotations I associate with "embarrassing" are indicators of my acquired value of conformity.

Appearance – For me is an acquired value. I know because I admitted I didn't want to be judged. I also, unfortunately, sometimes judge others on this insignificant detail. Judgement of yourself and others is a tell-tale sign of an acquired value.

I also value confidence. I have learned over the years I like to look a certain way and when I do, I feel like myself. No one said I had to look this way. I like to look this way. Some people don't like the way I look, and I don't care what they think. That tells me confidence is a core value.

Responsibility – This is 100% a core value. Even as a kid I was always responsible. My parents didn't care if I got a B on my report card, but I cared A LOT. I naturally gravitated toward helping others and actively involved myself (by choice, not out of guilt or shame) to help them solve their problems.

And yet, I acquired some components of this value as well. My extreme need to be self-reliant is partly acquired. Yes, it is responsible – and I can see how it naturally combined with this core value – but I know I can take this to the extreme. I worry about being a burden even though I would never consider others a burden. I also chose a career and multiple jobs because I was **never** going to have to rely on someone else. I vividly remember telling my cousin when I was in high school – *I will **always** take care of myself.*

This extreme belief, the worry, and the shame I feel when I am not self-reliant, is an indicator of an acquired component to this value.

I told you I could go deeper...

Conformity, appearance, and self-reliance all have true principles they represent. They are not "bad" values. They are only problematic because of the beliefs I hold about them. In their current form they are not serving me in my search for fulfillment and happiness.

Go Deeper

Why did I ask you if you uncovered a value you didn't realize was impacting your decisions?

Because we can acquire values on a conscious and a subconscious level. Messages can unwittingly get lodged in our subconscious and internalized as beliefs we don't realize we hold. We then start to act out of these beliefs automatically and unconsciously, potentially damaging our fulfillment in the process.

As a certified Values Coach and Values Coaching Instructor, my mission is to help people uncover their core and acquired values and empower them to make conscious choices about how they apply their values in their lives. If values drive all our behaviors, then understanding our values is the key to creating long-lasting behavioral change and achieving happiness and fulfillment.

We bring our subconscious acquired values to the surface by examining our behaviors (like our spending habits, our time management, or our toothpaste choices) and questioning the beliefs/values that drive those behaviors. We must make the unconscious, conscious. Only then can we **decide** if we want to continue allowing our acquired values to drive our behavior, or if we want to manifest long-lasting change driven by our innate core values.

The first step to uncovering your acquired values is to notice your behaviors. Take a critical eye to how you show up in a multitude of situations. I already gave you two options – reviewing your credit card statements and tracking your time – but the ways you can take stock of your behaviors are endless.

Second, question why you are behaving a certain way, just like we did with the toothpaste. Why this decision vs that? What beliefs are influencing your decisions? Where did that belief come from and what value is that belief representing?

Next ask yourself if that belief is true. Does this belief ring true for you on a visceral, gut level? If not, what do you believe or what do you want to believe?

Now ask yourself, does this belief/value truly serve me? Do you find yourself judging yourself or others because of this belief? Are you obsessing, feeling guilty or ashamed because of this belief? What *should's* show up around this belief/value?

Lastly, remember you get to choose. Now that you are aware of this belief you can control your subconscious, automatic thinking. You can decide to replace the behavior, the belief, or the value. You can set boundaries on how often or to what extent you will act from this value. You can even choose a new belief to associate with this value that serves you better.

Accessing your core values is a little bit easier. Simply ask yourself what you cannot help but be? You can also go through the exercise of writing down your top ten values. Yes, it is that easy, because when we consciously choose our values, we tap into that innate part of ourselves. Occasionally, a deeply ingrained acquired value makes it on to the list. If you think one of your stated values is acquired or partially acquired, go through the process above. What beliefs do you hold about that value? Does it ring true for you? What judgements, guilt or shame come along with this belief/value?

Your Values Are Your Business

How you choose to earn your money depends on your core and acquired values as much as how you choose to spend your money. No matter your position, you are still a person – a person with core and acquired values. You bring those values, both consciously and unconsciously, into everything you do every day, including your work and the investments of time and money you choose to make.

Increasingly you hear people say they want to work for organizations that align with their values. Some of us create our own businesses so we can more easily align our work with our values. The important question to ask here is…

Are you aligning your work with your core values or your acquired values?

A thoughtful answer is important for two reasons:

1. If you align your work primarily with your acquired values, fulfillment and happiness will be harder to find.
2. Your values influence your behaviors, and your behaviors influence others.

Reason 1:

I spent years changing jobs because I didn't "fit". No matter where I went, the grass wasn't greener, it was just a different shade. I chose jobs and made decisions based on an acquired value (security). The more I acted from that value, the more obsessive I became and the less fulfilled.

Now imagine pouring yourself into building a business (if you've started a business, you know the dedication it takes) based on your acquired value…I did that too. I created a hell of my own design. I not only reinforced my own obsessive and unsatisfying value, but I was also selling it to others. Meanwhile, I was doing it all alone, while my need for community ached inside of me.

I truly hope this does not sound familiar, but if it does, you are not alone.

Reason 2:

Regardless of our role in an organization, we all influence others. To some degree we are all helping our colleagues acquire new values. For leaders and entrepreneurs, this occurs to an even greater degree – we set the values and culture for our organization.

When we are acting out of *problematic* acquired values, we may not be showing up as our best selves. Our behaviors, demeanor, and attitudes reflect our lack of fulfillment and our frustration. We might obsess or judge our colleagues for not living up to our acquired values. *Don't they know better?*

We may also be less open to what others value – what others need to achieve fulfillment. We might be unable to see things from a different perspective. Our judgements get in the way of our communications, and everyone suffers.

As leaders and business owners, we might focus too heavily on feeding these acquired values and miss opportunities to see what our teams and our customers truly need. We might create metrics that drive behaviors antithetical to lasting success and fulfillment for us and the entire organization. We may even start to compromise on those stated, core values we envisioned for our businesses. As we become more and more unfulfilled, our businesses and organizations suffer.

What do we do?

You may or may not be able to completely change your organization depending on your role, but you can change you. You can:

- Compare your core values to those of the organization and highlight the alignments, overlaps and synergies.
- Find ways to feed your core values.
  - Reframe your perspective on certain organizational aspects from the point of view of your core values.
  - Find ways to perform more tasks that align with your core values, and less tasks that align with your acquired values.
- Change the beliefs that you hold to help your acquired values serve you better.
- Decide that an acquired value or behavior is necessary, but only up to a certain point. After that point, it is time to move on to something more fulfilling.

None of these suggestions are easy. I am happy to help you make sure your *Core Values* are your business. Reach out anytime.

Heidi Glunz

www.science2wellbeing.com

www.brainsquaredsolutions.com

https://www.linkedin.com/in/heidi-glunz-pmp-pcc/

Dr. Stephen J. Kosmyna, Ph.D.

 Dr. Stephen J. Kosmyna, Ph.D. is an Elite Level Success and Mindset Consultant, an Inspirational Speaker, Trainer, Author, Coach, Spiritual Leader, Entrepreneurial Adviser, Prosperity Teacher, Metaphysician, and an Ordained New Thought Minister. He provides inspiration, motivation, guidance, mentoring and coaching to individuals and small businesses, along with training in the corporate space, through an abundance of programs and workshops.

He has earned bachelor's and master's degrees in Metaphysical Science with a focus on the subconscious mind and visualization, and he also holds a Doctor of Philosophy, Ph.D. specializing in Holistic Life Coaching.

President of Success Ocean International, a personal and professional development company, Dr. Stephen is also a Certified Proctor-Gallagher Institute Consultant. With passion, and enthusiasm he facilitates classes and events that cultivate radical personal and professional transformation and quantum leap goal achievement. He is also the founder and voice of The Genesis Frequency podcast which also focuses on human potential development.

Dr. Stephen seeks individuals who would like to become entrepreneurs in this field of personal and professional development. He is looking for big thinkers who desire the freedom to work from anywhere with their laptop and phone, generating an executive level income. He works by appointment and conducts interviews prior to selecting individual candidates for his programs to determine qualifications and see if there is alignment regarding energy and objectives. Conversations and interviews by appointment. SuccessAppointment.com

Cracking the Rich Code - The Law of Infinite Potential

By Dr. Stephen J. Kosmyna

The code to enter the kingdom of riches is hidden right where you are. We are all participating with the code of manifestation whether we are doing it deliberately or not.

When we are unaware of the *code*, or the law of infinite potential, it doesn't mean it is not operating in our lives. The code is always at work and this chapter will show you how to work in harmony with it rather than simply moving through life unconsciously. There is no allowance for ignorance of these laws.

I will take you through a simple five step manifestation process that is the definitive *code cracker* which will allow you to experience everything you desire, personally and professionally. The objective is to satisfy any longing and discontent you may be feeling. This is also a real game-changer for entrepreneurs seeking to experience quantum leaps when it comes to goal achievement.

Cracking the code begins by knowing there actually is a code. By understanding it, working in harmony with it, and doing things in a certain way, you can be, do and have it all.

Being an author, trainer, consultant, and speaker, I love looking at different words and the variety of definitions they may have. Being a metaphysician, I love to explore the underlying nature of things, the laws of cause and effect.

Let's have a quick look at the words crack, rich and code and their definitions since we're learning about Cracking the Rich Code.

These are all according to Merriam-Webster's online dictionary:

CRACK: *to break through something, such as a barrier; to gain acceptance or recognition.*

So, we are unraveling that which may seem like a mystery in the beginning. We are learning to recognize then resolve the obstacles and break through the barriers that keep us stuck in the same place year after year.

RICH: *having high value or quality; well supplied; prosperous, abundance, plentiful, thriving, blessed.*

And the best part is that YOU get to define what RICH means for you! Rich means different things to different people, and we will explore this further as we move into the actual five step process of manifestation.

CODE: *a systematic statement of a body of law AND a system of principles or rules.*

For our purpose here, we are defining *code* as a system, a method, an established procedure to follow. Code means doing things in a *certain way* to achieve a specific outcome.

Cracking the rich code means to move into an understanding of the laws of causation which are responsible for making manifest all that shows up in our lives as our results. When we truly understand these laws and cooperate with them intentionally, we can truly create the rich life we would love to live and move into the realization of all we wish to be, do, and have. Make no mistake, this process to experience quantum leaps when it comes to goal achievement is the same for personal and professional objectives. The laws of infinite potential apply to individuals, small business owners and those in the corporate environment as well.

Rather than defining each of the seven primary laws of causation we'll move through a five-step process of manifestation that has been established based on these laws.

DISCOVERY

Where Are you Now, and Where Do You Want to Be?

You can only begin right where you are. I invite you to make an appointment with yourself. Find a quiet place and look at where you are in your life right now. Ask yourself the questions that follow and be honest. (Notice I said to be honest with yourself not hard on yourself.) This isn't an exercise in beating yourself up about what you haven't accomplished thus far. This is about bringing to the surface what you really want to experience in your life without placing any limitations on what you think is possible.

Where are you compared to where you were twelve months ago, twenty-four months ago and three years ago? Is everything pretty much the same? Do you appear to be stuck, not growing, not seeing the realization of *any* of your dreams?

Decide right now what it is you want. Keep asking. Has there been any growth? Have you seen your wildest dreams come true personally and professionally? In your business and/or in your corporate life? In your health and physical fitness? In your relationships? In your finances? Time and money freedom? Fun and recreation? What do you want for you? In what you would love to be, do, have, and experience in your life? What is your most outrageous dream? How do you define rich? Are you truly living the life you would love to live, the life that, up until now, you have only dreamt about?

What is missing if you have not yet realized your personal and professional goals?

Engage your imagination. Begin using it again like when you were a kid. Decide what you really want. Forget about the how, that's none of your business. And most of all, don't buy into any of your excuses for staying stuck right where you are.

It is so important to get this right. Do not consider the how. What is it that would satisfy any longing and discontent that you're feeling? What is the dream that is so big that it excites you and scares you at the same time?

In my work with individuals on their own personal development or when I work with small business owners or corporate teams and professionals, it comes down to understanding the mind, establishing the emotional state, followed by appropriate action.

You also need to understand the manifestation code; all the elements that are responsible for your results. Get these pieces right through study, adjust; and you will quickly move way out in front of the herd while holding the keys to *cracking the rich code.* You'll begin making quantum leaps into the realization of your most extraordinary life.

Let's continue to move in the direction of your dreams.

An Introduction to Manifestation - A Word About Paradigms

Paradigms are a multitude of habits that have almost exclusive control of your habitual behavior and almost all your behavior is habitual. In other words, your paradigms are always in charge. Paradigms have become your auto pilot system, your cruise control for living life. I have spent the last few years working with the late Bob Proctor and I currently work as one of his company's certified consultants. Bob used to say (and I'm paraphrasing), your paradigms keep you living life as an unconscious competent, walking around wondering what happened.

You must know and understand that it is your paradigms that keep you stuck. It's one thing to learn what a paradigm is and be able to define it and it's quite a different thing and an involved process, to identify what your paradigms are and how you go about replacing them. This work is best done with a mentor or guide, but you can begin right now by paying attention and becoming aware of all your habitual daily activities, your recurring thoughts, words, and actions.

It is so important to understand why you must consider paradigms in this process. You need to identify your paradigms and replace them because they influence the basic equation for what is showing up in your life. The formula is always the same; thoughts + feelings (emotion) + actions = results. Your thoughts are habitual, your actions are habitual, even the way you feel becomes a habit. These paradigms become your programming, your current operating system, and they dictate your results without fail.

Manifestation Preparation - The Genesis Frequency - Enthusiasm and Emotional State

As you begin this prep work, identifying your deepest desires, you must pay attention to your energy and emotional state throughout this entire process.

One of the laws of causation is the law of vibration. Everything is in motion. Nothing rests. To keep this simple, let's just say everything has its own frequency. Your goals, dreams and desires all have their own frequency. Their frequency was established the moment you created them using the power of your imagination as you designed them on the canvas of our mind. As you allowed yourself to get emotionally involved with the possibility of moving your dream from non-form to form, from the invisible to the visible, your own personal vibration and frequency shifted as well.

Think of this like the dial on your radio. If you have your radio set to an all-news format station, you're not going to hear smooth jazz or classical music unless you change the frequency by adjusting the dial. Likewise, as you're working with the law, you won't experience the realization of your dreams if you stay on the same frequency as your current results. All your problems and everything you don't want has its own vibration too. You move the dial by monitoring your emotional state. An emotional state that includes positive expectation, unconditional love, harmlessness, compassion, letting go, cheerfulness, faith, spaciousness, love, and generosity contributes to elevating your frequency.

By sustaining your higher frequency, you become more attractive to the energy of your objectives. You magnetize your condition. All your actions that are in supportive alignment with what you want to experience, receive a positive reaction from the energy field of the world around you. People, events, circumstances, conditions, and situations arise that accelerate and contribute to the process of manifestation.

In simple terms, every action causes a reaction from this energy field you're immersed in, the conscious universe. This is why you need not concern yourself with *the how*.

HERE'S THE PROCESS – A FIVE STEP MANIFESTATION PROCEDURE TO CRACK THE RICH CODE

1) Decision - Commitment

Decide what it is you really want to show up in your life. What is the one big, outrageous dream? Remember, however you define riches for yourself, whatever it is that you want to be, do, and have, already exists despite outward appearances.

You must commit yourself to this process. Set your intention to attaining it no matter what. Accept no excuses. Know that riches, however you define them, are within your reach. Make this process a priority. Choose only one thing (or two at most) which would be one personal goal and one professional goal. You're not doing S.M.A.R.T. goals here either, you're doing the outrageous!

2) Write it Out in the Present Tense with Gratitude

You must commit your desire to paper. Handwrite it out as an affirmative gratitude statement. Consider this; *'I Am so happy and grateful I Am now _____!'* Write it on a card, carry it with you. Read it out load many times every day, in front of a mirror too. Read it again before you fall asleep at night. Re-write it every day. I have my clients write it out by hand over one hundred times a day. All this will help to condition and reprogram your subconscious mind.

3) Visualize it and Feel it Real

Continue to use your imagination and engage with a vivid visualization process. Make your image clear and specific. Take time outs throughout your day to see and feel yourself experiencing the realization of your desire. FEEL the feelings of living your rich life. Feel and see yourself accepting all your good fortune. Engaging the feelings and emotions is key. We must live *from* the ideal rather than merely thinking of it. Simply thinking of it keeps it as a wish only and there is no movement. Feeling IS the secret.

4) Believe – Have Faith

Remember, you don't have to know HOW your good will come to you. There is a Presence and Power at work here that is beyond your human comprehension. In every moment believe and have faith that the law and this system is working for you. Stay committed to your vison feeling into the life you would love to live.

5) Gratitude

Every day, practice gratitude. How can you possibly want more if you're not grateful for what you already have? Practice past, present and future gratitude. Give thanks that you now have moved your riches from non-form to form by simply using the power of your mind, truly the gift has already been given. Thanks be to God!

REMEMEBER

Always take inspired action. When you feel that inner nudge to move and act, do it! That is the Spirit of Life, Love and Wisdom guiding you on your way. You must participate as you're directed. Find a mentor or coach. Feel free to reach out to me. We'll go deeper into this material. I would love to provide you the assistance you'll need along your journey.

Share your wins with others. Do so with gratitude and you'll attract even more good.

Manifestation Contamination and Degradation

The preceding has been a brief and basic synopsis of the manifestation process. We'll now take a brief look at what could potentially taint this process.

Back to definitions. Contamination is to corrupt or infect. Degradation is to degrade, to lower to an inferior or less effective level. You don't want either of these to take place when you are in pursuit of the desires of your heart.

Here are a few ways you might contaminate this process making it less effective. Beware, as you work with the law of infinite potential and allow this degradation to take place, you may end up moving things into your field of experience that you really don't want.

➢ Giving your energy to people, places, problems, circumstances, events, and situations that are not supportive of your desire for transformation. Energy flows where our attention goes. The equation remains the same; thoughts + feelings + actions = results. If you are constantly focusing your energy and attention on what you don't want, you will get even more of what you don't want.

➤ Giving your energy to your current results. Do this and you are affecting your frequency. Sometimes you may feel like your current situation is permanent and there's no way out. This changes your vibration and moves you further down the dial, further away from what you truly desire to experience. You must remain in the feeling tone of your dream fulfilled.

➤ Are you following the herd? Do you look to what everyone else is doing, how they're behaving; always asking them what they think and what they would do when faced with your choices? You must sustain the feeling of your highest vision being your new reality and you won't find answers in others who are living from the way things have always been. You must know for yourself.

➤ You must examine your self-image. You will never outperform a poor self-image. You must not give your energy to the stories of your life that you have bought into that are not true. It's time to create a new, ideal self-image that covers every aspect of how you want to show up in this world. This is powerful. It's all about energy, emotion, and enthusiasm. Begin at once and then energetically move into your new image!

Do this work and deliberately design your dream life, your dream business, or the corporate culture you envision. Don't let it remain just a wish. Be vigilant, making certain every thought, word and action aligns with your desires. Stay in the feeling tone of your dream being your reality now. Work with someone that will help you identify your hidden paradigms. Remember, the paradigms are always in control. You may have created a magnificent blueprint for the life you want to move into, but is your habitual behavior supportive? If not, you'll tend to desecrate the light you're called to shine by moving yourself, perhaps unconsciously, to being in a state of counter intention which is really moving yourself in the direction of what you don't want. You must take time to investigate your deep-rooted programming, your addictions and paradigms, and upgrade your operating system to one which is in harmony with all you want to be, do, and have.

Manifestation: Support System

Having just identified potential stumbling blocks, let's look at a few things that are supportive of intentional creation.

Understand that there is a law of gestation at work. You're moving your vison from the invisible world of non-form, your imagination, into the visible world of form and there is a gestation period before your vison is birthed. By replacing old worn-out habits that are non-supportive of your objectives with the manifestation support mechanics offered here, you will become less susceptible to distractions that delay the materialization of your desires.

Once you have moved through each step of this process you must then do each of the five steps simultaneously daily. The only difference is you have already decided what you want so you're not deciding on something new every day. In step one, you're simply re-committing to your intention to make manifest your objective.

Then:

- Continue to visualize and FEEL your new and improved life several times throughout the day. Be sure to vision from it, living it, not simply thinking of it.
- Continue with faith and belief in the process. It's law and it's always working
- Daily gratitude is so important. Keep a gratitude journal.
- Monitor your emotional state. Do what's necessary to maintain your genesis frequency.
- Don't keep score. This means you're not always looking for it, not constantly asking, where is it? You must stay in a ceaseless state of positive expectation. Absence of evidence is not evidence of absence. Have patience, your vison must be made manifest. If you are always wondering where it is, you are pushing it away and moving into the energy of counter intention.
- Spend time in the silence, practice mindfulness, meditation, and visualization.

- Turn off the negative news and other distractions that are non-supportive and operate on a less than desirable frequency. Spend time in nature, listen to beautiful music, enjoy the silence, become more aware of the omnipresence of the Divine, your Source.
- Develop your mental faculties. This will help you live from the inside out rather than from the outside in.
- Don't hesitate to reach out to me for assistance. I have modeled and demonstrated this process in my own life and business very successfully and it is my mission to help others.

Make no mistake, whether you want to experience more desirable results in your personal life or your professional life, or both, the process is the same as outlined in this chapter.

This process works and it works every time because it's law. To experience your biggest, wildest, most outrageous dreams, the ones that excite you and scare you at the same time; as an individual, a small business owner or in your corporate environment, it begins here and now with an understanding of these Laws of Infinite Potential and doing things in this *certain way*.

This is Cracking the Rich Code and it's calling you to begin at once to live the life you have perhaps only imagined.

It's time to start Cracking - the Rich Code.

***

To Contact Dr. Stephen J. Kosmyna:

Email: Stephen@SuccessOcean.com

Dr. Stephen's Calendar for no cost appointments - discovery - discussion sessions and inquiries, go to: SuccessAppointment.com

Websites: SuccessOcean.com - https://successocean.com/ AND www.stephenjkosmyna.com

Dr. Stephen's Podcast: The Genesis Frequency: https://thegenesisfrequency.com/ also available on Amazon,

Google, and Apple Podcasts; Stitcher, iHeart Radio, Spotify, Audible and TuneIn.

Turn your passion for personal and professional growth into your own lucrative business: http://www.successocean.biz/ (Work anywhere in the world with a laptop and phone; no selling, no convincing, no explaining, not mlm; must schedule interview.)

Join Our Social Platform for Cracking the Rich Code: https://www.richcodeclub.com/coauth/SuccessOcean/

Connect on Facebook:
https://www.facebook.com/steve.j.kosmyna/ AND
https://www.facebook.com/SuccessOcean

Private Success Ocean Inner Circle Facebook Group for Personal / Professional Development:
https://www.facebook.com/groups/SuccessOceanInnerCircle

LinkedIn: www.linkedin.com/in/dr-stephen-j-kosmyna-ph-d-12b822a5 AND https://www.linkedin.com/company/success-ocean-international-llc/

Twitter: https://twitter.com/StephenJKosmyna

You Tube: https://www.youtube.com/c/SuccessOcean/

P.Y. Nicole Chang

 P.Y. Nicole Chang is internationally recognized as a brand and growth strategist, helping entrepreneurs build creative, transformative business solutions to scale their corporations. With a background in finance, management consulting, and operations, Nicole has decades of experience leading some of the world's greatest companies and teams. She has developed an impactful framework for intention-based creative problem solving and vision creation, which harnesses individuals' untapped potential and innate inner wisdom.

P.Y. Nicole is a former McKinsey consultant, Morgan Stanley investment banker, and led Strategy and Corporate Development for a public commercial bank. She spent two decades in Europe and Greater China as COO/CFO for a media conglomerate; Global Vice President for DFS|LVMH, the world's largest luxury travel retailer; CEO of a SME content provider; COO of a wine distributor, as well as Founder of several companies. She is currently an active advisor/investor in socially conscious and technology-driven companies, including a kid's coding franchise. A sought-after speaker, Nicole has been featured at places like the Stanford Faculty Club and blockchain conferences where she speaks on business, mindset, and Web3-related topics.

PY Nicole received her B.A. from Harvard and her J.D. and MBA from Stanford. An expert on leading a life abundant in health, wealth, and happiness, Nicole is a powerhouse across many industries.

Six Words Can Change Your Life

By: P.Y. Nicole Chang

"Man is only limited by weakness of attention and poverty of imagination". **—Neville Goddard**

An apple and a piece of chocolate cake are in front of you. Which do you choose to eat? You know choosing to eat the wrong calories over and over results in excess weight, poor health, and other undesired consequences—and yet you still do it.

Similarly, choosing to recite the wrong thoughts in your head over and over can lead to undesired consequences; but you still do it. The subconscious mind controls 95% of your life. This means that the decisions you make, the actions you take, and your behaviors and actions rely on the 95% of the brain that is outside of your conscious awareness.[1] What if I were to tell you that by activating the use of six words, you could join the 5% Club of those who can use the conscious mind to steer the subconscious mind towards achieving their dreams.

I am someone who used to be part of the 95% Club (living a life driven by subconscious thoughts). I would eat cake and listen to internal thoughts that were misaligned with my dreams, even when I knew I shouldn't. I'd like to share with you how my life changed when I discovered the power of six simple words and applied them in different aspects of my life. Six words granted me access to the exclusive 5% Club.

SIX WORDS CAN CHANGE YOUR LIFE

"I don't like what I see." These are six words no expectant mother wants to hear from their obstetrician during a routine check-up. It was May 2, 2001, I was 7 months pregnant, and I learned that my unborn son had a life-threatening medical condition. I had already envisioned my son coming home, growing up, going to college, and changing the world. Now, I could only think of Ernest Hemingway's six-word story, "For Sale: baby shoes, never worn."

On May 17, 2001, at 9:30 PM, a month before my scheduled due date, my water broke just as I sat down to dinner with my husband. We rushed from our apartment in central Paris to the Necker Hospital for Sick Children. Twenty-five minutes later, the "on duty" attending physician arrived from his home where he had been finishing his dinner. After examining me, he said calmly, "There is a lot of fluid in your baby, so we must do a cesarean. If we do a natural birth, neither of you will live. With the complication of needing a cesarean and the challenge of it being a difficult surgery for your baby, it is better to wait until morning." In summary, "The A-Team shows up at 9 AM, which is still ten hours from now."

The attending midwife said the word that only the French could make sound so chic, "Impossible!" She informed that doctor that I was already four centimeters dilated and would likely give birth in a few hours. The doctor, who was in a hurry to get back to his dinner, left us with these parting words, "What must happen will happen. However, it would be MUCH better if we can wait until morning to do this. I am going home now. Call me if we need to do something tonight." With that, he bid us adieu and left.

The next ten hours were very long for me. I played meditation music and focused on doing the exact opposite of everything I had learned in the birthing classes for a speedy delivery. I was supposed to visualize the baby sliding down the canal; instead, I visualized him being sucked back into me by a strong force almost like a vacuum cleaner. I focused on envisioning everything inside my body happening in super slow motion. Somehow, I managed to make it through the night to 9 AM.

Minutes after delivery, my son was whisked away to undergo a long operation. My original fairytale visions of going home with my newborn son in my arms, wrapped in a blanket, faded into images of him in a little ICU bin attached to all sorts of monitors. There was a board in the ward with the babies' names on it, and every morning the names of the babies who didn't make it through the night were crossed off—a constant reminder of the fragility of life. I, or someone from the family, was with him all the time. Not only were we concerned for his condition, but we wanted to make sure he stayed safe from other dangers (we had witnessed a baby being dropped while being weighed, wrong amounts of medication given, and in my son's particular case, there was a night nurse who would literally tape his mouth shut when he cried too much).

I fought back tears as my son lay in his crib with multiple tubes coming out of him. One day, I looked him in the eye and shared my dream of him making it out of the hospital and eventually going off to college. I promised him that I would do everything in my power to make it happen. Three operations later, we were still nowhere closer to a solution. The surgeon was so desperate, he even asked me for ideas. This was not reassuring. However, the Chinese word for 'crisis' comes from the words 'danger' and 'opportunity'. So, I took the opportunity to read tons of literature and used a research-based approach to try different protocols. One of the protocols we came up with eventually worked (and I am happy to say that today, that same protocol is being used to save other babies). After three long months in the ICU fighting for our son's life—four operations and many prayers later—the miracle we dreamed about happened. He finally came home!

The ordeal of my son's medical condition, and my quest to find a way for him to live, inspired me to think a lot about **the power of thought and how it can be harnessed to change one's reality.** Those initial six words spoken by my doctor during the check-up— "I don't like what I see"—were a big wake-up call and forced me to dramatically alter the way I saw the world around me. His words forced me to confront the fact that I didn't like my reality and that I needed to do everything I could to **create a new reality**. My energy was entirely concentrated on a different set of six words: **Dream it. See it. Create it.** I focused on the desired outcome (a healthy child), envisioned what that looked and felt like, and consistently monitored my thoughts to stay optimistic (despite the odds); thus, aligning to a positive outcome. I harnessed the power of using my conscious thoughts (5%) to steer unconscious thoughts (95%) and create a new reality for myself.

I saw this codification work not only in my personal life with my son, but also, in my professional life. After graduate school, I lived in San Francisco, CA and worked for a consulting company called McKinsey. Although I loved my job and had a very comfortable life, I longed for more adventure. Instead of consulting the C-Suite, I wanted to be in the C-suite. Instead of living in San Francisco, where my life was 'too comfortable,' I wanted the excitement of working and living abroad. When I acknowledged that I didn't like what I saw, in terms of my life (as wonderful as it was), I became inspired by my dreams and was open to move in that direction. That's when my new reality unfolded. I would soon find myself living the coveted life of an expatriate in Europe and Asia. I worked in fulfilling jobs I was passionate about, broke a monopoly for the world's largest luxury group, and opened up a multi-billion-dollar Chinese duty-free market, led the first western-style IPO in Eastern Europe, and in my personal life, courted a romantic Parisian who would later father my kids and be my life partner (23 years and counting). I want to share with you the secret power behind these magical six words; and I believe that if people can master them, we can together co-create a better world.

REPLACE "I DON'T LIKE WHAT I SEE" with "DREAM IT, SEE IT, CREATE IT."

DREAM IT.

When you were a kid, you probably wanted to be an astronaut, or a doctor—that was me—or maybe a superhero. And then life happened. Right? One day, you woke up and realized you didn't become an astronaut or achieved that goal you had once dreamed of. Only three percent of people actually have a big dream (not to be confused with career aspirations), and only one percent actually write it down. That means, ninety-seven percent of people seem to have forgotten that they can make their dream a reality; they have let work and family responsibilities squash any progress towards accomplishing those earlier dreams.[2]

To "Dream it" means to have a big vision of an idyllic outcome in some aspect of your life, even if it seems very removed from reality. In the case of my son, I was dreaming of his full recovery, him growing up healthy, going off to college, and changing the world with his wisdom.

SEE IT.

To "See it" means to see the milestone goals (which will change as you act) with such clarity and focus that you feel as if you have already accomplished it. The mind can't tell the difference between imagination and reality. Have you ever woken up from a dream that's felt so real it was almost as if you were there?

Clarity comes from trying and sometimes failing forward and may require incorporating aspects of the OODA3 loop. To help visualize things, find ways to "live forward." You want to be driving a Ferrari? Go test drive one. You want that dream house? Go visit some dream homes on the weekend.

Focus is about having a "take no prisoner's" attitude. I learned about focus when I had a near-death experience. I was in sixth grade and was accompanying my dad on an out-of-town business trip. I joined my dad's colleagues' children on a school field trip to a local amusement park. Since I didn't know anyone in the group, I sat by myself on this new roller coaster which featured two double loops (the car would enter the first loop, stop for a split second at the top, then go in reverse and do the same for the second loop). Just before the ride started, I noticed that my seatbelt didn't work and the safety bar that was supposed to come down, didn't. I raised my hand to say something, but before anyone noticed, the ride started. I was so scared and held onto the side rails for my life. When the car was upside down in the loop, I could feel my body pull away from the seat. The only way I could stay in was to push my back hard into the seat and my feet hard into the floor. The whole ride probably only lasted two minutes, but in those few seconds that I was upside down, it was like time stood still and my only focus was to not fall out. I got off the car trembling and my back was black and blue for months afterwards.

Years later, when I started to work on the open-office space at the investment bank Morgan Stanley, I thought I would never be able to concentrate amidst all the trading floor commotion around me. However, much like that day on the roller coaster, I saw what needed to be done and tapped into my extreme focus to tune out things that were not relevant to the task at hand.

CREATE IT.

You look in the mirror and notice a bulging stomach and say to yourself, "I need to go on a diet." You start counting calories and 'eating better.' Three weeks later, those same bad habits creep back in, and you find yourself making that same New Year's Resolution again and again, year after year.

Conquer the **Knowing-Doing Gap**. Live as a thinner you, who does not gorge on fattening cookies. What habits are you willing to put in place to hit those goals?

"Create it" means taking the dream and detailed vision one has towards a goal and creating the habits and mindset to act on it despite all of the inconveniences that may come up (e.g., lack of funds, time, discipline, signs of success, desire, personal doubt).

THE ROLE OF CONFIDENCE

The experience of almost losing my son made me appreciate even more the gift I was given as a mother, and the responsibility I felt to raise another human being became that much more intentional. When my son was just a few years old, I was at my tenth reunion from Stanford Business School. Some of my female classmates and I were discussing life. This conversation was about our new second job—parenthood.

We talked about intentional parenting and the legacy we wanted to leave our children. Specifically, we asked ourselves the question, "If I were to gift my child one thing in this world, what would it be?" I thought to myself, *'Much of the knowledge and skills he will learn in school will eventually become obsolete.'* What children really need to learn is how to be comfortable with the uncomfortable, how to learn from failure, and how to believe in themselves when others don't. Confidence allows all this and so much more. Confidence allows you to decide when the choice is not clear; confidence allows you to persist even when the world seems dark. Confidence allows you to overcome your fears and turn "I can't" into "I can." Furthermore, to navigate in today's VUCA world (where the only constant seems to be change and where over eighty percent of the jobs have not been invented yet,[4]) confidence is paramount to thrive.

I asked myself, *'What makes me an authority on confidence?'* Honestly, it was out of necessity that I learned about confidence. I saw that without it, I would continue to be a guest at my own internal pity party.

It was confidence that allowed this short Asian girl (that was teased on the playgrounds in elementary school for her flat nose) to being proud of her Asian features and featured in Tatler Magazine.

It was confidence that allowed an asthmatic to become the first American to cross the finish line in the 1990 Helsinki Marathon.

It was confidence that allowed me to go from wearing hand-me downs as a kid to leading ventures worldwide for the world's largest luxury travel retail company.

It was confidence that allowed me to go from squabbling with my siblings to graduating from Stanford Law School and negotiating deals worth hundreds of millions of dollars.

It was confidence that allowed me to go from running my cookie business as a kid to leading from the C-suite for multi-national companies.

I circle back to my son. On December 6, 2019, when he was a high school senior, he told me the six words I had once dreamed to hear: "Mom, I got accepted into Stanford!" As he headed off to college, I shared with him my discussion from 15 years earlier and asked him what he felt was my number one gift to him. He thought about it and replied, "You gave me the feeling that I can do anything I want in the world."

In summary, the **SixWord© Methodology** to change any aspect of your life is:

Figure out which area in your life is where **"You don't like what you see."**

Dream it. Dream of a goal (ideally putting it into six words) that is worth striving for—not a goal you know you can do, or a goal you think you can do. Set a goal that is a Dream Goal. If you want to run a marathon, don't settle for running around the block. If you want to lose twenty pounds, don't settle for ten.

See it. See the potential—changing milestone goals with clarity and focus as if you already accomplished it. Live in appreciation for having achieved each one.

Create it. Put the systems and habits in place to move towards your goals. Don't let that inner voice of doubt, sabotage, or other subconscious habits get in the way as you work towards your dream.

What are the six words you dream to hear? Whether it is, "My book is a NYT best-seller!" or "I made a $100 million dollars" or "I met my dream man," believe you can get there. I believe that anyone can achieve anything with proper implementation and mastery of the **SixWord© Methodology.** I have seen individuals and corporations far exceed their wildest dreams—raising money with BN+ valuations, an entrepreneur creating a company he could not have dreamed of eighteen months prior, an eighty-year-old former schoolteacher making $1+ MN by trading stocks during the pandemic, a lawyer making partner at their law firm, finding one's soulmate. What is your wildest dream and are you committed to making it happen?

***

To contact Nicole:

Please contact me if this resonates with you and you would like to learn more about how to join the 5% Club. Go to the website below for a free Meditation to help you on your journey.

Website: www.pynicole.com

Email: info@pynicole.com

Endnotes

1. Gail Marra, <u>9 Interesting Facts about your Subconscious Mind</u>, Nov 11, 2021

2. https://authorvinod.com/people-who-live-without-dreams/

3. OODA Loop: 4-step approach to action-taking and entails observing, orienting, deciding and acting

4. According to a report published by Dell Technologies and authored by the Institute For The Future (IFTF) and a panel of 20 tech, business and academic experts from around the world, states that 85 percent of the jobs that will exist in 2030 haven't even been invented yet. Oct 28, 2018

Manny Lopez

Manny helps create & enhance speakers, coaches, authors, & consultants with strategic PR opportunities & dynamic systems of automation. A husband and father of 3, he devotes his time to creating a lifestyle of being #TooBlessedToBeStressed while creating opportunities for his network of over 30,000 business professionals worldwide!

Currently, he is a paid consultant on lead generation to over 1000 brands worldwide! Featured by INC. Magazine, Manny's work has been showcased on NBC, The Huffington Post, Bloomberg Radio, recently named "BEST NEW MEDIA" at Living Legends at Carnegie Hall, a CEO Space International graduate, and within just 2 years of starting his business, Manny was named "One of the Best" by Facebook when they hit 1 million advertisers!

Today, he uses his skills in building systems & brands to fund his passion project, "From Orphan To CEO" where Manny teaches MENTORSHIP, ENTREPRENEURSHIP, & FAITH to "DAY 1" entrepreneurs, at-risk youth & kids that age out of foster care using his revolutionary award-winning personal development platform, the MANNYfestation: SCHOOL OF BUSINESS! Currently the platform is active in 80+ countries worldwide, translates to 25+ languages, with 30,000+ global users and growing daily!

2 out of 3 kids that age out of foster care, within 1 year, end up DEAD, HOMELESS, or in JAIL! Manny hopes to see 2 out of 3 of these kids have MENTOR, understand ENTREPRENEURSHIP, & own their BUSINESS!

"From Orphan To CEO"

By Manny Lopez

The last time I shared my story in a published book was in 2017. A friend of mine on Facebook was putting together a book project to talk about their entrepreneur journey. I had been trying to write my "From Orphan To CEO" story into a book for some time.

I decided to jump in and in just one sitting, I had dived into every topic I could think of about my life. Things I have never shared with anyone. I left it all on the table & intend to do the same here.

From the most precious moments in life to some of my deepest and darkest secrets; my time in foster care after being left in a car at 18 months with my sister. Suffering from malnutrition, abuse, neglect, torture. My 3 near death experiences. My marriage to my high school sweetheart. My 3 beautiful children. My dad. The difficulties I had (and still have) with my mother.

As I write this, my first son, Isaac, is 15. My second, Xavier, is 12. My princess, Ava, is 7. I'll be married 14 years this year, together 17, with my queen, my rock… my everything.

Life can be quite interesting. Since submitting my story in late 2016, published in 2017, I've had a conversation with God, launched the "From Orphan To CEO" project, received a standing ovation at Carnegie Hall, collaborated with Tai Lopez & Les Brown, launched an award-winning free gamified school for entrepreneurs on how to start their own business, find a mentor, & how to put faith as a foundation into what they are building for the next generation.

The first time I shared my story, the book made me into a #1 Best-Selling author in 5 different categories; the ultimate reason why I joined the opportunity in the first place. I wanted my future projects to come out from the "Best-Selling Author" Manny Lopez. lol

That story was written before my 30th birthday. A very interesting moment in time where I was just a few months away from a checklist of promises I had made to my wife. Promises that were made after we had just become homeless for the 2nd time.

Before my kids could even recognize we had been left out on the street, a generous family had graciously welcomed us into their home where they converted part of their garage into a 1-bedroom for my queen, myself, and my 2 sons; one of which was still in diapers.

I remember having this overwhelming feeling of failure. I had gone all in, jumped from the cliff without a parachute, thinking I was smart enough to build one on the way down.

We crashed. Ending up homeless and nothing to show for it after years of collecting trophies, awards, and accomplishments everywhere I went.

The most important thing to me at that point, was to keep my family together. Things had to get serious. There is no way a man can feel worthy if he is unable to even provide the basic necessity of keeping a roof over his family's head.

I made a checklist. I made promises to my queen that by the time I was 30 years old, which was 6 years from this date we moved into this converted garage, that this is what would transpire:

1. We would NEVER be homeless again (my #1 priority)

2. We will have our daughter to complete our family

3. We will create a successful business

4. We will live in Lake Elsinore

5. Our home will be 2 stories

Up to that point, the best I could provide to her was an apartment in an area where we woke up to many mornings of gang graffiti on my kids' bedroom windows. At the time I made these promises, we are living in that converted garage.

The level of faith this woman had in me; I can't begin to imagine the strength she has had to endure. I really feel the test of a man is his ability to lead his family in uncertain times, but the test of a woman comes when her king needs her more than anything, when he has nothing. Does her loyalty still stand? Will she be the driving force of inspiration that he needs to succeed? I was at this point.

If she didn't believe in me, how could I even begin to believe in myself?

She's seen the real & unfiltered me since we were kids in high school, wandering through our journey of life, looking to understand ourselves in a world full of chaotic blessings.

But even though I was at my lowest, she still believed in my potential. I told her I would need time. 6 years to be exact. I was 24.

In this home, this converted 1-bedroom garage, is where I began my entrepreneur journey.

My story had left off just a few months shy of my 30th birthday, where I had only accomplished 2 of the 5 on the checklist of promises I had made to my wife:

1. I hadn't been homeless since (yay!)

2. Our daughter was born in 2014 (double yay!!)

As proud as I was, I still didn't feel I had a successful business, I didn't live in Lake Elsinore, and we weren't living in a 2-story home, I'm still in an apartment.

To say things were about to change would be an understatement.

It all began on a night walking my dog. It's January 27th, 2017.

We will call this day, "My Conversation with God"

To give you a little backstory, I've always had this idea of God as this incredibly busy "entity" that has no time for me. No time to look at my troubles and tribulations. If anything, He "delegates" it to a guardian angel. I've always seen God as this figure on a throne that just snaps His fingers to make things happen but never has the "time" to truly be there.

This day seemed to be a crossroads in life looking back 5 years later. I had received a call earlier that day from a friend that shook me to my core. I had to make a decision: continue on the path of least resistance and sacrifice every ounce of my moral being, or create a new path; something completely new, and put myself near a position I promised my wife we would never be again… homeless.

As a husband and father, I live to create a better world for my family and at times I get stuck in a never-ending cycle of self-doubt, wondering why I am not where I think I should be.

Can you relate to that?

I desire a world where we can live in peace, create abundance, while living with honor, respect, and dignity. Hopefully we wake up one day and as our life has flashed before our eyes, we can look back and smile at the memories we've made along the way & the people we were able to serve.

Being the provider is very important to me. It is what gets me up in the morning to truly make a difference in this world. I am an example to my children, while also racing against the clock to make something of this inherit wisdom before I leave this earth.

Becoming homeless was the last thing on my mind as I was looking to expand my growth back in 2017. I was already named "One of the Best" by Facebook when they hit 1 million advertisers, featured in INC. Magazine, a rolodex of hundreds of international clients I consulted for, but after this call I had received, life had been flipped upside down; and now it was time to make a decision.

I spent the rest of that fateful day pondering on that decision. The ideas kept spinning in my head on what I should do and how I should do it. Trying to fall back on my experience only gave me one route to consider, start all over.

I took the challenge to my queen. She's usually the level-headed one in the group and gives a great balance to my optimism. A man can truly benefit from a queen that brings an aura of consideration to the conversation. Sometimes we think our wives, spouses, and significant others don't understand our challenges, but in retrospect, after living a life of almost 2 decades with my own, she's been right far more than she's been wrong.

In this scenario though, she was quiet. There wasn't a clear answer in the room. I remember looking up at the ceiling laying on our bed, searching for a solution, wondering what that next step would look like. I'm mapping every scenario in my head to try and figure out this complex maze.

Still confused.

Around midnight, my dog starts barking. I've got a Maltese-Poodle mix that has a bladder the size of a peanut. If I don't' take him out now, he'll just keep barking until I do.

We get ready to go outside and as I start his walk, there is this voice in back of my head saying, "Put the dog away and keep walking."

At first, I try to ignore it. It's cold, I'm tired. I've got a lot on my mind and the last thing I want to do is walk around my neighborhood at midnight in the middle of January.

"Marshy" finishes his business and as I'm about to turn the knob at my front door to walk inside, the voice comes back, "Put the dog away. Keep walking."

Now I'm curious. Why would I be telling myself this? I have no interest in what this voice is saying. It can't be me.

At this point curiosity has won the battle, I put "Marshy" back inside and started walking around my neighborhood, noticing an uncomfortable silence.

Questions start to come up.

"What are you doing?"

"Why is this decision so difficult?"

I start to ask questions back.

"What am I supposed to do?"

"What is my real purpose?"

As clear as day, I can remember it like it just happened, the voice says, "HELP THE ORPHANS! YOU HAVE NO FEAR!"

Initially, to be honest, I was offended. I knew I come from foster care. I've talked about it. I've supported non-profits that serve the foster care industry. I felt I was already doing something.

I then got this sinking feeling I was barely putting a drop in the bucket to what was possible.

Thinking I'm just tired and not really thinking straight, I head to bed. This dream starts to bring my decision into focus. I look in front of me to a mountain on fire. People are running down the mountain, screaming with clothes torn, blood everywhere, and from what I can see, it has descended into complete chaos.

My instinct tells me to run up the mountain, for some reason. Go towards the chaos.

But the mountain is on fire.

Doesn't matter.

I start running, somehow getting this thinking that if I run fast enough, the fire can't burn me. Before long I'm at the top of this mountain and I see creatures attacking people. They're flying around unabated leaving destruction & bloodshed everywhere they go.

"YOU HAVE NO POWER HERE! LEAVE!"

Said with such conviction, somehow I knew they were powerless against my authority.

Then I woke up.

This flood of knowledge and wisdom comes, pieces of the puzzle start falling into place. The voice I was speaking to last night, the identity now known.

My wife is awakened by my excitement. I can't wait to share with her everything that had just happened. The voice, the message, help the orphans, no fear, the dream, the clarity!

As I'm sharing this, she's crying. Now I'm confused. Why are you crying? This is a joyous moment! I know what to do!

Then she starts to talk.

"Yesterday, when you were laying on the bed, wondering what you should do… while I was silent, I was actually praying for you. I was praying that God would reveal Himself to you and that He give you the answers you needed."

This was the day that changed my life forever.

I was now on a new path to find out what it meant to truly help the orphans, and to understand what it really meant to have no fear.

Initially, I looked at my skillset. What could already bring to the table that they needed? I was already a skilled consultant at systems & automation. I had a network of entrepreneurs I could tap into including industry leaders that we could potentially collaborate with.

I started there.

There was also the fact that I'm very analytical. Data is like oxygen to me. Started looking at the stats. The facts. The numbers. What was really going on?

Then I came across statistics that floored me:

- 2 out of 3 kids that age out of foster care end up dead, homeless, or in jail within just 1 year.

- 20% of kids that turn 18 are instantly homeless.

- 60% of sex trafficking victims come from foster care in America

We are failing these kids. Since I already understood the concept that change only comes from what we can relate to, I knew being homeless twice by the time I was 25 and suffering from similar experiences these kids have gone through, I could speak to them.

What inspired me to become an entrepreneur was seeing that Les Brown had created success in the avenue I was pursuing. He also came from foster care. He also had difficulties in school. So much of his life I could relate to. My first mentor told me to start listening to Les Brown and once I saw that there was someone like me that had created real world success, I now knew it was possible for me. Fear was thrown out the window.

Shortly after the conversation with God, I'm searching for a way to free up time to start dedicating to my "orphan" project. Still clueless as to what I will create or bring to the world.

In the business realm, my specialty is automating or delegating a process that gets a specific result.

How could I use that to help orphans? Is there something I create? Is there something I do? A month later into this endeavor and I'm still drawing a blank at what I am able to do.

My phone rings. It's a friend of mine from years ago when I spoke at an event in Chicago. Someone I've been serving for quite some time, and he felt the need to reciprocate. He had just joined a mastermind group of entrepreneurs and extended an invitation for me to join as his guest for one of their events. They were meeting a little over an hour from where I was at the time. I showed up and it happened to be Tai Lopez's home in Beverly Hills!

A conversation about mobile apps turns into an opportunity to solve the challenge I had in needing to create more time to build my passion project. Within a couple weeks of that invite, I'm collaborating with Tai Lopez where I'm teaching a course on mobile apps which helped completely automate my prospecting time so I could start building my "orphan" project. I knew that had to be the first sign I was on the right path.

A couple months later I get a call to do media for an entrepreneur event in Las Vegas. At this event, things clicked. A presenter had shared a concept on building a "Tom's Shoes" business model where you can create a product or service that can benefit more than 1 person each time it's sold... just like Tom's Shoes! Every time someone buys a pair of shoes from them, they donate a pair of shoes to someone in need!

Why couldn't every business do this? At that moment, I headed home early from the event as I had work to do. It was time to start building the "From Orphan To CEO" program!

I'd create a school for entrepreneurs where the teachers were active in the industries they teach. They would teach on the topics of mentorship, entrepreneurship, & faith. The 3 pillars that hold me up every day to go out and serve my way to success!

Mentorship: Find someone that has already been where you are trying to go. They have accomplished what you are looking to accomplish, and they are willing to teach you from the experience they have learned along the way.

Entrepreneurship: This is your vehicle to stop waiting for permission to build someone else's dream. It's time to build your own.

Faith: You are building something that will last generations. The life you have lived, the chaos you have overcome, will one day become someone else's survival guide.

Within a few months, I had developed a process to implement this strategy. The concept of teaching kids that are aging out of foster care how to start their own business. How to find a mentor, and to put faith as a foundation to their success.

I wanted to make sure what I built was a gift to the world. No cost to my students. No subscription. No credit card required. No matter your background or financial situation, you can learn from same people I'm a sponge for knowledge every time I can be in the same room to hear them speak. I knew what I created for the orphans would need to be free, but I also knew I needed a way to fund it. That's where the "Tom's Shoes" business model fit perfectly!

To fund my idea, I'd create a service in my business where I could use resources from every new client I brought in to bring even more resources to the students in my program!

I also knew that by giving it away for free, it would be very hard to get our students to show up, so we integrated a way to gamify the process, meaning to reward our users to show up and continue to show up!

In 2017, we launched an ERC-20 token called MannyBUX! These MannyBUX are used to collaborate with our members. They are worthless outside of our community so you can't use them at your local grocery store or to fill your gas tank, but you can use them in the MannyBUX Network to unlock opportunities with our members to find a mentor, start a business, or grow your existing business!

It all starts with education & collaboration. Our school rewards our students in MannyBUX to show up to school, attend classes, engage in class, & show up to LIVE events!

The LIVE events are where we capture the education & introduce the community to the collaboration!

From the founder of the Make-A-Wish Foundation, Frank Shankwitz, to the "World's Most Dangerous Man" Ken Shamrock, to the man who inspired me to start my entrepreneur journey, the world's #1 motivational speaker, Les Brown, I've built powerful relationships to get hundreds of superstars to share their message of hope to our students, foster kids, & day 1 entrepreneurs.

As I write this, we have hundreds of hours of interviews our students can get rewarded in MannyBUX to watch, my award-winning school is now active in over 80 countries, over 30,000 global users, and has been translated to over 25 languages so far!

To think… we are just getting started!

The vision I have is to one day see the foster care system produce adults that by the time they age out of foster care, we are not seeing 2 out of 3 kids dead, homeless, or in jail within a year, but rather 2 out of 3 of these kids have a mentor, understand entrepreneurship, and own their own business!

We all have a God-given purpose. Sometimes you find it facing a crossroads in life, looking to find a solution to problem that is just a miniscule part of your journey, like me.

That same year where I only checked off 2 of the 5 accomplishments, I promised my wife we would experience by the time I'm 30? I can proudly say we checked off the other 3 that same year:

3. We will create a successful business: *I'm now a paid consultant to over 1000 brands worldwide.*

4. We will live in Lake Elsinore: *I'm writing this story from my home in Lake Elsinore. We moved in 2017.*

5. Our home will be 2 stories: *I'm writing this from my room, on the 2nd story.*

You have a genius within you. Have you discovered it yet? Are you nurturing it? Are you feeding it?

Become a sponge for knowledge. Find that next mentor in life. If you can't find a mentor, start with Jesus. Once I looked at Jesus as a relationship & not a religion, the world changed all around me. It almost becomes like an extra sense to what happens to you.

In my experience, everything happens for a reason. If it is meant for me, I will receive it. If it is not meant for me, no matter how hard I try, it never seems to come to pass.

I have taken that philosophy to almost every interaction I now have. So many times in life I've seen a situation or an opportunity that I thought was mine, only to find out God was taking me in a new direction, a new path, even better than I could have ever imagined.

This is why I always say I am too blessed to be stressed! I have faith that what I am supposed to do will become clearer and clearer the more I desire to walk in that direction. That He will always provide for what I need. Not always for what I want, but always for what I need.

I'll never say it will be easy, but just know if you put your faith in Him, it will always be worth it.

To contact Manny:

www.MANNYfestation.com

Ken Steven

Ken Steven is an entrepreneur, consultant, coach, author, speaker, and former marketing and advertising executive for Fortune 500 companies.

He envisions a world where everyone eagerly embraces their work, feeling passionate and purpose-driven by what they do. It is his passion and his life's purpose to help at least one million people get unstuck from a job they don't enjoy and discover one that fuels their passion and inspires their purpose.

Ken spent most of his career working in jobs he disliked, chasing opportunities for bigger paychecks to fund a better lifestyle he ultimately became too miserable to enjoy. He desperately wanted to find a job he could feel passionate about, but he had no clue what his passion was.

Frustrated that conventional passion discovery methods were fruitless for him, Ken spent 16 years researching, developing, and testing a better way. The result was his invention of the DreamJob Type Indicator (DJTI)™. It's the only career assessment specifically designed to identify the type of work you'll naturally feel passionate about doing and the specific job titles to pursue to have joy, meaning, and fulfillment from your work.

Ken is the author of DREAM JOB DISCOVERY – How to Find a Job That Fuels Your Passion and Inspires Your Purpose (Even If You Don't Know Your Passion or Purpose).

A Problem Too Big to Ignore

By Ken Steven

One day when I was 34 years old, my alarm clock went off at 6 a.m. like always. Normally, I'd be looking forward to sipping on a freshly brewed coffee while I planned my day. But on this particular morning nothing felt normal. There was a sick feeling in the pit of my stomach. I'd been awake, tossing and turning most of the night with a million thoughts racing through my mind. I was having a tough time dragging my butt out of bed. I didn't want to get up, not if it meant that I had to go to work.

Looking at my life at that time, you'd think I had *"cracked the Rich Code"* and was living my dream. I was a vice president in a global corporation, earning a generous salary with excellent benefits, including a company car and an expense account for wining and dining clients in the city's finest restaurants. Best of all, I had a fantastic boss who was mentoring me to take over his position. Even my team was ideal. They were talented, friendly, and always ready to give 100 percent without complaint.

"Ugh," I thought. If this situation was so ideal, why was I pulling the covers over my head in a state of dread? Why did I want to hit the snooze button and escape reality for another ten minutes? Why wasn't I happy? *It didn't make sense.*

According to a study of workers in 155 countries published by Gallup in 2017, job dissatisfaction like I experienced is rampant. Only 15 percent of full-time employees worldwide are *"engaged"* in their jobs.

What does engaged mean? Gallup defined engaged employees as being highly involved in and enthusiastic about their work and their workplace. These are the people who are driving performance and innovation for their employers. I call this group the *"Passionate and Purpose-Driven."*

Sadly, the remaining 85 percent of workers have no such love for the work they do. Of this group, 67 percent are *"not engaged,"* meaning they are psychologically unattached to their work and their company. You know the type. These people are the clock-watchers. Like prisoners, they are doing their time instead of investing energy or passion into their work. The remaining 18 percent of employees are *"actively disengaged"* at work. These people are like rotten apples. They are so unhappy that they make the work environment toxic with their displeasure and even undermine the advances that their engaged coworkers strive to achieve.

The United States and Canada reported the highest level of engaged employees at 31 percent, with 52 percent not engaged and 17 percent actively disengaged. So, in the best-case scenario, the bottom line is that *seven out of every ten* workers in North America feel no joy in their job.

That's a problem too big to ignore.

You don't need to read a study to know this is true. You probably know people who are unhappy at work. You might have family members who fit this description. And perhaps you too may be struggling in a job you don't like, let alone love.

So, what is it about *your* job that *you* don't enjoy?

If you've ever played the murder mystery game, Clue, you know that players take on the role of one of six characters: seductive Miss Scarlett; smooth-talking Mr. Green; proud, adventurous Colonel Mustard; brilliant, scatterbrained Professor Plum; proper, extravagant Mrs. Peacock; or domestic, persnickety Mrs. White. The game's backstory holds that all the characters were inside a mansion when a murder took place. The object of the game is to gather clues to determine which of these characters committed the murder, in which room, and with which weapon. It's always one of them.

Now, imagine you're invited to play a slightly modified version called *"Clues to Why I Hate My Job."* There are six characters in this game too, and the point is to figure out which one is unhappy at work for the same reason you are. Without further ado, meet:

1. ***Miss Bored.*** Miss Bored's workday is a monotonous routine. She has many valuable skills and a lot of talent and ambition, but her current job role lacks opportunities for her to use all her gifts. She craves a job that challenges her and offers more opportunities to learn new things. She feels she's stagnating with no chance for promotion or pay increases. Of all the reasons people hate their jobs, isn't boredom a pretty good one?

2. ***Mr. Invisible.*** Poor Mr. Invisible. He's capable, he works hard, but it's as if his boss and coworkers don't even know he's there. His daily tasks are necessary but easy to be taken for granted. Though he meets his deadlines with competent work, his accomplishments go unnoticed. And what's worse is that he longs to do something that makes a positive impact, but his job doesn't make a difference. Who could blame him for being unhappy at work?

3. ***Colonel Cause.*** Colonel Cause and his employer do not share the same values. He cares deeply about sustainability and the environment. And yet, the company he works for engages in activities that destroy our environment. It clear-cuts forests and pollutes rivers in their manufacturing process. He now realizes that there's no way he can continue to work for them and feel good about it.

4. ***Professor Picked-On.*** Professor Picked-On has a boss who steals his ideas and takes all the credit. Beyond being a bully, his boss is overly demanding, and Professor Picked-On is his favorite target. As he leaves the office at night, he dumps a new project on Professor Picked-On with instructions to finish it by morning. He expects him to work all night if that's what it takes.

5. ***Mrs. Coworker.*** The unfortunate Mrs. Coworker is a good apple in a basket of bad apples. She enjoys working for her boss and her company. But the people in the surrounding cubicles either don't like her or feel threatened by her ability. They are not only unsupportive and uncooperative;

sometimes, they undermine her progress and success. These toxic teammates make her life miserable.

6. ***Mrs. Faraway.*** Mrs. Faraway lives one county over and getting to work each day is becoming a major hassle. Her commute is 90 minutes each way on a highway with bumper-to-bumper gridlock. She's spending a small fortune filling up her gas tank, not to mention the wear and tear on her car. If only she could find a job closer to home, or even better, one that she could do from home.

So, which one of these characters do *you* most identify with right now? What's *your* reason for disliking your job? Is it boredom, feeling invisible, having values that clash with those of the company, a bad boss, toxic coworkers, or too much hassle getting to work?

You may think that the best way to escape your current situation is to find a new job—making a fresh start at a new company with a new boss and coworkers. Surely, that would solve your problem of unhappiness at work, right? But what if it doesn't? What if you keep hopping from job to job and still can't find happiness?

That's what happened to me. I kept changing jobs to escape situations of boredom, a terrible boss, and a huge hassle getting to work every day. Then I started working for a company that I really liked, with a boss who was the greatest guy on the planet, and coworkers who were all amazing team players. This is the job I told you about earlier—the one I hated so much I didn't want to go to work. *It made no sense to me.*

After several sleepless nights trying to figure this out, I finally realized the *mistake* I'd been making. And maybe this is a mistake that *you've* been making too. And you might never have thought that this could be a mistake.

If you're anything like me back then, the *real reason* you hate your job right now may have nothing to do with being bored, feeling invisible, having values that clash with the company, a bad boss, toxic coworkers, or too much hassle getting to work. It may be because the *skills* upon which you have built your entire career success so far have been systematically sabotaging your chances of ever being happy at work.

In a nutshell: The stuff you're good at doing could be the stuff that's causing you grief right now.

Beware of the Sabotaging Skill Set

Envision someone who graduated college and landed her first job at a good company. Let's call her *Ms. Capable.* She's like the seventh character in our modified game of Clue that you never knew existed.

Ms. Capable's job pays decently. The benefits are solid. Her employer likes her and provides her with training and opportunities to grow. She works hard and gets good at what she does. Over time, she develops solid *skills.* Her boss notices what she's good at doing and promotes her into a new job role where she can make greater use of those skills.

In her new job role, she becomes responsible for training others in acquiring and developing those skills. And she adds a new layer of complementary skills to her repertoire.

This is great, right? Ms. Capable is a model of corporate success. What a happy story!

Not so fast. One day, Ms. Capable wakes up and feels bummed out, empty, and sad. *She doesn't understand why.* She should feel grateful, right? More time passes, and anxiety sets in. She's miserable, even though she earns good money and has a lot of responsibility. It seems as if her entire life lacks joy.

Ms. Capable decides to make a fresh start and begins looking for a new job. She enters the job market and leverages the *skills* and experience she gained at her first company. She lands a new job at a new company with a new boss and new coworkers. She even lands a higher salary.

Now she's set, right?

Not exactly. After six months, the novelty of her new job wears off, and the same old feelings return. The emptiness, the sadness, the anxiety. All of it.

A year goes by, but nothing changes. Ms. Capable decides it's time to shake things up again. Because she's so capable, she leverages the *skills* she's good at doing to land a new job somewhere else. All those skills go on her resume, along with all the accomplishments she made using those skills. And the new company that hires her is so delighted to acquire that skill set that they pay her more than she was making before.

Wow, more money, more happiness, right?

It's not hard to imagine what happens next. The novelty of this new job wears off as quickly as the last one. Ms. Capable notices that the feelings of anxiety and misery she felt in her previous job are growing even stronger. She has become trapped in a never-ending sequence of job-hopping, like running on a hamster wheel.

If *you're* like Ms. Capable and feel stuck in a never-ending job dissatisfaction sequence, it's likely because the *skills* you've continued to leverage to advance in your career are ones that you have zero passion for doing.

In my case, one of the skills I excelled at in my first job as a marketing assistant was analyzing reams of data to forecast sales for my product line. It was one of the skills I leveraged to land myself a job as a marketing manager at another company. I also had to analyze research results about consumer attitudes and usage of all the brands in my category for that job. So, in both of those job roles, I was good at doing activities that fit the DreamJob Type™ of *"Analyzing or Calculating."* (This is a teaser—you can learn all about the 21 different DreamJob Types in my book *Dream Job Discovery.*)

My DreamJob Type (job passion type) is *"Improving or Perfecting."* This is the only type of work that I can feel deeply passionate about doing. So, everything I had been learning to do skillfully up to this point in my career had nothing to do with my job passion type.

Then I got good at creating Gantt chart critical paths to schedule the various tasks required to develop new products. That kind of work fits well with the DreamJob Type of *"Organizing or Coordinating."* Again, I was developing skills in areas that had nothing to do with my job passion type.

After being promoted into more senior roles, I had staff to manage. I became responsible for their professional development, and it was something I did well. But that's a skill set that fits within the DreamJob Type of *"Teaching or Training."* It, therefore, was not an activity that made me happy.

Can you see how easy it is to move from job to job, acquiring new *skills* that have nothing to do with your job passion type?

So, if *you've* been job-hopping and you still aren't happy, it may have nothing to do with having a bad boss, toxic coworkers, or a conflict with corporate culture. It could be that the strengths and *skills* you've been developing and leveraging to get ahead in your career are the things you have zero passion for doing.

I'm going to give you a quick and simple exercise to help you determine if this is what's happening to you:

Step #1—Grab a piece of paper and write down all the tasks you're *good* at doing in your current job. (See the list of *Tasks You Might be Good at Doing* below for thought starters.)

Step #2—Review your list and circle only those things that you really *enjoy* doing.

If you don't circle many things on that list, it's a sure sign that you're not happy at work because *you* have no passion for the work you do. And if *you* have no passion for something, it stands to reason that *you* won't be feeling enjoyment. Without enjoyment, how can *you* expect to feel happiness? And, without happiness, there can be no *"dream job."*

Tasks You Might be Good at Doing

Acting, Singing, or Dancing

Appraising Things

Assembling Things

Assessing Quality

Bookkeeping

Cardio or Strength Training

Caregiving

Carpentry

Cataloguing Things

Cleaning

Conducting Surveys

Cooking or Baking

Creative Writing

Customer Service

Data Analysis

Designing Things

Diagnosing Things

Driving a Vehicle

Drywalling

Farming or Ranching

Forecasting or Estimating

Interior Decorating

Interviewing or Recruiting

Investing or Financing

Masonry

Networking

Operating Heavy Equipment

Operating Machinery

Organizing Things

Painting or Drawing

Painting or Wallpapering

Persuading or Negotiating

Planning Events or Travel

Playing a Musical Instrument

Playing a Sport

Plotting Strategy

Plumbing

Proofreading or Copy Editing

Public Speaking

Purchasing Supplies

Repairing Things

Resolving Disputes or Grievances

Sculpting or Carving

Sewing or Tailoring

Socializing or Hospitality

Software Development

Solving Problems

Teaching or Training

Testing or Experimenting

Welding

Wiring

Writing Emails, Minutes, or Reports

Yoga or Meditation

Why Job Passion Matters So Much

After countless hours of research and plenty of real-life experience, I believe that if you want lasting happiness in your life, *the single most important thing is to find a job you love to do.*

I know that may sound like a bold claim but think about it for a minute. The only time we have the chance to enjoy our lives is the time that we're awake. For most of us, that's probably between sixteen and eighteen hours a day. And on average, we spend at least eight or nine of those hours each day doing our job. Many of us also put in extra hours on weekends and during our vacation time. So, it's not an exaggeration to say that we'll all be spending at least *half of our lives at work.*

If you aren't doing work that you love, that means you're missing out on 50 percent of your opportunities to be happy!

And, if you aren't happy at work, it can create conditions that compound your grief. When employees aren't happy, they aren't motivated to perform at their best, and their productivity might be only half as good as it could be. So, they might get passed over for job promotions and pay increases. Even worse, that lack of performance and productivity might lead to them losing their job. You might even know some people who have experienced this misfortune. *You* might be one of them.

Any of those situations can create an incredible amount of stress. Numerous studies, which you can easily find in a Google search, conclude that workplace stress makes us sick. It contributes to health problems like high blood pressure, heart disease, diabetes, depression, burnout, and substance abuse. If *you* aren't healthy, it's tough to be happy, right?

Sooner or later, all that unhappiness will spill over into your home life. It creates tension between you and your spouse or your partner. Suddenly, you find yourself at the dinner table, snapping at the smallest of criticisms. It makes you less present with your children, or your dog, or your cat. You'll be way less fun to be around!

So, if you're not happy at work, you can see how your life might begin to spin out of control.

That's why finding a job you love is the single most important thing you can do.

And that's why I've made it my mission to help a million people achieve this outcome.

***

To Contact Ken:

Discover more about Ken Steven and his innovative programs to make the world a happier place for everyone to work.

Websites:

https://www.dreamjobdiscovery.com/

https://www.kensteven.com/

LinkedIn:

https://www.linkedin.com/in/kennethsteven/

Facebook:

https://www.facebook.com/coachkensteven

Rich Code Club:

https://www.richcode.club/home

Susan Welton

Susan Welton is an internationally bestselling author, speaker, healer and intuitive who lives in Madison Wisconsin with her husband Kurtis and their extended family. Susan was adopted at the age of seven from South Korea and recently reconnected with her biological family. She is proud to be an American and is grateful everyday she lives in the best country in the world. Susan has been an entrepreneur for almost 20 years and has owned numerous businesses and assets including real estate. She went to the University of Wisconsin- Madison and received a Bachelor of Science. She has a passion for helping people heal from trauma and loves inspiring others to manifest their dreams!

From Enslavement to Freedom:

A story from spinning to co-creating

By Susan Welton

My hope is to inspire entrepreneurs to face their own unhealed early childhood traumas. If left unresolved they can have the power to enslave you. In this chapter I will share action steps, to get to the other side of healing traumas, which will allow you to co-create and manifest the life of your dreams. One of my favorite quotes from Carl Jung is "Until the unconscious is conscious, it will direct your life and you will call it fate." I feel empowered to share my repressed early childhood trauma and experiences so that individuals with unresolved traumas can relate and learn from my experiences and can navigate their entrepreneurial lives better.

Below please find an excerpt from a book I had published in December 2021.

"SLAM! The door crashed in my face again as I heard her scream my name. "Sung Eun, get out!!" was still ringing in my ears. Alone in the dark, trembling and shaking with my heart racing, I faced the dirt road again. At least tonight it wasn't snowing. Was it true what my aunt told me, that nobody loves me? That nobody wants me?

As I clung to the coins in my hands, I started to walk down that familiar dusty road in South Korea. The rocks cut into my bare feet. The pain of the beating from my aunt joined with the pain in my feet. It helped mask the pain I felt from my uncle's abuse; abuse an innocent little 5-year-old girl couldn't begin to fully understand.

This walk started like the countless other times I'd been sent out to get supplies for the baby. I didn't know it at the time, but this night was going to be different and would forever change the future trajectory of my life.

As I stumbled down the road, chaotic thoughts swirled through my mind: *"What did I do wrong to be hated so much? Why was I such a bad person? Why did I have to suffer so much emotional, physical, and mental pain every day?"* It wasn't my fault my parents died when I was a baby or that I was sent to my aunt and uncle to be taken care of. My hopeful, innocent heart didn't know any better than to keep trying to prove my worth and play my part.

I started to panic as I returned to the house with the supplies. Was I going to be met with more hate, rage, and abuse? Was I going to be safe and left alone, or was I going to get thrown out again? I never knew. Why was caring for me such a terrible obligation for my aunt and uncle? Why did they despise me so much? I was their slave, and I resented the baby, their baby. The baby they treated like gold while they treated me like dirt. No child should have to go through this much abuse.

I was alone in the dark and in the depths of despair and hopelessness. The pain from the physical and emotional abuse made me want to cry. Agony enveloped my entire being, choking tears from my eyes one cold drop at a time.

With nighttime encroaching, and a lonely silence, I lingered to avoid returning home. That's when I felt this incredibly comforting bright Light surrounding me like a soft blanket. It hugged me and brought me out of the darkness. I wanted to stay with this nurturing Light forever. Suddenly, I felt it communicating with me, the message was, "Little one, you are going to be okay." I felt the Light and knew for a brief moment what love was—such comfort and peace in my heart. It didn't last as long as I would've liked, but it left me with hope for my future. It was a defining moment in my early life that forever changed me.

(Susan Welton. Ignite the Hunger in You. Dec. 2021)

I repressed these traumas most of my adult life. Despite some success in the business world, I did not face my unresolved traumas from childhood, nor did I face the fears that controlled me until my early 40s. I want to share how some of my early childhood experiences created more trauma in my professional life. I was a striver or what I call a plate spinner. Imagine holding a series of rods; you set one plate spinning, then let it go to pursue the next plate until about 10 plates are continuously spinning on each rod. I would keep spinning and spinning until I was physically exhausted and miserable and that's usually when they all crashed! I didn't realize the obligations I was responsible for until I realized I put more time, effort, and energy into making others successful. It suddenly dawned on me how much I was carrying the other partners.

In 2008, I was very fortunate to have a business mentor (Jeffery Combs) who called me out on my stuff. I was frantically spinning plates during this time (most of them for other people), all while wearing a smiling mask. My mentor pulled me aside at one of our real estate events and we had one of the most important conversations of my life. He told me, "You are an incredible woman, Susan. But are you happy? Why are you carrying these low energy partners, and frankly, the entire team?" During this time in my life, I was generating more income than the others, which often caused me to feel guilty, and so I tried to do for them what they failed to do for themselves. I had a rescuing and fixing nature to my personality; so, instead of focusing on myself, I attempted to help others find success regardless of whether they earned it or not. My business mentor was right! I was miserable, filled with guilt and a sense of obligation to help others on my team achieve success. So much so I often enabled them. I felt unworthy of the type of money I was making. It made no difference that I worked harder or longer hours than everyone else. If I was going to succeed, I wanted everyone else to succeed as well. I wanted to share the wealth as sharing had always come naturally to me.

The wound of abandonment I received as a young child created unequal partnerships in my early business life. Partnering with men, and doing way more than they did, was fueled by my lack of self-worth as a woman. This stemmed from being sent out of a culture where my biological family kept my two older brothers and gave me away for adoption. How could I not translate this to mean that I was not valued? So, feeling inferior as a woman, I was hell-bent on proving my worth to the world; therefore, willing to overcompensate both financially and productively. It was not until I recognized my pattern of fixing and rescuing others that I was able to acknowledge how exhausted I was. My partners never appreciated what I did for them, and I had built up a ton of resentment during these years. I had become an unhealthy helper, forcing my help on the world—giving help when no one asked, choosing less than quality partners, and giving more energy/effort than everyone around me. I was literally "throwing pearls before swine." I now know this deep abandonment wound attracted anyone instead of no one, so I was not alone. This was a tough lesson because I did this unconsciously.

It was around 2007 when I first learned about *The Secret* and the Law of Attraction. I will go into this later, but this revelation left me feeling invincible. I was able to transition from plate spinning, wearing a mask, repressing and exhausting myself every single day, to healing, letting go and now living out my dreams. It's been quite the ride! We will dig into this more in a bit.

I was adopted at the age of seven from South Korea into a white family with 4 older brothers in Madison, Wisconsin. Very early on, my adopted father taught me I could do anything a man could do! I absolutely believed this and made it a reality. Unbeknownst to me, I had a lot of anger energy from my unresolved past. I pushed forward into 80-hour work weeks right after college. My father taught us an extreme work ethic from early on in my life and so this felt natural to me. I never realized that 80-hour work weeks were unusual and when I first became an entrepreneur, I worked until I was physically exhausted. I often slept only 4 hours a night, from 2 AM to 6 AM, and easily put in 18-hour days. I was a workaholic, which became a huge part of my independent striver lifestyle. I was all about working to ensure my past was buried; I never slowed down enough to let it come up. I made sure I was physically exhausted and flew out of bed when the alarm went off each morning.

I was also in toxic relationships that I attempted to rescue in my free time. My personal relationships tore me down regularly. I never even thought to stand up for myself. My pattern was always to rescue someone from their depression and negativity. It gave me a great sense of purpose to help people; I just didn't realize I was enabling those around me in an adverse way.

Trust issues have followed me my entire life. I had a protective wall around my heart and no idea how to let people in. I wore a mask of positivity everywhere. Most people had no idea about my past because I always told them my life started once I was adopted at the age of 7 and brought to America. I am truly grateful for my life of opportunities. I had already been through hell in my early childhood, so I knew how good I had it. All I wanted to do was to move forward and never look back.

When I pushed and was forcing things to happen, wearing many masks of perfection, feelings of needing to prove, as well as feelings of unworthiness and shame showed up regularly in my life. There were many things I needed to face. I had some amazing moments and many phenomenal months of being on stage selling real estate education and the American Dream—telling people that real estate was an incredible vehicle to build long-term wealth. In February 2007, I had a month of over $72,000.00 just from the sale of real estate education (not including rental income, flip income or any other). I was convinced the money was going to flow endlessly as long as I spun the plates. I converted duplexes to create more affordable housing in the area. I acted as the bank on numerous real estate deals and ended up taking back a couple of properties—which was not my intention. I even went as far as buying a teeth-whitening business that included a lease at the mall. Although I made great income during these early years as an entrepreneur, I had many lessons to learn. It is not how much you make but how much you keep that is the true sign of wealth and prosperity.

It was only a few years later that I got this crazy notion: if I could make over $72,000.00 in one month, then that should be my standard for every month. So, I went to a different real estate market (about 5 1/2 hours' drive away) and bought properties at a big discount. I thought I could buy 100 of these houses, fix them up, and rent them out. Then, after paying off the notes on the mortgages, I would have gobs of cash flow. To make a very long story short, I dealt with several dozen calls from unethical contractors that did not have integrity. My dream of owning cash flow from a project of this magnitude quickly morphed into needing to liquidate everything. I had to face the reality that without a trusted team, I had nothing more than a bunch of failures and more trauma and red ink as a business owner. I'm sharing this experience so that entrepreneurs really understand that one must face all the fears and traumas of their past in order to find success in the future. There are patterns to be broken and one must understand the root cause of why we do what we do.

I finally had to look in the mirror and see who the constant variable was in every experience. Of course, it was me. This was a painful reality I had to face. I had co-created my life and I knew it! I only had myself to blame. Even though I lent money thinking I would be repaid, I trusted individuals that were unhealthy and untrustworthy. I had no boundaries. I didn't even know what a boundary was at that point in my life. I was so addicted to helping others that I failed to help myself. My cup was constantly empty and yet I still had the addiction to want to help others. This was my mode of operation even before I entered the business world. I knew deep down I had a lot of traumas, but I never had the courage to face them. I lived by the Zig Ziglar model: "If you help enough others get what they want, you will get what you want."

Breakdowns in the business world were costly—over $1.7 million worth of valuable insights, lessons, and experiences all earned by going through the school of hard knocks. Am I grateful? Yes! In a short few years, I gained clarity about my unhealthy, unhelpful behavior patterns; I thought I was helping but I was actually enabling and entitling others. There is a huge difference. I attracted toxic, jealous people who lacked self-awareness and often played victim. I drove hard, knowing hard work and studying personal development right out of college would help me become successful. I researched and studied how successful people think. Success leaves clues!

Thank God for this part of my life! It was my saving grace. Let me share some of my adult trauma so that you can better understand the reality I faced in my late 20s and 30s. I was a workaholic—striving, needing to prove, self-sabotaging, mistrusting, without boundaries, stuck in toxic relationships, experiencing financial abuses and breakdowns, lacking worthiness, doing more for others than myself, needing control, feeling miserable, without faith, unable to surrender, repressing to the point of exhaustion, subconsciously pushing into flight-or-fight and chaos energy, constantly spinning plates, and forcing things to happen by constantly staying busy. Can you relate?

As I mentioned earlier in college, I studied successful people like Tony Robbins. I'd read Napoleon Hill's *The Law of Success* and researched the Mastermind concept for decades. I knew about the Law of Attraction but around 2007, I had the opportunity to see it in action. I saw how the Law of Attraction works—but not in a good way, meaning I was subconsciously attracting what I didn't want and allowed my unresolved trauma to recreate more trauma. It was shortly after liquidating my various properties and investments that I realized I had an opportunity to co-create the life I wanted, rather than the life my childhood traumas were attracting.

I went through a period of being single for several years, focusing and visualizing a future of everything I wanted. I began writing in a journal all the qualities of the kind of people I wanted to actualize in my future. I was specific and very detailed as to what I wanted to surround myself with in my future. *The Law of Success* by Napoleon Hill taught me well. The Mastermind concept—the blending of harmonious positive energies—was very important to me. No negativity or playing victim allowed! I had learned through the school of hard knocks in both business and in my personal life. Journaling, co-creating, and visualizing my future and the life of my dreams were extremely important actions. This particular process was very easy for me because I had lived through everything I did not want.

Today, I am grateful and thankful for living my wildest dreams. Every entrepreneur knows success and wealth is not an easy path, nor for the faint of heart. My life and personal experiences are a testimony of what is possible! For those that have had a great deal of early childhood trauma it is imperative to face your biggest fears and heal your trauma. There are patterns to be broken. By facing your trauma, and healing, a person can vividly embrace their most ambitious dreams! I am now living out my dreams. I have trusted teams of people, going in every direction, that are appreciative of what I bring to the table. I'm very fortunate to have overcome my traumatic experiences so I can speak about them in the hopes they will help others embrace their healing process.

I no longer have a rescuing mentality when it comes to success. It is a journey and not a destination; those that want to attain success have a lot to learn on that path. I am the happiest I have ever been in my life. All the years of striving to make things happen, needing to constantly prove my worth, caused me to sacrifice a family of my own. But God has provided what is most important and that is an incredibly godly family. My husband, who lost his first wife in 2011 to cancer, was brought into my life by God's grace. I have his 5 adult children as friends and 5 wonderful grandchildren (so far) in our lives—along with 12 brothers and sisters-in-law and their children (over 25 of them). I have received the close family I was always seeking, and I am thankful. I also have reconnected with my biological family from South Korea and have a lot of them yet to meet. I am blessed beyond measure, and I can say I had faith in knowing my future was bright. I knew I could co-create the life of my dreams if I could get past the unresolved traumas. Now, I get to help others face their traumas and embrace healing. The best part is, I'm living my passion to inspire others to manifest their dreams… just like I have!

How can I best support you on your journey toward healing? It would be my privilege to connect with you.***

To contact Susan:

Susan Welton

Internationally Bestselling Author, Speaker, Healer, Intuitive, and Empath

Phone: 608 443 6341

www.susanwelton.com

susanw@buildtosuit.com

Lou Vickery

My life has been an incredible journey. I have had four distinctively different careers. I have been a professional baseball player, a stockbroker, a sales trainer/motivational speaker, and a radio and TV talk show host. My avocation over these years has been authoring sixteen books on a variety of topics. The movie rights to my only novel, A Touch of Gray, have been secured.

Pro baseball and/or speaking engagements have taken me to every state in the union. I have spoken in every city with over 150,000 in population. I have seen all the great sights in this country, from coast-to-coast. Hundreds of thousands of people have participated in my seminars and development sessions. I have rubbed shoulders with highly successful people from all walks of life—from athletes to businessmen to world leaders. On my TV show, UPTALKTV.com, I hosted guests from a Pulitzer Prize winner to a clown. My legacy: sixty-three years in the workplace and still going strong!!

I have been blessed by so much great exposure to those who found the secret to living life to the fullest. These individuals created a higher capacity for improvement…expanded their intellectual curiosity…enlarged their creative imagination…and rearranged their lives to grow beyond what they were before. It's their stories I want to share with audiences everywhere.

Thrive in Chaos

Lou Vickery

A prominent question asked: "Lou, what is the biggest single challenge an individual faces today?" There are many answers, with each containing the same base word—chaos. My small-town bank even titled a position as *Chaos Coordinator*. How applicable for this modern age!

The emotional upheaval chaos can bring about is a mixture of stress, pressure, and anxiety. To get a clearer picture, toss in the *dis*—as in distress, disarray, disorganization, along with disruption. The turbulent nature of today's society has been an outgrowth of unprecedented demands to compete and succeed. An increase in chaos is the norm the higher the expected advancement.

When amid chaos, differences may occur relative to the circumstances. A grand experiment illustrates differences "under fire" when the heat is on and action is required. Take small amounts of meat, sand, clay, and wax, along with a stick of wood. Throw them into a fire. What happens? The meat fries... the sand dries up... the clay hardens... the wax melts... while the wood burns. Each item subjected to the same external prompt—the fire—reacts differently.

Under chaotic circumstances, human beings resemble the articles in the fire; they react in distinctive ways. It rests on an individual's true make-up.

REAL-LIFE CIRCUMSTANCES

The one constant in life is its unpredictability. To enhance life's journey, a daily mindset should explore possibilities that might arise amid real-life circumstances. That mindset allows accessibility to more deliberately examine the opportunities presented within chaos.

Each person receives life on different terms. Even life itself on occasion begins in chaos. A prime example is my wonderful mother,

Anna Ruth Vickery. Mother has celebrated ninety-eight (98) birthdays. When the weather is nice, you might find her working in her garden. A blessing indeed to be that fortunate.

Mother was the sixteenth child born to William and Emma Wise. That's right, number 16! All single births. They estimated she was born around three months premature, weighing less than two pounds. This was in 1923 long before incubators or top-notch neonatal care. The doctor told my grandparents their daughter probably would not survive.

Stunned by this news, my grandfather was determined to keep his daughters alive. Poppa William created an incubator from a big-mouth gallon jar. He stuffed cotton in the bottom, placed his newborn daughter in the jar, then put a kerosene lantern for heat next to the jar. Daily he refreshed the cotton. With Poppa's help, Granny Emma fed their baby girl with an eyedropper. After many chaotic instances with months of extreme care, Mother survived to become a healthy, successful woman.

On the doctor's advice, my grandfather could have given up, but he didn't. My mother survived against insurmountable odds of complete disarray and uncertainty.

FEAR-BASED CHAOS

One of the more pronounced factors of chaos is stress, a by-product of fear. When fear is absent, stress becomes virtually nonexistent. It is human nature to become uptight over finances, careers, health, relationships, in addition to a ton of smaller, less significant areas of life. The greatest chaotic challenges stem from many self-imposed fears. Instead of the fear itself being of greatest concern, the thoughts created by that fear takes center stage. Among those most prominent are the fears of failure, loss, rejection, poverty (lack), inferiority, control, loss of freedom, and inability to manage success.

For example, people willingly risk tackling an original design, but fear the consequences if they are unsuccessful. People adore admiration yet fear the next time may produce a change in the outcome. People may feel comfortable presenting a potentially effective idea. The fear is the possibility others might dislike the idea. When people say they fear the future, they fear what the future might hold. To embrace someone comes naturally but what if that embrace is not returned? That is the fear.

Fear often develops from illusory thoughts that come across as real. A unique description of fear is through the acronym F.E.A.R., "F.alse E.xperiences A.ppearing R.eal." The more "real" these fears become, the larger the role they play in life. Regardless of how, when, or why they appear, they seem real!

Research points out two natural fears: fear of loud noises and fear of falling. All other fears are learned. Thus, they can be unlearned. Anyone who aspires to reach a greater level of satisfaction must strive to master the chaos emanating from fear. Certain fear is ultimately a part of life, no way to avoid it. The goal would be to lessen it, so it has minimal control over those important decisions in life.

Fear-based chaos intensifies with anticipation of what lies ahead. Certain individuals simply cannot handle the weight created by chaotic fears. Chaos hampers their productivity and peace of mind. These individuals wrestle earnestly with fear. They either consider giving up, or have already given up, on their dreams and goals. What they leave behind is crucial to a better life.

The paths to success are many but there is only one path to failure— to surrender or give up. To quit is the easiest route to follow. It takes no talent to fall by the wayside, throw in the towel, or simply walk away.

Is fear causing chaos in your life? At a particular point, you have probably let fear in one form or another get a grip on a part of your life. Rarely does anyone reach the pinnacle of success without experiencing some form of fear that hinders chances for developing a more productive future.

Controlling fear-based chaos is a challenge. The first step in getting a handle on the fear is to be realistic and acknowledge its existence. Evaluate your experiences where fear rears its ugly head. Explore options that will help you better manage fear thus minimizing chaos. Most importantly, remain mindful that controlling fear requires action. Ralph Waldo Emerson said: "Do the things you are afraid to do, and the death of fear is certain."

CHAOS MANAGEMENT

What is your current effectiveness in managing chaos? Do you need a tune-up for dealing with stress, and its two siblings, anxiety and pressure? All three can become tangible negatives in life. That's where chaos management begins.

Stress can affect you in both positively and negatively. The majority of the defensive mechanisms used to manage chaos are unproductive. A hard worker will tend to labor harder at the same job. Blaming others for creating chaotic circumstances, leads to intensifying the blame of others. To sweep things under the rug so to speak, results in their denial with even greater force. Having a dependent nature, creates a tendency to lean even more heavily on others. As long as these defenses are employed, nothing constructive is learned about managing chaos. Continuing to use prevailing reactions without creating further helpful actions seldom results in an optimistic outcome.

Managing chaos solely comes from the inner self. Developing positive thoughts, beliefs, and strategies instinctively build chaos-related defenses. Thriving in chaos goes beyond any drawback by establishing a foothold on the constructive side of a challenge. Often, right in the middle of every chaotic position is a productive solution leading to a more enjoyable life.

A stressful climate can be an incentive to move toward the emergence of a better outcome. This requires a tough mental approach that puts accent on positivity arising from chaos. Such mentality views the negatives at the core of chaos as challenging and exciting, instead of overwhelming and daunting.

A few important lessons learned during my professional baseball days are adaptable to real-life chaotic matters. These include, but are not limited to:

- One play (task) is seldom more important than another play (task).
- One game (important event) is never more important than another game (important event).
- The first contest (challenge) of the season is just as important as the last (challenge).
- There are no pressure situations...only situations where an individual succumbs to pressure.

Translate these aforementioned important lessons into your daily affairs, the last one particularly. You need a demanding form of mental discipline when the chips are down, as well as when the rewards are high. Thoughts influence actions, whereas actions influence thoughts. This never-ending cycle clarifies that chaos brought on by the internal factors of stress, pressure, and anxiety is mental. Being mental is essentially 100% manageable.

PRESSURE TOLERANCE

Fear creates stress, while stress produces pressure. Crucial decision-making and life-changing measures yield times when people flinch or retreat. Why? Often at pivotal points in life, pressure is one of the most notable opiates known to humans that alters perception.

Think of how you react under stressful circumstances. Does your heart pound more than usual? Do your palms become sweaty? Does a big lump develop in your throat? Do you have doubts whether you can meet the stress head-on to create the desired outcome? Those who handle disorder with *pressure tolerance* are the ones who have the upper edge on elite life status.

Succumbing to pressure can bring out a person's best or worst qualities. Stress is not, after all, what happens but is the reaction to what's happening. Stress is a negative force when internalized. It produces distinct physiological adjustments in the body and mind. Blood vessels constrict, which reduces blood supply to the brain, influencing cognitive proficiency. Concentration is affected, limiting the extent to stay focused. The result is predictable: pressure has retarded the ability to work at peak performance.

There is also a brighter side to stress. The right level is essential to well-being. Managed correctly, stress carries awesome potential. It can be a highly productive force when its power is exerted outwardly. Stress used correctly can bring depth and meaning to daily activities.

When you find yourself under pressure, fixate on the powerful intensity that can be drawn from effective tolerance. Think of how a stressful state can be an incentive to provide potent motivation for performance at an optimal level. Stress assures the presence of vitality, zest, and a sense of challenge. Use it to your advantage.

CAPACITY TO CHANGE

Necessity has been called the mother of invention. It is also the mother of change. *Re-imaging. Redirecting. Reinventing. Retrofitting.* These modern terms refer to the capacity to modify and adapt the way matters are presently addressed. Every change doesn't lead to growth, but for growth to occur change is imminent.

Expansion begins by desiring the benefits of *re-imaging* more than the continuation of the status quo. This mentality explores unfamiliar territory and expands into the unknown. In the beginning, venturing outside the comfort zone may seem intimidating. However, once that first step is made, the next comes strikingly easier.

The root of *redirecting* and the catalyst to accept any newness is simplistic. Completing a mission in the same way expecting different results is a formula for failure. To experience diversity calls for varied procedures. It is important on occasion to complete matters you dislike to bring out points you like.

Reinventing goes beyond the adverse attitudes associated with repeating the same behavior expecting another result. It calls for delving into innovation. A modification may be slight, but often has a tremendous impact on the outcome.

The adventurous nature of *retrofitting* is recognition. Nothing can move from the present until attempting something new. To foster a career, even life itself, calls for possessing a *"but now"* attitude. My mother was given little hope at birth, "but now" she is on the threshold of celebrating her 99th birthday. These two simple words indicate difference in the future. "But now" carries with it a huge responsibility of constantly retrofitting.

The final phase in your capacity to change is the action phase. Is there nothing more to learn? Are all skills developed? Challenges no longer existent? Modern tactics and techniques at a standstill? The difference-makers in answering these questions are: *re-imaging, redirecting, reinventing,* and *retrofitting.* Make them a part of an innovative process in your world.

MENTAL FOCUS

Mental toughness holds the formula for managing the chaos created by stressful pressure. During my years as a baseball pitcher, comments recurred, such as, *"Stop thinking and just pitch." "Relax out there; you're thinking too much." "Concentrate more on the pitch."* Those statements center on one effort: maintaining focus.

The inherent ability to focus on execution—rather than the result of the execution—optimizes probabilities for superior results. This keeps mental focus *maintained* on the task, instead of being occasionally *attained.* A steady focus always exceeds a wavering one.

If you are asked to concentrate, what becomes the centerpiece of that concentration? Do thoughts of expectations expressed by others take precedence? Does concern of making a mistake or miscalculation override effective action? Is your focus on the end result instead of how to get quality results? Concentration outside the immediate project shifts the focus in the wrong direction.

It is important to stand firm in the present. Too much thought that swings to the past or looks ahead to the future weighs on performance. This leads to mental tiredness, which makes you increasingly prone to more mistakes and minimal success.

It's easy to get caught up in a day's busyness. Similar to a ping-pong ball in a windstorm, you may bounce from here to there. It is important to learn to disconnect from what's going on around you and connect to what is going on within you. Be sensitive to the importance of gaining a broader perspective on the challenge at hand, especially when presented in a state of urgency. By taking a wider view, you might uncover opportunities that otherwise could be overlooked or abandoned. Once that is achieved your commitment to stay focused is an invaluable skill.

"Wherever you are, be there!" Your ability to follow this advice could be the accurate measure in doing your best within the midst of a chaotic state of affairs. Discipline yourself to focus thoroughly on every undertaking, regardless of circumstances. When each situation is as important as the next, they all carry the same value.

FORGETTERY

In professional baseball, success often came to players who put a past play behind them and kept their attention on the present. This was true whether they executed the play or just royally messed it up! Either way it was done, over, kaput!

Those involved showed excitement or disappointment, depending on the results. They displayed an immediate favorable or unfavorable reaction and employed their best *forgettery*—putting the past in proper perspective to highlight ventures moving forward.

Memory is an important trait, but forgettery may be just as significant. At times, moving on becomes difficult. The secret of forging ahead is letting go. Employing forgettery allows complete focus on the next challenge. Learn by intention, let it rest, then get ready to tackle the next challenge. Stop thinking of what should or could happen if done differently. When thoughts center on an earlier performance, it will affect the next, then the next, and so on.

Applying forgettery helps to keep you on an even keel, neutralizing the propensity of emotional swings. A real value of a good forgettery is that it conserves mental energy. Reaction with powerful emotion to either good or adverse circumstances soon takes a toll on any mental approach.

Is the ability to move on past the chaotic nature of a big mistake or failure a challenge for you? It takes a conscious effort for *forgettery* to allow attachment to the next activity. By engaging forgettery, mistakes lessen as the level of productivity heightens. This will alter the future outcome of whatever is to be accomplished in a manner conducive to greater success.

In exercising *forgettery*, the door opens for adventure. Instead of being imprisoned by the past, you work around the theory that your strength lies in the present. You face challenges, especially those surrounded by chaos, with a staff in your hand instead of a crutch.

ACTION WITH COURAGE

The banner of courage shines on numerous facets of life. Nowhere is this clearer than when facing chaos. A mental picture confronting chaos courageously trains your mind to work at being fearless. Ultimate success in a chaotic position revolves around acting with courage following a well-designed mental plan.

To tap into your deepest resources rising above the norm takes courage. It creates an atmosphere conducive to intellectual, physical, and emotional growth. When facing life's chaotic moments with courage, they vanish as suddenly as they appear.

Courage is not all-encompassing. Carryover value may differ from one encounter to another. For courage to become a constant companion when confronted with chaotic confrontations, this requires tackling each one on its own merit. Consistency is a key element in facing with courage the varied challenges that need to be overcome to reach the pinnacle of success.

Living courageously transforms the whole complexion of chaotic situations. Action with courage creates the environment for higher achievement, greater happiness, plus an overall appreciation of your capabilities going forward.

Understand the value of *focus, forgettery*, and *courage* in making the most of chaotic conditions. They strengthen the resolve needed to overpower the challenging side of chaos. The more you employ these three great attributes, the sooner you put chaos in its proper place. This shifts the spotlight directly to a more meaningful and productive life. You will spend your days enjoying the greater reward of what can be.

To Contact Lou:

Socaplife.com

louvickerybooks.com

Teon Singletary

God-fearing, Military Veteran, multiple #1 Bestselling Author, Executive Director and serves on the President Advisory Council for the Maxwell Leadership Team, and a prodigy of Les Brown, Coach Teon Singletary brings magnetic energy, inspiring you to live the best life you can. CEO of two businesses: SP Serves LLC, which is a graphics and video designing base business and Book Publishing Company. And the second business is TS Leadership Empowerment, which specializes in Professional Teaching, Speaking, and Coaching others to become their best self.

Teon believes that you have the potential to be great and everyone have a story to tell. His passion is supporting driven leaders and speakers who desire personal, empowering coaching to gain clarity so they can lead with practical systems. Having served in the military capacity for 20+ years and leading thousands of people to excellence with precision, Teon's coaching ability has developed into a useful, compassionate, and no bs way of helping people get what they want.

He's known as "The Coach":

- Coaching Leaders to level up

- Coaching individuals to inspire their lives

- Coaching speakers to Spark audiences

- Coaching entrepreneurs for excellence

Teon's favorite saying is: "You don't know what you don't know, and in order to go up, you must grow up." The power of choice is yours.

Conquer Your Fears-Five Steps to Success

By Teon Singletary

Every morning, I wake up and say, "I am greatness made from greatness." Why, because today is a great day to be alive. Now, not every day is great. We all travel on this life journey. And on this journey call life, we will have some troubles and issues that will come our way. Some fear will enter into our lives. How many of us can say that we have some fears that are holding us back from reaching our greatness? Perhaps, that's you. However, I believe, you have the potential inside of you, to conquer your fears. In this chapter, I am going to provide you the five steps you can use to conquer your fears. Make sure you have a pen and paper to take notes. I'm about to share some things with you that will change your life for the best. Say out loud to yourself, "I am greatness made from greatness. And today is a great day to be alive." Before we go into the first step to conquer your fears and achieve success, I want to share with you a story.

Facing Fears

There I was, just arriving at a new high school in 9th grade. I was on lunch break from class. In the JROTC Parade field were some cadets with a rifle in their hands, spinning and throwing it up in the air, catching it and spinning it behind their backs.

I remember this moment vividly, and I made this statement, "I want to be part of that team." What they were doing was beautiful to me. They called themselves Drill Masters. And in order to join that drill team, you had to first join the JROTC Program. Now, you had a choice, to do PE or join JROTC. Yeah, that was an easy answer for me at the time. I went to JROTC.

First day in the program, we were in formation outside. It was a little chilly that particular morning. A man was at the doorway, and it felt like he was only mean mugging me. The cadet in charge of the formation guided us newbies in the building to our prospective classrooms. We recited a cadet creed and we sat down. Then, that same man with the mean mug came charging in the room and started talking to us that turn real quickly to yelling. I was like ok, maybe I'm in the wrong place. I don't remember signing up for the military. Fear immediately entered into my heart. I was ready to get out of there.

The class session went on and before the bell rung, he asked the question I was waiting for: "Who wants to join the Drill Team?" I immediately raised my hand and asked with a big smile, "is that the guys with the rifles". He looked back at me with an evil smile and said, "You are correct, you want to join." I shook my head yes, not knowing what I was getting myself into, because first practice was right after school that same day.

So there I was at practice and they gave me this rifle and I almost dropped it because it was so heavy. I looked at them, then at the rifle, back at them, back at the rifle, back at them again, and said, "you want me to spin this, are you crazy." They said with a grin on their faces, "Yes and Yes."

Ok, ok, ok, I really did not sign up for this.

For the next couple of weeks, they only taught us basic movements and exercises with the rifle. No spinning or throwing in the air at all. I was starting to get frustrated. I joined to spin the rifle. Not to march around with my arm and shoulder muscles hurting. I did not sign up for this. As soon as I started thinking this way, the very next week, they began to teach us basic rifle spinning and throwing movements. See, they were conditioning our bodies to be able to perform these difficult movements. That's preparation.

Now, I found myself practicing my craft during my lunch breaks, in the JROTC parade field. Trying to become the best Drill Master. Guess what, I did and I still am. That focus and determination provided me the courage to join the military when I was a junior in high school in 2004. Now, I am an Officer in the Army National

Guard as we speak, and I perform rifle drill shows at different events from time to time.

The moral of the story is this, sometimes we not going to completely understand what we sign up for. However, if we stick with our decisions, greatness is waiting for us on the other side. The goal is to not give up on what you want to achieve. You must persevere to the end. Persistence produces results.

Awareness

The first step to success is you have to be aware of your fears. Why? Because awareness is key. You cannot conquer your fear if you not first aware of your fear. When I first joined the military, my fear was the Drill Sergeants. They immediately place fear into my heart, just like the instructor in JROTC.

"Fear is just false evidence appearing real".

I thought they were my fear, however, it was false evidence. The Drill Sergeant's goal to make you fear them. With that fear, they use it to break you down. Once they do, their mission changes to building you up to become the best soldier you can possibly be.

There were plenty of times I won't to quit and go home. Getting four to six hours of sleep every night, waking up 5 o'clock in the morning, and running everywhere we went was starting to wear me out. Sometimes I will wake up toeing the line wondering when I got up and how I got there. Those were some funny times I must say now.

There was a turning point for me, and I can remember this like it was yesterday. I found myself laying in my bed thinking why am I here and why do I fear the Drill Sergeants so much? I begin to analyze the situation. To my finding, I realize that I was there because I wanted to better myself and get away from the poverty mindset. I was raised in poverty and had a lot of limited beliefs. My goal was to change that. I also realized that I should not fear the Drill Sergeants because they are human just like me.

Preparation

Once you realize what your fear is, then and only then you are able to complete step two. Which is prepare yourself. See preparation is also key. And preparation starts with your mind. You have to create the mindset to win. There is a Lion or Lioness, lying dormant, waiting for you to let it roar. My preparation was to work on my mind; mentally, spiritually, and physically. When I came to this realization, everything changed. I begin to enjoy my time in basic training and learn everything I can from the Drill Sergeants. I also begin to reach back and use the tools I was given when in JROTC. See, I was made and prepared for this moment. I just had to realize it.

The more I submitted myself to the training, the more I grew. When I failed and fell face first to the ground, I got back up and did it again. With every blood sweat and tear moments, I got stronger and stronger. Every obstacle and training event was preparing me for the life with the military. What's your Drill Sergeant within your life?

Believe

Step three, is believe in yourself. The Drill Sergeants were my fear, and I knew that. But I also knew that I had superpowers. I had to believe in myself and my capabilities. Because of my life growing up, I was built to never give up, never give in, always persevere to the end. What superpowers do you have that you can use to conquer your fears?

Believing in myself and my capabilities provided me the confidence to endure. When I was the platoon guard for my group of 30+ recruits like me, I had to believe that I had the leadership skills to lead them each and every day. Which I did. I was the Battalion Commander for the JROTC program my senior year and I had the capabilities to lead. I just had to remind myself of this fact.

Les Brown says that "too many of us are not living our dreams because we are living our fears". Sometimes you will question yourself. Sometimes you will ask the question why. When your why is strong enough, you will fight through your fears. Eric Thomas says that you got to want it as bad as you want air to breathe. Fear makes us second guess ourselves. What I want you to do is this:

"Face everything and rise". John Maxwell says this, "Effective leadership requires the ability to stand up, stand out, and the conviction to do it." Again, I ask you, why are you afraid?

You got to have this thing call grit. Day in and day out, dig deep for that grit, for that Lion inside of you, to get up every day and do it over and over again each day for the rest of your life.

Say this to yourself, "I believe in me." This thing is a process. And it is a scary process. However, you can do it. Believe in yourself that you have the ability to reach the finish line.

The Process

When you are able to believe in yourself, you are able to move to step four. Which is trust the process. See, the process is what's going stretch you to the next level, to become bigger, to become better. It's going to help you to become the person you need to be in order to master your fears.

No one is stopping you. The only person that is stopping you is you. Why are you stopping yourself? Let me tell you something, "success is not when you achieve it, success happens when you take the first step towards that achievement." My first step was when I decided to join the JROTC Program. When I did, I was fearful, however, I faced it head on. This first step gave me the opportunity to do something different. Joining the Drill Team gave me the opportunity to learn and grow. Joining the military gave me the opportunity to create a better life for myself and future family.

There is one common denominator is this. That brings us to the final step. Are you ready for step five?

TAKE ACTION NOW!

One of the things that we learn within the Maxwell Leadership Team is this: do it afraid. Jump and grow your wings as you fall. You have to have faith that everything is going to be ok. All odds may be against you. Everything that can go wrong will go wrong. Whatever the case may be, you must face your fears and take action now. When you take action on something you are supposed to, the way forward becomes clearly for you. This is something I had to learn personally.

As my military career began to build momentum with every small win, I found myself thinking about how I can better myself and others more. That's when I decided to embark on a self-development journey. This was an area I needed tremendous help in. To be honest, I never read a book from cover to cover until I was overseas in 2012. I regret the lost opportunities I had to read more when I was younger. I laugh at my stupidity for not taking action on reading. However, that is history. Now, I have read close to hundred books. How? Because I took action on my shortfall.

My Growth Period

When I was younger, reading was not a strong point for me. I feared reading in front of people because I was not good at it, and I stuttered. Being picked on by students and teachers didn't help me to face that fear. It wasn't until I was introduced to a marketing business in college that encouraged and empowered me to read. It also taught me that coaching is important as well. This marketing business was Amway. The learning system they encouraged us to tap into was the Leadership Team Development. It increased my awareness of why I was where I was, and the way in which to get to where I wanted to be in life.

I followed the five steps above and didn't realize it at that time. Once I was aware of why I was where I was, I begin to prepare myself every day to face my fear of reading. I started small by reading a few pages with belief that I can do it. Trusting the process was fundamental during these early stages. And by taking this small action every single day, I grew a love for reading. At the end, I faced my fear of reading and I'm thankful that I did. It allowed me to become the man that I am today.

If you are aware of your fear, you can prepare yourself. Part of preparing yourself is believing in yourself. When you believe in yourself, you have the ability to trust the process. When you have all of these within your DNA, you will have the courage to take action now and your results will be conquering your fears.

When you don't conquer your fears, you are causing someone else not to conquer theirs. Your bravery can help someone reach their greatness. It is time for you to remove that fear out of the way, allow your greatness to shine, and show the world you can't be stopped. This takes strong faith and hard work.

The Next Step

In the Bible, James 2 tells us that faith without works is dead. With this statement, I have three things I would like to share with you. How you apply these concepts into your life will determine your movement to conquering your fears.

1. Step Out in Faith

The first step is everything right. Just like a baby, once you take that first step, the rest is history. If you want to change your life for the best, take the first step in faith. Whatever your first step may be, just take it. It could be writing gratitude statements every morning and night. It could be redefining your purpose and core values. It could even be seeking out a mentor or coach to assist you within your growth walk. I had to do all of the above. You need to just take action and step out in faith.

2. Follow the Process

Above, I told you to trust the process. After you trust the process, you now have to follow it through and through. Everything in life has a process that you must follow. How well you follow that process will determine the outcome of your future. Just like a caterpillar, you have to follow the process to become that beautiful butterfly. Once you face your fears and learn all you can within the season that you are in, it is time for you to level up to a greater and better you. However, you have to follow the process. Within every process, there are lessons that we must learn to grow ourselves. When we decide to skip steps, we miss out on learning something we need to know for the next step. Trust and follow the process. It will do more good than harm.

3. Be Willing to Learn & Grow

When you have the spirit of always learning, your perspective on life changes. Willingness to learn helps you to move from a fearful mindset to a growth mindset. Brian Herbert made this statement, "The capacity to learn is a gift. The ability to learn is a skill. The willingness to learn is a choice." Will you choose to be persistent in your willingness to learn and grow? If you do this, I guarantee you will learn how to conquer your fears and grow even more.

Again, say to yourself, "I am greatness made from greatness. And today is a great day to be alive."

Yes, you will have people that will try to stop or even will not support you in conquering your fears. I like to call those folks the naysayers and dream crushers.

"Let your naysayers become your motivators."

Some of those people will be your family and friends. They may have genuine concerns for you, however, do not allow those concerns to steal and push you away from your dreams. Some may try to hinder you from your growth. What you have to do is push through and persevere with concrete action. When you decide to walk this walk, I will see you at your peak on the mountain top.

Before you leave, I want to share with you some tools that will change your life for the best.

- 12 Month Leadership Newsletter - https://bit.ly/TSLeadershipNewsletter.
- 12 Month Building Stick-to-itiveness - https://tsle.leadingthebest.com/BSTE0001.
- Online training - "Five Steps To Success" - Email a photo of this book to bless@teonsingletary.com, and I will grant you free lifetime access. Guess what, the five steps are above, however, more content is available.
- Follow me on Facebook, Instagram, and Twitter @teonsingletary.
- Visit the site, www.teonsingletary.com, for another free gift on the 15 Laws of Growth taught by my mentor and coach, John C. Maxwell himself.

I genuinely want to see you succeed. The question is, will you seize this opportunity and conquer your fears? The greater you is waiting on you to move. Be great in you and the things that God has empowered you to be, do, and have in life.

***

To Contact Teon

https://linktr.ee/TeonSingletary

http://www.TeonSingletary.com

Nanci Lublin-Good, CHPC

Nanci gets women promoted, playing more, and sleeping longer. She knows it's not only possible, but necessary, to cultivate strong relationships, hobbies, and health when planning to land a corner office.

She coached continuous improvement efforts using Lean / Six Sigma principles while creating mindset and behavior shifts that ensure the balance needed to avoid burnout. Nanci guides clients in implementing a personalized roadmap to achieve their most important aspirations at work and at home.

Personally, Nanci's walk and talk are congruent with her values of collaborating and serving others...imparting her knowledge to improve people's lives through getting to know what makes them tick, what they want from life, and their best way to achieve it. While she's known for asking the 'hard questions,' Nanci loves helping women discover what brings them joy and how they can make more room in life for those moments. Nanci knows everyone can have a life they enjoy by focusing on meaningful work, targeted personal-development, and consistent achievement.

Nanci lives in Texas with her husband and three dogs. She gives back in her community with efforts that honor military personnel and empower women. Her hobbies include veggie gardening, dancing, and reading. Nanci attended the Women's College at the University of Denver and has a tender heart for strong women who meet life's challenging circumstances with integrity, grace, and grit.

Turning Career Sequels into Box-Office Hits

By Nanci Lublin-Good, CHPC

Some film critics say, "Every story has already been told." If so, why do we keep spending time and money on new films, not to mention sequels? Admit it. Your favorite film franchise just flashed through your head...James Bond, Hunger Games, Star Wars, Wonder Woman, Harry Potter, Rocky, Indiana Jones.

Imagine if they only made the first film in each franchise. What if Sean Connery was the only James Bond? What if Jennifer Lawrence played Katniss only once? Think of all the technology we enjoy today because of sci-fi films: cell phones (Star Trek communicator), jet skis (The Spy Who Loved Me), tablets & video conferencing (2001: A Space Odyssey), motion sensor gaming (Minority Report)

Take it a step further and there would be no films to show us how strong, clever individuals outsmart the villains. I suggest to you that films mimic life in that we need to see repeat performances, in similar yet varied situations, where good conquers evil. Where the underdog wins by overcoming extraordinary obstacles.

How often have you faced a villain and come out the victor? What sacrifices did it require? When did you realize you'd learned something in the process? Who did you share that wisdom with? Take a moment and contemplate a defining moment, a story, when you powered through obstacles and came out stronger on the other side.

As leaders we must be selective for our own personal watch lists. Just like Netflix makes recommendations based on what you've already watched, our brains can be very persistent with shoving episodes through our minds daily.

Which stories from your past keep popping up on your feed as recommended viewing? Images of those stories continue to play in our minds like movie trailers. We each have a list of *What's Trending...*

- I'm not smart...I didn't finish college.
- I'm not creative...I can't waste time on hobbies.
- I can't eat healthy...I'm too busy.
- I'm not a good parent...I work too much.
- I'm divorced...I'm just not loveable.
- I didn't get the promotion...I'm not valuable.

If we keep rerunning these episodes, we start thinking, "Why bother? It never works out for me." In other words, evil wins. Create your watch list of wonderfully epic moments where you are the conqueror and binge watch them every chance you get.

When our personal movie trailers trend toward dramas and tragedies, we spend millions of dollars and decades of time creating bad sequels. If you or someone you know does this, I'm here to tell you that your remakes or sequels can be bigger hits than the original releases.

A second marriage can be a phenomenally loving and fulfilling experience, even if the first marriage left you feeling unlovable. You can learn more in college as an adult finishing your degree than you would have if you'd stuck with it as a teen. You can be a better grandparent than you were a mom or dad with your added life experience.

One minor shift makes these possible. You must stop playing supporting roles in your life and take the lead in your epic story. So, what's involved in jumping into the spotlight and channeling your best self for a box-office hit? It's the same as what works in the movies.

There are five key components to making a great film franchise, leading a successful business team, or enjoying a happy family.

- ➢ **Great Leadership**
- ➢ **Top Talent**
- ➢ **Compelling Projects**
- ➢ **Time Together**

> ➤ **Fun in Failure**

<u>**Great leadership**</u>

A director who can articulate a clear vision is worth their weight in gold. Virtually all leaders believe their vision is right for the organization. But many have difficulty understanding why others don't just get on board with their ideas. This is a sign that leaders failed to connect the dots from task to purpose. Those with a gift for seeing the big picture may feel that it's a no brainer, but not everyone can see the path as clearly.

Remember that your team hasn't been in attendance for the full thought process taking place in your head. Start with describing your vision in tangible ways that incorporate the five senses. Use examples that you can see, hear, touch, smell, or even taste.

Follow that immediately by explaining your reasons why this vision feels so right for you. Notice I use the verb *feels* here. Share the emotions that are driving you to this decision. Be sincere and as open as you can. While logic is easy to defend, emotions move people to action. That's why movies that make us feel that we're part of the scene stick with us so much longer. When others hear your vision, they should also feel the emotions. Others need to determine for themselves that you absolutely believe in your vision before you can help them find their compelling reasons to do what you're asking of them.

Spoiler alert...their reasons for doing what you ask do not need to be the same as yours.

If the vision is clear, what's driving others to accomplish it can be completely different from yours. Be aware that you may have biases toward different motivations. I've worked with leaders who are strongly against employees doing something strictly for monetary gain. But what if that employee grew up in extreme poverty and now works tirelessly for the money to ensure their family will never experience that? Or they need money to care for special needs children or aging parents? Others may just want shiny new things. If you have proper oversight in place and your metrics and controls limit the risk of abusing the system simply for monetary gain, then someone's reasons for doing what you ask is irrelevant. It's the ultimate win/win scenario. They work hard with integrity, and you achieve your vision.

Once you express your vision as clearly and genuinely as you can and help others find their compelling reasons for moving forward, stay engaged with the team as they work. A director doesn't explain to the cast what they want and then go back to the office during filming. Continue to paint vivid pictures of the future you expect. Use tangible examples to help everyone connect with what they're working toward. Be honest about the challenges you expect to face while achieving this vision. Tell the team frequently that you have confidence in their ability to meet those challenges. A leader who knows her assets and is open to alternative solutions to each new problem is resourceful. Studies show that more than 60% of employees are more motivated by leaders who keep them informed, are resourceful and easy to talk with, than they are by money…especially when things are going wrong.

Top Talent

Which brings us to recruiting and retaining top talent. You'll be amazed at the innovative solutions teams create and problems they solve as you stay engaged and remain easy to talk with. Allow each team member to bring their strengths to the project. You don't need to hire the most expensive or the most well-known person for the job. Recruit people who collaborate and challenge each other to take their work to the next level. They bring their A game every day and build an expectation that others will do the same.

I've seen new departments built by selecting the top 10 to 20 individual contributors in an organization. First, all that ego in one room is exhausting. Second, it creates a team with skill gaps. For example, a team made up of top salespeople can push the product, but when it comes to working with product development, customer service, or training new hires you'll struggle to get the team to step up in those areas. Instead, look for individuals with different talents that complement each other and meet all the requirements you want to deliver. Diverse tasks need diverse people to lead them. Letting people leverage their strengths allows them to become superstars quickly, enjoy their work even more, and gives you a team with a lot of momentum. If you already have a team with skill gaps, leverage development plans to close them.

Development Plans That Work

Have your team members pick three activities that will help them develop skills you both agree will enhance their performance and improve the team results. You may need to guide them a bit on selecting activities that will truly help take their performance to the next level, but it should also match their desires on what they want to develop.

1. A daily/weekly nibble that keeps them in a continuous improvement mindset. It can be a podcast they choose or a newsletter on the topic of interest. Touch base with them frequently to see what they're learning, how they're applying it, and who they share the lessons with.
2. Something significant like a college course, a multi-day conference or workshop that provides information and techniques to try and evaluate within your team. (Tip: make sure these happen in the first half of the year, so they have time to apply it before year end evaluations.)
3. Something really juicy that no matter how busy or crazy things get, they're going to make the time for this one. It could be attending a keynote address by someone they admire, or a weekend adventure on how kayaking teaches leadership skills.

Investing in your team and their development also means investing in your own. As the leader, you are part of your team and need to role model what you expect. Setting aside time for your own development shows them that you take this seriously, and so should they.

Compelling Projects When the story or project resonates with the cast, you hear interview soundbites like, "I fell in love with the story" or "I knew I just had to be part of this" or "I was made for this role." When it happens in the office, you see 100+ applications for three open positions, and you hear employees talking about what's exciting for them. This allows you to be selective and gives you visibility to people you may not have known. So, what makes a project compelling? Vision and Purpose.

Millennials now make up about half of the US workforce. Collectively, they're known to express a desire to be part of something that will make a difference in the world, something bigger than themselves. One of my early jobs was in a corporate office for a fast-food chain, and their motto was "If you're not serving the guest, you better be serving someone who is." This means your vision needs to include a purpose that is meaningful to your customer and will impact more than just those involved in the project, you should all be "serving someone" or making life better somehow.

Many employees are voluntold into project teams because there is a distinct lack of compelling reasons, or purpose, to draw applicants. I've had employees ask to be released from projects because they just didn't see the point. That's great feedback that leaders did not clearly communicate the mission. It's difficult to keep working through challenges if there is no purpose to your effort. If you went to the gym five days a week for a month and saw zero results, how compelled are you to continue? If you have a class reunion or a wedding coming up, you might keep going. But you'd find alternate solutions to try because you're fully invested in getting results. You will push yourself a bit harder in the workouts or change your diet. If, however, your vision is to live to be one hundred years old, you need strong visualization skills and an extensive list of milestones to meet along the way.

Compelling projects have milestones to achieve, so members can see the progress they're making. They also allow the team to pivot as necessary to ensure the trajectory is on target to match the ultimate vision and ensure success. When a cast or team achieves this kind of success, they want to come back and be part of the sequels. They want more of you and what you bring to the table as their leader. This means you have people you already know, like, and trust when you have a new role, project, or idea that needs support. Most of us know someone that if they started a team or project and asked us to join, we'd jump on board immediately. Be that person, often.

Time Together Work is intense, so celebrating each milestone and completed project isn't a nice to have, it's a necessity. I don't mean that everyone gets a trophy, but everyone does need time to enjoy each other and their collective progress away from the trenches. I once sat in a conference room observing ten colleagues who were there for a staff meeting. Everyone had their laptops and were tapping away on work waiting for the VP to arrive. Nobody said a word other than a brief hello as newcomers filed in to take their seat, open their laptop, and start tapping away. This fascinated me. Here we have a few minutes where we could decompress some stress, transition from one task to the next, or just enjoy each other as human beings. But the culture was one of task over relationship.

Employee engagement has become a much larger topic with the issues surrounding COVID lockdowns and remote workspace. Employee Experience Professionals are working feverishly to develop events that entice employees to come back into the office. If you have a culture of task before people, getting anyone to commute and spend more time away from family just to sit in a conference room and tap away on their laptops is going to be a significant obstacle to overcome.

Organizations that spend time developing a culture where colleagues know each other, enjoy spending time together, and collaborate are having greater success with much less expense in this arena. It was also easier for them to move to a remote or hybrid workforce because the employees cared about what their colleagues were experiencing during the lockdowns. They stayed in touch with technology just to check in with each other. For some employees, this also reduced the mental stress created by isolation.

Whether you plan large company events for employees to attend, provide comfortable breakrooms where they can watch TV or play ping pong, or just set aside time at the opening of meetings to chat for a minute, the expense is well worth the outcome. Loyal, engaged employees who feel appreciated and valued for more than just the bottom line they can deliver are also more willing to step up when things go wrong.

Fun with failure Blooper reels or the vignettes at the end of the credits are my favorite part of a film. I love seeing these perfect actors, who dress exactly right and say fantastic lines, get stupid silly over making mistakes. It helps me to look for the humor in setbacks.

It's my practice to share my leadership philosophy in writing with each new team member. It includes the phrase, "I promise to never shoot the messenger." For those not raised in a military town, this means I'm not going to lose my mind and attack you as a person when you bring me unwelcome news.

As a leader, we need those working with us to tell us the good, the bad, and the ugly. We need to create an environment where anyone can feel confident that when they share a mistake or tell us something isn't working, we won't attack them, we attack the problem. And we do it in a way that allows everyone to maintain their dignity.

Assuming positive intent is a fantastic way to maintain focus on the problem and not the person. Nobody wakes up thinking, "What can I mess up today?" When we stay curious about the situation and help others do the same, we show people around us that they are valued, and we are confident that together we can overcome mistakes. If we fail to do this, mistakes get covered up until they implode, and everyone stops taking even the smallest risks to move forward. The result is flatlined careers and companies that die slow agonizing deaths. On the other hand, when we can see the humor in our errors, we can quickly convert the laugher into fuel for taking the next calculated risk. I'm not suggesting that you don't hold people accountable for negligence or failure to perform, but you do it with an eye toward developing them, not destroying them.

As you move up the ladder of success, your ability to incorporate these five common keys will boost your career into a box-office hit. When you move up in the organization, you'll have fan clubs popping up across the organization just waiting to get into a new project with you. The people will have different titles and the projects will look a bit different, but the passion, motivation, and success are the same. Especially if your watch list includes your epic moments of…

- **Great Leadership** articulating vivid details about the vision and staying engaged with your team.
- Encouraging **Top Talent** to live from their strengths and continue to develop them.
- **Compelling Projects** where you're inspiring a deeper purpose that generates commitment to team and taking risks.
- **Time Together** enjoying and appreciating each other as fellow humans.
- **Fun in Failure** when you found the humor in the situation and used it to fuel your next try.

Take a couple minutes to determine which of these five key components you need to develop for your current project to be the next box-office hit. Write them down, post it somewhere you'll see them daily, and then share with at least one person on your team why you feel this is critical for

***

To contact Nanci:

Facebook	https://www.facebook.com/nlgcoaching
LinkedIn	https://www.linkedin.com/in/nancilublingood/
Instagram	https://www.instagram.com/lublingood/
Twitter	https://twitter.com/LublinGood

Mega R. Mease EHP-C, RMT

Mega R. Mease EHP-C, RMT, known as the "Everyday Ordinary Healer," is a Holistic Health Entrepreneur Manifestation Coach, founder/owner of the Center for Advanced Energy Therapeutics and the CAET Community Wellness Volunteer Program in Tucson, Arizona. As a board member of the National Alliance of Energy Practitioners, she works with others to share information about quality energy practices, educate the public on the styles of energy work, their use, the research on energy practices, and the limits of what a professional practitioner can do. Mega is nationally certified by the National Certification Center of Energy Practitioners.

People from all walks of life seek her for guidance, stress reduction, and relaxation. These include mental, emotional, and physical challenges and life-threatening diseases. Her rare deep-seated wisdom regarding manifestation can be experienced in the energy healing, health, wealth, relationship, and business arenas.

Mega's longstanding involvement in Energy Healing, Nutrition, and Self–Empowerment led to the creation and development of HeartRay™ Energetic Therapy, Bone Energy Re-Pattering™, FootFlex™, and the Mega Method™ of Healing.

When asked, "Who are you, and what do you do?" she answers with an ear-to-ear grin: "Today, I am fully engaged in a life of joy, authenticity, and fulfillment. Holistic health isn't only a professional path; it's my lifestyle. My family and friends are my greatest treasures; my work is my play, and service is my nurture."

Rich Man. Poor Man. Beggar Man.

A Lesson in Duality

By: Mega R. Mease

Light and darkness. God and Devil. Brahma and Shiva. Batman and Joker. The universe exists in opposites that balance, compensate, and supplement each other. Duality permeates every aspect of life. Some might believe that these opposite powers compete. You may experience this in your own life as a consistent ebb and flow of circumstances—some that bring blessings of abundance and ease and others that generate strife and hardship. Even so, duality should be perceived as an efficient instrument, setting progress in motion and contributing to global balance. Would the world be a better place to live if it had a single, infinite day? Would the beauty of the stars shine as radiantly against anything other than a dark velvet sky? How could we marvel at awe-inspiring natural beauty if we've never experienced ugliness and destruction?

A closer look will reveal the existence of competing forces everywhere. Some can be easily detected. Others require comprehensive analysis, out-of-the-box thinking, and an innovative approach to examine an object, process, or idea from an atypical angle. This chapter is a humble attempt at grasping the depth of duality. My intention is to invite you to embrace life's complexity, diversity, and uniqueness in all its forms and manifestations. To begin, let us consider the following three archetypes.

Rich Man

When asked for the definition of a 'Rich Man,' most will agree—a person with great monetary wealth. An extended answer would more than likely include a long list of desirable material gains (i.e., massive home, luxurious car, holidays beyond your wildest imagination, brand-name everything, access to the best money can buy, and so forth).

However, closer consideration would bring to light a duality that isn't always immediately recognized. Not all wealthy people need or want to dazzle others with external attributes of their material success. There are those who, often feeling insecure and undeserving of their abundance, seek to give it away—perhaps using it as a tool to secure their personal value instead of their financial value.

On the other hand, there are those who store up their treasures on earth—unwilling to spend a dime unless absolutely necessary. This is a very different kind of Rich Man, one who is much more interested in holding onto his wealth for the sake of having it, as opposed to enjoying it. The way to prosperity is not strewn with roses alone. Success is a two-sided coin, with hard work and sacrifice looming largely.

Poor Man

In line with an opposing likeness of the Rich Man, the Poor Man is one who is often thought of as impoverished, needy, or disadvantaged. A Poor Man lacks money or other material possessions. A diversity of opinion is mainly dependent on the financial standing of the one who seeks to evaluate the economic status of another person. For example, entrepreneur Richard Branson's wide variety of middle management and wealth-building strategies can be easily categorized as an outreach opportunity to those he views as the Poor Man.

What about the Dalai Lama? He doesn't have any fortune, but do we consider him a Poor Man? A Poor Man's identification does not feel right when applied to those possessing priceless wisdom, reasoning, or kindness. Their intellect and insight are worth millions of dollars whether they elect to retain them or not. The same ambiguity of definition arises from another, less visible side of poverty—spiritual bankruptcy. The iconic "Jerry Maguire" movie, featuring Tom Cruise, is an excellent example of a person making significant money while still being profoundly miserable inside. Jerry needed to lose his material wealth to fully understand the value of love, friendship, and genuine support.

Beggar Man

Society often perceives the Beggar Man as asking unscrupulously for money to supply alcohol and drugs, fueled by a lazy, "I don't want to work mentality." This makes all beggars an easy target for social protest. However, not every Beggar Man needs money. Consider the people forced to leave their homes, who ask for nothing but food, clothing, or an employment opportunity. They may live in the same cardboard boxes on the street and possess the same human dignity, but the judgment is different based on what? Asking for the rod rather than the fish? How do you decide which person begging on the side of the road is worthy of receiving your gift of resources? Who are you to decide? Regular philistines hardly have the time or the wish to distinguish between people whose belongings can easily fit in one box and whose address is not limited to a single house. What about being poor in spirit? What would you call such a person? Is the only difference between a Poor Man and a Beggar Man the fact that one is willing to ask for what they need, and the other isn't?

It is curious to ponder, isn't it? This is the reality and the complexity behind the dual nature of the universe as a whole and of humanity as a species. We live lives that are simultaneously in conflict and in harmony. When you are struggling with feeling misaligned, either within yourself or in relation to the world around you, it is because you have not yet discovered the neutral existence between the two extremes you are encountering. The anecdote to this misalignment is a deeper understanding of duality.

Duality: What It Is & What It Isn't

According to the Merriam-Webster Dictionary, duality is defined as, "A quality or state of having two different or opposite parts or elements." Essentially, there will always be a battle of opposition in and around you. No matter what. Without fail. Despite the harshness of this truth, duality is not simply a force that happens to you without reason. It is not chaotic nor fundamentally out of your control. Duality is a powerful system of universal checks and balances, and it is possible to establish a harmonious balance between the opposing elements. It is possible to foster a complementary interaction where there once was conflict.

Please take a moment to consider the duality of Up and Down. They are opposite realities of one another. Being Down in life carries negative connotations and consequences while being Up in life is represented by prosperity and well-being. Both extremes can occur in prolonged or brief seasons of life. And yet, there is a third option—a middle ground that presents a peaceful opportunity for neutrality. Understanding what contributes to and withdraws from each extreme will make it easier to locate the middle ground and more comfortable to reside there both consciously and physically.

Learning to Embrace Duality

As I discussed above, determining the neutral center of your circumstance is an essential step in achieving balance. However, please hear me when I say that neutrality does not equate to the avoidance of decision-making. This in itself is a paradox that is a struggle for most. We can become so afraid of choosing one way or another that we allow inaction to become a glaring, nonproductive choice. There will be positive and negative consequences no matter which path you take; harmony comes when you accept this truth and have peace with the inevitable outcomes. Your circumstances won't always be perfect. The good news is that when you honor your choices, acknowledging that you made the best decision for you based on your understanding and experience of the opposing elements you are encountering, you will have balance in your body, mind, and soul!

It will benefit you to keep in mind the examples that were introduced at the beginning of the chapter. We wouldn't appreciate light without darkness. We wouldn't recognize beauty without ugliness. We wouldn't seek out what is good without the desire to avoid evil. The crucial lesson is that we could never find balance without a wide-swinging pendulum, and we could never find joy in the blessings of life without the hardship of life. Duality is a powerful tool for perspective and a motivating force for progress, especially when the extremes knock us off-kilter a bit. Be proactive in regaining your equilibrium.

Prepare to push the limits of your spiritual comfort zone if and when equilibrium is not possible. This is when the universe is calling you to fully embrace one extreme or the other for the deep-seated purpose of your highest good. There will be seasons in your life when you will be required to stretch yourself and become profoundly uncomfortable as you become whole. I return to my example from Jerry Maguire. Jerry was comfortable in his own skin, career, and the lifestyle it afforded him; however, he was severely off balance with his personal life—sacrificing his relationship with his wife and children. He didn't want to lose everything, but he needed to embrace the loss of material value to gain the profound value of developing into a kinder, more compassionate, spiritually rich husband and father.

Achieving Harmony

First and foremost, concentrate on the things above. Focus your thoughts and intentions on the things more significant than yourself (i.e., love, compassion, generosity, peace, unity). Set your personal development around the elevation of your consciousness. Revel as you allow the ripples of your light to expand out from around you in every direction! Our longevity in this life and the life we consciously seek to leave for future generations depend on our ability to harmonize. It's a lot of pressure, I know!

Nevertheless, it is a special responsibility that we must take seriously. It starts with seeking and finding unity within yourself— that sacred equilibrium within you. As I mentioned before, duality isn't just a force that happens to you. It is a substantial force you can tune into, harness, and use in a meaningful way.

Journaling is a powerful exercise for understanding and self-discovery. If this isn't currently a routine practice in your life, please consider it. It is often astonishing to look back and see patterns in your thought process and decision-making that were completely hidden from your awareness. Valuable insights can be gleaned from seeing specific priorities and fears so clearly spelled out on paper.

Reflection is one of the most potent teachers there is. Gaining this deeper level of insight into your own heart and mind will better equip you to align your intention with the swinging pendulum of duality. You will be better able to reconcile the conflicting elements of the circumstance you face to restore harmony in your life.

Another critical and helpful tool to achieve harmony is to avoid an 'either/or' situation. Walk away from locking your consciousness in this box of limit and lack. Instead, remain open to the art of unlimited possibilities. As a reminder, the intention always needs to be to have peace regardless of the outcome. When faced with a trying circumstance or a challenging decision, write all opposing viewpoints on a piece of paper. Mindfully ponder the potential consequences of each side. "If it goes this way, I can expect this to happen...." "If it goes that way, I can expect that to happen...." Stretch yourself. "Is there anything that could happen that I'm not expecting?" Thoughtfully explore all the possibilities, tell yourself that you are open to all options, trust the outcome, and embrace that it will be okay no matter what. Allow the two lists to become one list in your mind—further cementing the notion that all possibilities are available, accessible, and acceptable. This is the key to inner peace, harmony, and alignment.

One final point on achieving harmony, if I may. As I have alluded to, you will not only be combating duality externally in terms of your environment. Duality exists within every single member of humanity as well. I believe it is fair to assume that most of us struggle with the battle between our hearts and our minds. Some of us may be challenged by what we say versus how we feel or what we think versus what we do. Misalignment can significantly impact your relationship with yourself and your relationship with others. With that said, I cannot emphasize strongly enough the importance of unifying your heart and mind. Explore the depths of who you are without trepidation. Again, you must understand the reality of Up and Down before you can align yourself in the center—just as you must first achieve internal harmony before you can work to attain external balance.

In conclusion, embracing the duality of the world and the complexity of human nature is the first step to a fulfilled, balanced life. At times, every person is individually driven by confronting urges and emotions. We all possess both internal and external power to withstand evil thoughts and embrace seeds of goodness and kindness. If Dr. Jekyll could acknowledge his weaknesses, there would be no need to breed the ruthless, evil Mr. Hyde. The need to be more understanding of one's imperfections and more merciful toward the human habit to err paves the way for openness, tolerance, empathy, and acceptance. A balanced life is inextricably connected with the ability to listen and respond, question and advise, and appreciate diversity. Stand on your own ground and be grateful for the darkest night, giving rise to the brightest day with new hopes and aspirations.

There comes a time when you "know" that the life you are living is no longer aligned with who you are, and it doesn't resonate with your evolving soul. A voice inside is whispering, "Take control and responsibility for your health, begin a happier, independent, more productive, peaceful existence.

It is my great privilege and joy to serve others by helping them connect with their passion and find new ways to live a more fulfilling life. Guiding people with effective tools to learn to listen and say "YES" to their heart's desires is a humbling and rewarding experience.

When you are ready to design your new, improved, empowered YOU, I invite you to come along and walk awhile with me. You deserve the gifts of Happiness, Contentment, Wealth, and Wellness. Energy Healing, Manifestation Coaching, and Holistic Health care can pave the way to being the best you can be at any given moment.

If it's time to Live larger, Smile often, Love profoundly, and Laugh Louder…

Schedule a complimentary 15-minute phone consult: AdvancedEnergyTherapeutics@cox.net

***

To contact Mega:

www.AdvancedEnergyTherapeutics.com

www.caetWellnessProgram.com

www.facebook.com/groups/Abundance

AdvancedEnergyTherapeutics@cox.net

Monique Elliott

Monique Elliott is the Consultant Founder/Chief Executive Officer of S.A.V.Y. (Success Achieved when Visioned by You), LLC, and Savy Counseling Services, LLC. She is a licensed clinical social worker with expertise in the areas of mental health and wellness. She is a motivational speaker and an internationally recognized published author of *My Sister's Arms, A Guide to Structuring Your Vision, 7 Steps to Discovering Your Dreams, and Zoey's Dream Adventure.* She is a TV/radio personality, television host, and producer of Mind Health Matters.

In her role as CEO, Monique brings over 30 years of experience in training leaders and growing businesses. Monique works with executives, professional athletes, entertainers, individuals, and organizations to increase their capacity for change and growth.

Her passion for touching lives and empowering others is evident in her spirit of philanthropic giving to impact mind health around the world. Monique and her team of coaches have developed programs that bring solution focused strategies, visionary planning, and wealth building while helping to develop work life balance.

The Wealth of Mind Health

By Monique Elliott

You are your best commodity! You are flowing with greatness throughout your entire being. There is no other person in the universe like you. Yet millions of us struggle to understand our worth. We are constantly competing and comparing ourselves to another's greatness. We are secretly worried or afraid that someone will take something that was meant for us. We believe that our worth and value is connected to another person's success. I ask how can another take what is already yours? How can another steal your greatness? Your ability to soar and create wealth of mind, body, and soul were in you before you were born. The desire to obtain more greatness is impossible because you are already great! Financial wealth means little if you do not have mind wealth. Many obtain remarkable success but continue to live with anxiety and sadness. Others decide that financial wealth alone will bring them everything their heart desires. But unfortunately, things of themselves do not satisfy the soul. There must be a purpose fulfilled, a life changed, a moment of love given, and a place for mind wealth to grow.

Mind wealth is the secret to living with peace. It is the mindset of being enough. It is knowing that no matter what happens today in my life, I will thrive. Mind wealth helps you to understand that your success does not depend on the greatness of others. Mind wealth helps you to stay focused in the moment while preparing for your future. Mind wealth slows you down just enough to listen to your thoughts and to create brilliance. Mind wealth takes away the fear of not being enough or feeling like an imposter and replaces your fear with power and confidence.

How do you get mind wealth? First, you must take the time to explore what it is you really want in your life. What are your short-term desires? What do you want your future to become? How do you envision the steps along your journey? Do you want to have happiness? Do you want to spend more time with your family? Do you want a business or a job that brings you peace? Do you want to live a balanced life with laughter and flexibility? The ultimate question is what is your end goal? These questions are something only you can decide. Your mind wealth must be cultivated by you and the choices you make. When was the last time you went outside and felt the wind on your skin? When was that last time you sat and enjoyed the laughter of someone you love? Every moment of your life is a series of choices. You give yourself absolute permission to experience joy. You give yourself permission to take the tiny moments of a day and view them as miracles.

The most important role you can play in your own mental wellness is to listen to the themes of your thoughts. You must receive the fact that you are a spiritual being who has the capacity to have a healthy and meaningful life. What are the thoughts that you consistently ignore? Do you find yourself ignoring your emotions and pushing them aside? Are you suppressing past pain or a situation that needs your attention? It is often the ignored thoughts in your mind that hinder some of your happiness. You have become so used to ignoring yourself, that you do not truly know how to find the root of what you are feeling. Here is an exercise I would like for you to try. The following steps will assist you in decreasing anxiety in many ways. It will also provide a space for mind wealth.

Step one: Observe your body cues and sit with your thoughts. What is your body experiencing while you are thinking about a situation or when you are in the presence of others? Does your heart rate increase, or your shoulders begin to tense? Take notice of what your body is saying to you.

Step two: Identify the feeling. Sometimes this may take a moment, but you will begin to know if you are feeling fear, embarrassment, anger, sadness, anxiousness, or any other feelings. Remember feelings are neither good nor bad. Feelings are there to tell you something is going on.

Step three: Understand why you are experiencing this emotion. I believe in looking at triggers around you. There are words spoken that can trigger a not so pleasant memory. The person speaking may not truly be the target of your anxiety. It may be a past emotion creeping in from your subconscious mind.

Step four: Acknowledge the emotion. Acknowledge that you are feeling an emotion and refuse to ignore it. It is a good thing to acknowledge that you have feelings.

Step five: Experience the emotion. Do not be afraid to experience what you are feeling. It is all right to cry. There is strength in your tears. Experiencing the emotion helps to move you forward in wellness. Many people are mature in taking on responsibilities and meeting their commitments, but they become stuck emotionally. Their emotional intelligence is hindered by ignoring their own feelings.

Step six: Limit the time you spend on the emotion. Do your best to experience your emotion or feeling about a situation but limit the amount of time you ruminate about it. What I want you to understand is that the more you ruminate without making a change in your mind, the more you will stay in your emotional cycle. Take time to speak with a counselor or life coach about your experience if you cannot move forward. However, know that it is possible for you to move forward and have mind wealth.

Step seven: Make a change. Decide to make a change in your life. You are the only one who can. Unfortunately, for better or worse, we cannot change the past. We must learn how to live in our moments and make them better. We acknowledge that pain hurts. We acknowledge that life is not always fair. We also acknowledge that we can make our mind health a priority starting today.

You have the power to take the negative patterns in your life and replace them with great possibilities. Take the stories of your past and share them with someone. Use your voice to make a difference in the world. I have worked with individuals who have become happier and resilient when they have used their voices to speak up for what they need. When your voice is suppressed, you have a challenging time growing as a person. Things that happened to you as a child do not disappear because you are a successful adult.

Many of these past experiences must be shared to rid yourself of the hold the past may have on you. Moment by moment as you find an emotional safe space to share, you will start experiencing mind wealth. There is an amazing freedom in sharing our stories.

I honestly believe, it is possible to grow everyday of our lives. Life has many more lessons to give us. Hope is deep inside of us all. I believe that if you can change your thoughts, your thoughts will change your life. Every new day gives us the opportunity for a new beginning. You are more than capable of turning your circumstances around. Your very presence has an impact on someone near you. We are forever learners and forever teachers.

Mind wealth is all around you beautiful one. When you decide that a peace of mind is the most important gift you can give to yourself, the world's river of wealth in many forms will begin to flow to you. How is this possible? It is because you will become a magnet for positive people. Opportunities to use your greatness will come to you. Your natural inspiration, your smile, your strength, your confidence, and your heart of kindness will shine through without saying a word. The amazing gift of having mind wealth is that it changes your focus.

Your gift of greatness is all about accepting your ultimate assignment to love yourself and to know you are loved. The more you accept yourself and your own greatness, the more you will be able to appreciate and value others. Your expectations of others will also begin to change. You will love others but will have the courage to set boundaries. You will refuse to tolerate people or situations in your life that do not bring peace. You will set a standard of mind wealth in all areas of your life. You will value the time you spend with yourself and others. Yes, mind wealth is the key to clarity and calmness.

We become what we continually focus on in life. If you constantly complain about people, our job, the world, then people, your job, and the world will continue to disappoint you. Find solutions to the things that present themselves as challenges. Become mindful of those situations that are in your control. I am not asking you to ignore the challenges. I am merely encouraging you to purposely be a part of your life narrative. Daily you are painting the portrait of you for others to see. Daily you will show the picture you want others to experience. The more knowledge you have regarding your mind health, the more impactful your Picasso will become. How do we achieve a greater understanding of our needs and mind health? How do we obtain mind wealth? It is through cultivation.

Mind wealth cannot be bought, it can only be cultivated. Cultivation is created through the next seven principles:

Clarity - Clarity is knowing what you want in this phase of your life. Take steps to find out what you enjoy. Clarity helps you to hear your heart. Clarity of the mind lets you know your how and your why. Clarity will assist you in understanding the reasons for your life choices.

Peace - Peace is recognizing you made the best decisions possible with the choices you were given. Peace is going to sleep without worrying coming into your dreams. Peace is feeling good about how you treated yourself and others.

Joy - Joy is living your life aloud! Joy is laughing, smiling, dancing, playing, and having a mind of gratitude.

Gratitude - Gratitude is saying thank you to others. Gratitude is saying thank you to the creator for all things. Gratitude is being aware of the impressive privilege of just breathing on your own. Gratitude is speaking with appreciation to others for being a part of your life's journey.

Forgiveness - Forgiveness is letting go of the thoughts of punishment and revenge. Forgiveness is sending love to someone through your thoughts and prayers. Forgiveness is asking the Holy Spirit for the strength to move forward without expectations from the one forgiven.

Truth - The truth is communicating your thoughts with your heart. The truth is wanting the best for yourself and wanting the best for others.

Love - Love is accepting others for who they are and wanting the best for them.

I challenge you to sit still for a moment and take a deep breath. Give yourself a moment to breathe in peace and breathe out fear. Breathe in joy and breathe out anxiety. Let your mind overflow for this moment with all the possibilities of newness that waits for you. Mind wealth will not flow if you are in the cycle of running. Be purposeful in sitting still for 2-3 minutes a day. Listen to the voice inside of you and take notes on what comes to your mind.

If you become tempted to get back to business as usual, come back to this chapter for a moment and remember your why? Remember why you have decided to make a change in your life. Remember your why to live more joyfully with others. Remember the greatness that is already inside of you. Remember that you have chosen to live a life of Mind Wealth! It's the passion inside of your spirit that will forever change the world.

***

To contact Monique:

www.savyvision.com

savyvision@gmail.com

Ladymoniqueelliott@instagram

Moniqueelliott@LinkedIn

Brenda's Editorial Services

Greg Andruk

Greg Andruk is a CPA, MBA, CGMA (Chartered Global Management Accountant), and a CPC (Certified Professional Coach) who works with executives and business owners to help them resolve their business issues and achieve their goals.

Greg has managed cash flow, vendor relations, financial planning, staff recruitment, marketing, and mergers/acquisition for companies such as Continental Airlines, Dart Industries, Jack LaLannes' Health Spas, and many other companies prominent in their industries.

Greg is a licensed CPA in California, received a B.S. in Accounting from Utah State University, and an MBA from the University of Southern California with an emphasis in Finance and Marketing. He is a member of the American Institute of CPAs, and a member of the California Society of CPAs.

Greg is an Energy Leadership Master Practitioner, a designation issued by the Institute for Professional Excellence in Coaching, which is one of the largest and most reputable coaching institutes in the world. He finds that helping others use their energy to be successful is rewarding on many levels. Greg's many years of hands-on business experience makes him unique as a coach, where he brings the added dimension of first-hand knowledge to each business coaching experience.

When Greg is not helping others with their business and life endeavors, he enjoys riding his motorcycles, working on his six classic Cadillacs, swimming with a Master's team, and gardening.

You Cannot Make a Mistake.

IPEC Foundation Principle

By Greg Andruk

This is one of the thirty plus Foundation Principles of the Institute for Professional Excellence in Coaching (IPEC). It was the first one presented to me. We are starting to hear this all the time. I remember that John Wooden, the famous UCLA basketball coach, emphasized this in his pyramid of success. Don't dwell on your mistake, get up and make something good happen, and he ONLY won ten NCAA basketball championships, IN A ROW!

What is a mistake anyway? What is a mistake to one person could be a victory to another? If we get so hung up on the outcome or the process, we limit our opportunities. Are there really any mistakes? In our journey to get to our desired outcome, don't we limit ourselves by putting a negative connotation on a result? Isn't a "mistake" just an outcome we don't like? Don't all of the outcomes to our actions lead us to our eventual destination? The outcomes that we classify as mistakes may be the most memorable.

I was recounting to a friend my experience with the draft board. Remember the draft? Can you imagine it today?

My parents were divorced. I was born in Jackson Heights, Queens, New York. We lived in the basement apartment of my Grandparents house. When I was three, my parents split up, divorced when I was four, and when I was six, my mother and I moved to Southern California. My Mother, who didn't drive, landed a job at a company named Garrett Airesearch, which is now part of Honeywell. She was a clerk that supported the Contact Administrator for military spare parts. The office was on what is now part of Terminal One for LAX. Because of that we always lived near the airport until my mother learned to drive, which was several years later and part of our family folklore.

When we moved to Southern California, I would be sent to stay with my father in New York during the summers. He would park me with my Grandparents, which meant it was mostly with my grandmother, which wasn't too bad because I was surrounded by seven cousins, all boys. If I had stayed in Southern California, I would have been in some day care facility all day long. With my cousins, we basically ran the neighborhood all day, and I would wind up at the end of the day at Grandma's. This lasted four about four years, and my father remarried, bought a house on Long Island, and my days were spent with my new stepmother, who is not the friendliest person in the world, at least not to me. I think she resented my existence, oh well.

Each year when I would come home from New York, my mother would have moved to a new apartment, which meant a new school. I went to six elementary schools, one junior high school, and two high schools. I was always the new kid in school, and usually the youngest because my birthday was right after the cut off for which year you were with. Fortunately for me, I was one of the larger if not largest kid in the class, even though I was six months to a year younger than most of the kids in the class.

Twice my mother moved to a new apartment while I was in New York because she had gotten married during the summer. Just a touch of emotional instability there, but I never felt insecure, or that she was going to abandon me.

When I was in fifth grade my mother married Dick Hewitt, who was from a wealthy family in Vermont, and several times was the number one TV salesman in the country. Dick, who was in my life the longest, five years, was wonderful to me. I have a great love for him. However, he felt boys should go to boarding school, and I was entered into Mt. Lowe Military Academy. I was allowed to go home for the weekend every other weekend. It was the sixties. My parents would drive me back to Mt. Lowe each Sunday night, my mother crying all the way. To get home on the weekends off I would have to take the bus from Altadena to the Green Hotel in Pasadena, and take an airport bus to LAX, which was near our apartment. Talk about character building! At the time, we lived in an apartment at 99th and Crenshaw. Century boulevard is the entrance to LAX, and

I developed the skill of getting the bus driver to let me off at Century and Crenshaw, much to the consternation of the other passengers.

Those experiences of a new place to live every year, a new school, a new man in my mother's life, and consequently mine, a change in my Father's life that wasn't particularly friendly to me, and the isolation from the rest of my New York family, are occurrences that I think it is safe to say that no child would welcome. Because of those circumstances I was always the new kid at school, and just as I would establish some friendships, off to New York I would go, and be thrust into another new set of kids when I got back. These experiences built a skill and a strength in me to see things as they really are. Groups of people build patterns and a history over time that may not necessarily continue to be real. I learned to look at people's actions and not their reputation or statements to get a feel for how to interrelate with them. It's not something I consciously developed. It is something that happened out of necessity. My power of discernment was sharpened to a razor's edge when I spent the fifth grade in military school. Kids can be vicious, and in a closed environment like a boarding school, where there is nowhere to hide, upper classmen can be particularly predatory. Seeing how thing really are surely helped me to survive the experience of military school.

Back to our story in New York. While I had this situation of constant change in Southern California, I would have to deal with my father and Stepmother on Long Island during the summers. I no longer saw my cousins, or my Grandparents in Queens because my father didn't get along with his siblings or his father. That's understandable. My Grandfather was from the old country, and you didn't mess with Grandpa. My most vivid recollections are from around the kitchen table in his house, and I did something that angered him. Once or twice his belt bucket was whizzing by my ear. He could get his belt off in a flash, and I was lucky that I have been blessed with fabulous reflexes and speed. My other recollection was my uncle Matty was visiting Grandma at the end of the day. Uncle Matty was a giant of a man, particularly to my eight-year-old self. He was six three or four and two hundred fifty pounds of muscle. Not someone to trifle with. Grandpa burst through the front door of his house, which opened to the kitchen, saw Matty, and in a rage punched him in the mouth. The two men tumbled into the parlor which was beyond the kitchen. Grandpa had clearly built the house without an architect. The two men wrestled in the parlor with Grandma screaming, and when Grandpa had made his point, Uncle Matty got up and left like nothing had happened. I thought to myself, humph, these adults are wild!

So, back to the staid environment of Long Island, my Father would lecture me that my grandfather, who had passed away when I was twelve, would have paid for my cousin's college education, but my cousin had decided to become a New York City cop, and didn't go to college. My Father was now managing my grandfather's properties, and he would tell me on a rather regular basis that he would pay for my college, along with telling me a lot of other stuff teenage boys love to hear from their fathers. I think he felt pretty safe making these pronouncements based on what he thought my chances were of going to college.

Well, when the time came, I had applied to several colleges and was accepted by two or three. My first choice was USC, which at the time cost around $3,000 per year. This being the moment of truth for my Father related to the statements of paying for college, he pronounced USC too expensive, and that I should go to The University of Colorado, my second choice. I think HIS real first was choice Santa Monica City College, a local junior college that was $3 per year, but my Father lived in New York and didn't know community colleges at the time were $3 per year. Yes Bernie Sanders, college was nearly free in the old days. Pretty much everybody could afford the $3 for a year of college education. So, my Father made a deal with my mother, and agreed to pay $100 per month as his HALF of what it would cost for me to go to The University of Colorado. So, off to Boulder for me.

I was 17 when I started college. At Boulder, when running for classes the last stop for us male students was the draft table. The draft started when you were 18, and there were various deferments, but the draft and the Viet Nam war were coming under increased scrutiny, and deferments, specifically student deferments, were on the way out. The lady at the draft table told me not to worry about the draft, and she told me that when I go home to LA for Christmas break, I should go to the draft board and register for the draft. Sitting behind the table and looking pretty official, I took the draft table lady for her word, and I would register for the draft when I got home for Christmas.

That semester in Boulder was pretty tumultuous for me. My Father never sent any $100 checks to my mother, and in fact, when I turned 18 in October, mid-way through the Fall semester, he broke off all contact with me. It would be five years before I would speak to him again and resume our on again and off again relationship.

It wasn't any better on the home front with my mother. While I was in Colorado, she split up with my stepfather Dick, whom I adored, sold the house in Pacific Palisades, got rid of my cat, dog, and most of my possessions I didn't take to Colorado, and moved about forty mile south to an apartment in Torrance. My first night "home" in the apartment in Torrance, my mother had invited her new boyfriend over for dinner, and he was so drunk, he wretched into the planter box outside the front door of my mother's apartment. Welcome home!

We are getting to the heart of this story now. The next morning, after my memorable dinner with my mother and her new boyfriend, I traveled to the draft board in Gardena, which is near Torrance. The whole process with the Draft Board was so demeaning. It involved a lot of paperwork and a physical exam. The Army felt it helped the process for us new registrants to do this in our underwear. You went from station to station either being examined or completing paperwork in your underwear. When I got to the end of the process, I was asked why I didn't register for the draft within the time limit in the law, which was something like ten days from your birthday. I told the Draft Board person that I was told at the University of Colorado to register when I got home for Christmas, well, the Draft Board person informed me that I had broken the law and that I need to stand in the line for those that had broken the law. Well, you can imagine what I felt like at that news. I trooped over to the scofflaw line, where twenty or thirty young men in their underwear were milling around.

When I got to the person at the scofflaw table, I was nearly in a panic, no, I wasn't NEARLY in a panic, I WAS in a panic! You see, they could have declared me 1A, and put me on a bus for boot camp right from the draft board. The person at the table told me I had made a BIG MISTAKE and wanted to know why I hadn't registered in a timely manner. I told him the story about the lady in Boulder when I was running for classes, and that she said it was no problem to wait until I came home to register. He said, you're a college student. I assured him I was by showing him my CU ID, and he lit up like a Christmas tree, it WAS Christmas time, and he sent me to the student deferment table. Apparently, I was the only person that day that was NOT either resisting the draft or had been in jail for the reason of registering late. I trooped over to the student deferment table, got my draft card, which I carry to this day, put my clothes on, and went back to my mother's apartment in Torrance.

Even though I had turned eighteen two months before, I mark that day as the day I became an adult. NONE of those experiences I would call a mistake, not even the bad advice not to register for the draft. Those experiences have shaped who I am today.

Ok, those of you who have made it this far are probably wondering, what has this got to do with business or ME?

Well:

Ever have a professional give you advice that didn't work out?

Ever have something or someone you counted on disappear?

Ever have your entire world change, like being fired from your job, company go bankrupt, your job moves to a different location, lose a major customer, or have the operation you work for moved to a different country, or your spouse tell you they were in love with someone else? Millions of people experience this EVERY day.

The Draft Board was a real lesson in taking responsibility for what happens to you, and what one needs to take care of. I could have been on a bus to Fort Ord, and Vietnam thirty day later. If that had happened there would have been a new set of opportunities to deal with.

Chaos is here to stay, and really has never left us. The one thing all of us can depend on is that change is going to happen. All an outcome we don't like does is set us up for the next experience, and if you are living in the moment and process orientated rather than outcome orientated, it becomes easier to get things going in the direction you really want.

Richard Nixon is my favorite President. Not for opening China, getting us off the gold standard, or ending the Viet Nam war. He's my favorite because right after my narrow escape from the draft board, he eliminated all deferments to the draft, and established a lottery system. The new system was based on a random drawing of birth dates, and he promised he wouldn't go over number 156 with the draft. My number was 159. Less than six months from nearly being shipped off to basic training and Viet Nam, I was permanently dismissed from military service. It was amazing.

I was on a track to go another year at Santa Monica College and then attend USC, my original first choice, on a Navy ROTC scholarship. I tell people that had I continued on the path to the Navy, which required five years of service after college, we probably would have gotten into a war with China, and we would still be at it. Instead, Nixon ended the Viet Nam war, and the ROTC graduates had to do 30 days of active duty with the National Guard and were released from their service obligation. Do I have any regrets? Not a one. It would have been nice to go to USC. It made a pretty large impact on my career as a CPA not attending there, but I made other choices that have served me well. A lot of people would have thought it was a mistake not to go to USC on the Navy's money, but that is hindsight, and I have made a lifetime to looking forward.

Making things happen when others don't think a positive outcome is possible is a valuable skill to have. I don't always succeed, but I always take responsibility, and like John Wooden advised, I don't dwell on the outcome because there is always a tomorrow.

Not being tied to an outcome as good or bad, but instead as a guidepost for the next decision or situation is quite freeing. The freedom from a specific outcome opens up the possibilities of taking different paths that can lead to even greater outcomes than one specific outcome one can be stuck on. That demon disappointment clouds our vision and causes us to label the results of our efforts. I have received some really nice rewards because I took on projects and was willing to risk failure. It probably goes back to the new kid syndrome. By being willing to disregard the potential negative effect on my position in the group from failure, my stature soared within the organizations I have been a part of. Did I know I was going to succeed, no. Did many of my projects have a different but still beneficial outcome, yes. All because I am constantly willing to have different outcomes, which are never labeled as a mistake. I urge those who read this story to shift their outlook to the non-judgmental and self-forgiving outlook that "You Cannot Make a Mistake".

***

To contact Greg:

https://www.linkedin.com/in/greg-andruk/

https://www.powerandperformancecoaching.com/

https://www.linkedin.com/company/power-and-performance-coaching

greg@powerandperformancecoaching.com

(800) 287-9971

Seonad Cook

Seonad Cook is CEO of Executive Growth Coaching. She's an educator, a certified personal growth coach, an entrepreneur, and a 7-figure salesperson.

Seonad has a Bachelor of Science Degree from the University of Glasgow, Scotland and a master's degree in Education from the University of Cambridge, England. Seonad's extensive career in education and personal development started in The Gambia, West Africa with the Voluntary Service Overseas (UK's equivalent of US Peace Corps). Over her career, Seonad has travelled the world extensively as an educator, coach, senior education executive and education sales consultant across the USA, the Middle East, Europe, China, and Southeast Asia.

With a commitment and desire to make a difference in the world through education and personal development, Seonad has trained and assisted over 56,000 senior professionals around the world make the most of their untapped potential and impacted the lives of over 4 million children globally.

Seonad believes we all have unlimited potential and no matter how successful you are in your business, career, or life right now, you are only scratching the surface of what you can achieve. Seonad's mission and passion is to help ambitious entrepreneurs, individuals, and teams bring more of their potential to the surface and take a quantum leap to achieve their personal and professional goals so that they can live the life they truly desire.

The Mindset of Selling

By: Seonad Cook

Selling is an essential skill for any entrepreneur to master, and it starts with having the right mindset. In fact, I believe that success in selling is 95% mindset and 5% strategy. Master your mindset around selling and watch your sales skyrocket!

In reading this chapter, my hope is that you will gain insight into how much your mindset around sales and selling impacts your business' success and I will share with you, based on my own experience, what has helped me to become a consistent 7-figure salesperson. Finally, I will introduce some practical tasks that you can implement right now to help you master the mindset of selling and achieve greater success in your business.

I am an educator, a personal growth coach, an entrepreneur, and a lifelong salesperson. That last one may surprise you. "What is a lifelong salesperson?" you may be asking. We will arrive there in just a moment. First, I want to share a bit of my background with you.

In the field of Education for over 30 years, I was constantly selling— selling my ideas, curriculum, and initiatives to children, parents, teachers, school leaders and owners, as well as regional and national government officials. Over the span of this time, I trained and assisted over 56,000 senior professionals around the world achieve their personal and professional goals and had an impact on the lives of over 4 million children globally.

A few years ago, I ventured into a very unfamiliar environment. I entered the corporate world as an International Sales Consultant with a multi-billion-dollar global corporation. Please understand that I possessed no formal sales training whatsoever. I secured this position with nothing but a belief that the skills I had gained throughout my years in Education were both valuable and transferrable. Sure enough, I very quickly rose to become a top International Sales Consultant and a consistent 7-figure earner for the organisation.

Whether we recognize it or not, we are ALWAYS selling, always negotiating our next deal. To varying degrees, we are all salespeople. Think of your family and the discussions that go into where you want to go on holiday or which restaurant to eat at. Consider the negotiations with your kids: what time they need to go to bed or which vegetables they need to eat in order to justify having dessert. We are always involved in some form of negotiation. One of my favourite quotes is, *"Raising kids is like being constantly surrounded by a tiny sales team. They're always trying to persuade you into doing or buying something. And they assume everything you say is just an opening offer."*

I have a distinct memory of a time when I was homing in my negotiation skills. At 13 years old, I was devastated when my parents refused to let me go on a cruise around the Mediterranean. It was a school trip, and there was no way I was getting left behind while my friends all had a blast. So, I set about 'selling' the idea to Mum and Dad. I thought that washing, drying (and putting away!) the dishes every night for a family of six (no dishwashers in those days!) and vacuuming the whole house every weekend for the next year was a good trade off to be allowed to go on the cruise, but unfortunately, it didn't work. I needed to think about what would be more important to them if I stood any chance of going on the trip. I always knew that my parents expected me to do well at school and that my education in high school was very important to them. So, I decided to take a different approach and emphasize the once in a lifetime educational value of the trip. That's what ended up winning them over, and even though we hit stormy waters on that cruise, and I wished I had stayed at home on solid ground, I had achieved my goal; I had made the sale. I realise now that selling the idea to Mum and Dad was about developing skills that would serve me well throughout my working life.

No business can survive without a successful salesperson, and yet so many entrepreneurs struggle with selling. There can be several reasons for this and one that I see most frequently with my clients is limiting beliefs. What is a limiting belief? A limiting belief is a false belief you hold about something or someone (including yourself) that can hold you back from achieving success and keep you stuck. Limiting beliefs are usually passed onto you when you are very young by the people around you, your parents, grandparents, family, and friends. In many cases, limiting beliefs are passed down through many generations; you would need to go a long way back down the family line to see who first made the decision to do many of the things you do now. Unfortunately, unless consciously replaced, false/limiting beliefs can control many aspects of your life and your results.

For example, a limiting belief about money can keep you from earning the income you truly desire. Your relationship with money, and how much money you believe you can earn, will impact how much revenue you generate in your business. A person doesn't earn $50k because they want to earn $50k; they earn $50k because they don't believe they can earn $150k. This applies to entrepreneurs as well. If you don't believe you can earn the amount of money you would really love to earn in your business, then chances are you will undervalue yourself and your product or service and set sales targets that are way below what you could potentially achieve. A limiting belief about sales and salespeople can sabotage your potential sales. If you feel apprehensive or hesitant about asking for the sale, your prospect will pick this up from you and will probably not buy, no matter how great a presentation you delivered. Limiting beliefs are very powerful and can really hold you back from achieving the great success you are capable of achieving.

There have been many times in my own life when limiting beliefs have held me back. I grew up in a working-class family where no-one had ever gone to university. The belief at home was that the only way to be successful in life, after high school, was through sheer hard work in a trade—not through studying. This limiting belief almost kept me stuck—and could have resulted in me living a completely different life.

When I was 17 years old, a small handful of my friends were applying for university. As someone who grew up in a working-class family, I didn't think university was an option for me. I honestly didn't think I was even smart enough. However, my life completely changed direction when my guidance teacher, Mr. Wright, asked me why I wasn't applying for university. When I discussed with him my family's belief around higher education and work, he helped me see the limiting belief I'd bought into. With his help, I applied, and a few months later, was accepted to study Mathematics at the University of Glasgow in Scotland. With a mix of excitement and trepidation, I once again went about 'selling' an idea to my parents, who were going to have to fund my studies.

Thankfully, I was successful and managed to win them over. Four years later, I graduated with a Bachelor of Science Degree from Glasgow University, and subsequently went on to study for a master's degree in Education at the University of Cambridge in England. Being able to sell an idea, a dream even, had served me well once again. Let the lesson to you be, if you are carrying around limiting beliefs about yourself, about money, or about sales, this is going to significantly impact your ability to sell and will ultimately impact the success of your business. If Mr. Wright had not helped me to recognize the limiting belief that was holding me back from going to university, how different my life would have been! Not only that, but I may not have had the opportunity to serve and help thousands of people around the world bring more of their potential to the surface and achieve their goals.

The great news is you can do something about your limiting beliefs; you can develop new beliefs around selling that will replace your current, limiting beliefs.

As I mentioned, there are other hurdles that entrepreneurs face when it comes to making consistent sales in their businesses and I work with my clients every day helping them to overcome these hurdles.

Here are four practical things that you can do today to strengthen your mindset around selling and improve your business' success.

1. Set Clearly Defined SALES GOALS:

Do you find yourself going around in circles and not making much progress? Do you sometimes get to the end of a day and feel you haven't achieved very much? As Robert Heinlein says, "In the absence of clearly-defined goals, we become strangely loyal to performing daily trivia until ultimately we become enslaved by it." Having a clearly defined sales goal is very important for the growth of your business. Otherwise, you can easily "…become strangely loyal to performing daily trivia" and get lost down the rabbit hole of distraction and 'busyness.'

How do you set the right type of GOAL?

a). The purpose of a GOAL is to grow, not to get. When you set your goal, if there is no growth in going from where you are now to where you want to go, then that is not an adequate goal. There is no growth in going after something you already know how to do.

For example, if you are just starting out on your entrepreneurial journey, maybe your goal could be to attract and close your first five clients. If you are a more seasoned entrepreneur, and you increased your sales revenue last year by 5% or 10%, why not go for a QUANTUM LEAP this year and increase your sales income by 100%. Now, that might seem illogical and impossible to achieve, especially if you have always improved your sales each year in incremental steps.

As Price Pritchett says in his fabulous book, *YOU2*: "It's time to start focusing on possibilities, rather than on limits or obstacles. Making a quantum leap means moving outside your mental boundaries. If you will rethink how you're thinking, you can multiply your performance potential. You must let your desires guide you, instead of allowing yourself to be boxed in by perceived constraints."

The way forward will reveal itself once you start acting towards your goal. In the words of Steve Jobs: "You cannot connect the dots looking forward, you can only connect them looking backwards. So, you have to trust that the dots will somehow connect in the future."

b). You must really WANT your goal. Making a committed decision to achieve your goal is key. As soon as you commit to going after your sales goal, you flip your thinking onto the frequency of your goal, and as Einstein said, "Match the frequency of the reality you want, and you cannot help but get that reality. It can be no other way. This is not philosophy. This is physics." Whatever your sales goal, mastering the mindset of selling is essential.

2. Step into the IDENTITY of a Successful Entrepreneur.

You have two images of yourself, one that you present to the outside world and one that you have inside, which is called your self-image. The important thing to note is that you cannot outgrow your self-image and whatever you believe to be true of yourself determines the level of success you will achieve in your business and in your life. So, if you want to be a successful entrepreneur, you must see yourself as that person now and replace the image you currently hold of yourself with the new image of a successful entrepreneur. Now, that might seem illogical but as Neville Goddard said, "It's not what you want that you attract, you attract what you believe to be true." You need to develop the proper mentality and become a successful entrepreneur now in your mind so that you can attract what you need to achieve your sales goal.

Here are some questions to think about to help you create your new self-image of a successful entrepreneur:

a). How do you FEEL now that you have achieved your sales goal with ease?

b). How has the success impacted your business?

c). How has the success impacted you family?

Hold the image of who you are when you have the successful business you've been dreaming of and feel all the benefits this success brings to your business and to your life.

3. Take ACTION.

You must take action every day that will drive you towards your goal.

Think of all the daily activities you do on a regular basis. Are there any activities that you would regard as non-productive?

Do you regularly carry out activities in your business that don't take you towards achieving your sales goal? Write down a list of six activities you did yesterday that were non-goal achieving activities.

Now write down six goal achieving activities that you could do today to move towards achieving your sales goal.

4. Develop HABITS of a Successful Entrepreneur.

Forming good habits around selling is essential if you want to make consistent sales.

Examine your habits around selling:

a) Do you focus on answering emails or planning just to avoid having to make sales calls? This can take you down a rabbit hole, and before you know it, it's the end of the day and you haven't been very productive. A better habit to form here is to start each day with goal achieving activities that will take you towards your sales goal. For example, decide that you will make three sales calls before you open your emails.

b) Do you avoid following up with prospects because you don't want to appear pushy or salesy? You could be leaving $1,000s on the table because you do not follow up with people you have already spoken with over the previous weeks, months, or year. Having a tracking system in place for regularly following up with prospects will make a significant difference to your sales success. Decide that each day you will follow up with three prospects you've spoken with previously.

c) Do you have the habit of allowing yourself to buy into the prospect's limiting beliefs as to why they can't purchase your product or service? Be aware of your prospect's limiting beliefs and don't allow yourself to buy into them. When you know that your product or service is a solution for your prospect's problem, and you get an objection, find another way to show them how it will solve their problem and the transformation it will bring about for them.

d) Do you ask prospects to buy your product or service? It's incredible how many people do not ask for the sale. I love what Bob Proctor says on this point: "If you don't ask for the sale, all you're doing is research!" When you are confident that your product or service is a good fit for the prospect, and it will give them the transformation they are looking for, ask them to buy!

When it comes to selling and prospecting, the reason many entrepreneurs have not formed good habits around this is because it can feel uncomfortable; it doesn't feel good. If you are responsible for sales in your business, you feel uncomfortable selling your product or service, and you are not making consistent sales, you've got to get beyond this if you want to have a successful business.

As Albert E. N. Gray states in his book *The Common Denominator of Success*, "The secret of success of every man who has ever been successful lies in the fact he formed the habit of doing things that failures don't like to do......unless you have deliberately formed the habit of calling on people who are able to buy but unwilling to listen, then unconsciously you have formed the habit of calling on people who are willing to listen but unable to buy."

Develop new habits around selling and watch your sales soar. You have unlimited potential, and you can achieve the success that you want in your business and in your life. Don't shy away from selling; embrace it.

I have given you some ideas and practical tasks in this chapter, which if you implement them, will help strengthen your mindset around selling and will help set you up to make consistent sales in your business.

***

To contact Seonad:

Email: seonad@executivegrowthcoaching.com

Linkedin: www.linkedin.com/in/seonad-cook

Website: www.executivegrowthcoaching.com

Bonnie Kowaliuk

 Bonnie Kowaliuk is an eclectic mindfulness coach and transformational leadership consultant focusing on the mental health and wellbeing of men and families. Bonnie's inspiration for this life path has been her children and in particular her son, who like so many young men struggle in silence and shame, relative to accessing effective and empowering mental health resources. Healthy and whole men support & nourish health and whole families. She has background designations as a registered social worker, accredited music therapist and business leadership consultant, who over the course of the past 10 years has been exploring brain-based approaches to learning, transformational leadership, health and wellness. She completed her designation as a Fellow of the Bonny Method of Guided Imagery and Music which employs music assisted mindfulness and psychotherapeutic approach to help address a range of issues from mental health and wellness to optimal learning and performance. Bonnie is a coactive certified coach and has a certification in mindfulness via Royal Roads along with a certification in Mindfulness Based Stress Reduction from the Center for Mindfulness Studies in Toronto. As a lifelong learner & change catalyst, she hopes to inspire growth, change and evolution in others and in organizations through her own example and her love to learn, live authentically and discover her true self.

SOS: Leader Alert! Mindfulness and Resilience are Essential to Your Thriving (Not Just Surviving)

By Bonnie Kowaliuk

We are castaways washed up ashore

While we continue to manage the harrowing reality of a pandemic and ongoing global conflict, many of us feel like castaways on isolated islands.

It's been quite inspiring to witness how entrepreneurs, small businesses, and corporations continue to adjust to the changing socio-economic and cultural climate. Many have come together, supporting their communities and neighbours, and looking for ways to reinvent themselves.

A recent survey (**1**) performed by the Angus Reid Institute suggests most Canadians believe COVID-19 has pulled the country apart instead of bringing it together. The survey also shows that 79% believe this crisis has brought out the worst in people, while 61% state their level of compassion towards one another has deteriorated.

Gratitude, kindness, and solidarity have been present. But what seems to have prevailed is a sense of frustration, hopelessness, and uncertainty. People have lost faith in their leaders—CEOs, owners, directors, managers, and government officials.

What can erode people's trust in leadership? Lack of awareness, purpose, and values; reactive versus proactive actions; arrogance and selfishness; disconnection from reality and people's needs; an unhealthy pursuit of power; and an accountability deficit.

How can leaders become more resilient during these turbulent times?

How can they gain back people's trust and hope while adapting to change?

I believe the answer is in **<u>mindful and resilient</u>** leadership.

What is mindful leadership?

Mindful leadership is the art of adopting mindfulness as you guide teams, organizations, and communities.

According to Jon Kabat-Zinn, Ph.D. (**2**), **mindfulness** is the "awareness that arises through paying attention, on purpose, in the present moment, non-judgementally."

A mindful leader embraces moment-to-moment awareness to pay attention to their environment, thoughts, feelings, and behaviours. They are open, curious, compassionate, and make decisions based on their mission, vision, and values.

How can mindfulness support leadership capacity and development?

According to a 2019 study (**3**), mindfulness training may help improve mindful task management, self-care, self-reflection, and the capacity to relate to others and adapt to change.

Let's look at how mindfulness can also support other specific leadership skills according to research:

Mindfulness may reduce stress and anxiety

Evidence (**4**) shows that reduced stress is one of the most noted psychological benefits of mindfulness, which seems to be consistent across job types, mindfulness training, and employee stress levels. Likewise, according to the American Psychological Association (APA) (**5**), Mindfulness-Based Stress Reduction (or MBSR) programs have been associated with decreased stress and anxiety levels.

Mindfulness may increase awareness

Mindfulness refers to intentional and non-judgmental awareness. As leaders become more mindful, they develop a greater sense of self-understanding, observing their ideas, decisions, emotions, and actions relative to how they might impact themselves and others.

This 2019 (**3**) study also sees workplace mindfulness training as a favourable intervention to increase "awareness of the way they manage their tasks, lead tense conversations, or react to change."

Mindfulness may help develop emotional regulation

Research (**4**) suggests that a lack of emotional self-control can be a crucial roadblock to leadership success.

As APA states (**5**), mindfulness can help develop effective emotion regulation in the brain, even in periods of stress, which may help mitigate said leadership challenge.

Mindfulness may promote acceptance

A 2017 study (**6**) claimed that mindfulness might reduce stress reactivity by training acceptance. Mindfulness (**5**) enables leaders to accept what they cannot control without attachment, judgment, or the need to change it.

Mindfulness may enhance resilience

A 2018 systematic review (**7**) shows that mindfulness may positively impact resilience, which has been associated with easing the adverse effects of stress, trauma, and adversity.

Another 2018 (**8**) study examining human service professionals concluded that "mindfulness-based interventions may effectively replenish resilience, reduce states of burnout and traumatic stress, and improve psychological well-being."

A leader with **reduced stress and anxiety, increased awareness, enhanced emotion regulation, acceptance, and resilience** is better equipped to surf the waves and navigate through the storms of life.

A closer look at resilience

Resilience is our capacity to recover or spring back from hardship. APA (**9**) defines it as "the process of adapting well in the face of adversity, trauma, tragedy, threats, or significant sources of stress."

The word resilience (**10**) was first used in the 1620s, deriving from the Latin "resilire," which means to recoil or rebound. By the 19th century, the term had evolved to include the meaning of elasticity and flexibility. Later, it was used to describe being resistant or not susceptible to something.

As Dr. Steven Southwick discusses in this psychotraumatology paper, resilience is a complex concept that may exist in a continuum—varying in levels, showing up in different parts of our lives, and changing over time.

Multidisciplinary experts point out that specific childhood factors may help you develop resilience, including:

- Healthy relationships and caregiving

- Emotion-regulation skills

- Self-awareness

- Capacity to visualize the future

- Motivation system that encourages you to learn, grow and adapt

Ideally, we foster resilience before setbacks happen. Yet, specialists also suggest we can enhance it during or after stressful situations, highlighting a healthy family and community environment as one of the key ways to do so.

While external factors may help, there are moments when you are the primary source of resilience in your life—your grit, moral compass, and personal values. For example, a British survey (**12**) revealed that 75% of employees felt the most significant drain of resilience resulted from managing relationships or workplace politics and that an astounding **90%** were getting resilience from within themselves. Not from their organization, relationships, or work. **Themselves.**

This brings up a valuable question: **How can organizations help their teams become more resilient so they can rebound from adversity and thrive?**

As Brent Gleeson states (**13**): "You can't build resilient teams without resilient leaders."

What is resilient leadership?

Resilient leadership refers to the ability to bounce back from difficulties and lead with agility without engaging in negative habits of mind and dysfunctional behaviours.

Resilient leaders are focused, authentic, and innovative. They leverage their experience, purpose, and values to reframe failures as temporary setbacks or opportunities to grow and become better human beings.

But they can't do it alone. Resilient leaders need to foster resilience within their teams so organizations can fully recover and succeed abound.

Resilient leaders typically:

- Align teams to a shared purpose, vision, and set of core values

- Build awareness and a growth mindset

- Exhibit emotional stability under stress

- Navigate setbacks with equanimity

- Accept uncertainty without getting attached to "what ifs"

- Adapt and persevere through changing scenarios

- Count on a support system to manage difficult times

An outstanding portrayal of resilient leadership is **Nobel Prize winner Nelson Mandela,** who was sentenced to life in prison in 1963 after devoting his life to ending apartheid. While incarcerated, Mandela suffered cruel isolation and contracted tuberculosis, but that did not stop him.

As he eloquently said: "Everyone can rise above their circumstances and achieve success if they are dedicated to and passionate about what they do."

The intersection between mindful leadership and resilient leadership

Mindful and resilient leaders...

- Have open **awareness** of themselves as leaders, their organizations, and their environment.

- Recognize the concept of **impermanence**—everything is changing all the time—and **accept** hardship without clinging to the past or future.

- **Manage stress** and **regulate the challenging emotions** that may come along during high-stakes situations.

- Adopt a **beginner's mind,** looking at the world with curiosity and inventiveness.

A co-active coaching approach to resilient leadership

Co-active coaching is one of the methods I implement as a coach, which focuses on helping clients deepen the meaning and forward the action.

- **Deepening the meaning** refers to tapping into your being, your why, and all the lessons learned along your journey.

- **Forwarding the action** consists of moving forward, achieving goals, or implementing new practices to support your capacity to thrive.

Both **being** and **doing** are essential to embracing resilience. You must deepen your purpose and take aligned action to steer yourself and your teams.

As Henry Kimsey-House et al. state in their book, Co-Active Coaching: Changing Business, Transforming Lives (**14**), "it's the cycle of **action** and **learning** over time that leads to sustained and effective change. Clients take action and learn, which leads to more action based on what they have learned, and the cycle continues."

Imagine you are a body of water. When you are being in the present moment, you are like still water—you are very reflective and deep. But when you transition into doing, you are more like the waves in the ocean—there's a force behind you; you can move ships, marine life, the earth, and more. The goal is to move out of stillness into waves of action.

Let's take a co-active look at the **essential qualities (being)** and **best practices (doing)** of a resilient leader.

Becoming resilient: Qualities of a resilient leader

Awareness

Resilient leaders are aware of their strengths, biases, and areas of opportunity. They have a clear grasp of their organization's internal and external reality and their team's operations and needs.

Hay Group performed a study (**15**) on more than 17,000 individuals worldwide, revealing self-awareness in 19% of the women versus 4% of the men interviewed. So, there's certainly room for improvement in this area for all leaders out there.

Curiosity

Resilient leaders are innovative thinkers, visionaries, and creators. They hone the power of imagination and reinvention to feed their growth mindset and aim for transformation.

A clear example of a curious leader is Albert Einstein. Leveraging his wild creativity and wonder, he pushed the boundaries and changed the world with his many contributions to the scientific community.

Purpose

Resilient leaders are fueled by a higher purpose or why. As author Simon Sinek (**18**) defines it, you're why refers to "WHY does your company exist? WHY do you get out of bed every morning? And WHY should anyone care? (...) All organizations start with WHY, but only the great ones keep their WHY clear year after year."

Leaders rooted in their purpose have the potential to transform people and entire countries. Look at Martin Luther King Jr., whose dream drove him to lead the Civil Rights Movement in the U.S. and resulted in the passage of the Civil Rights Act in 1964.

Taking resilient action: Best practices of a resilient leader

Value-based action

"Beliefs underlie every single thing we do, both individually and organizationally. Beliefs are like the root system of our lives. In my metaphor, I started to look at organizational culture as the soil. The quality of the soil will have a huge impact on what's planted—new ideas or new people—in the organization." —Ari Weinzweig (**16**), co-owner and founding partner of Zingerman's Community of Businesses.

Your beliefs or values represent the moral compass that informs your decisions and keeps you true to your purpose.

Perseverance

Resilient leaders persist with tenacity and determination, despite the challenges. They fail forward, transforming misfortune into a source of strength and inspiration or a chance for reinvention.

Think of Oprah Winfrey, a BIPOC woman who overcame sexual abuse as a child and navigated racial discrimination throughout the years. She is now one of the most successful African American women around the globe. Her TV show, book club, and countless charitable initiatives continue to uplift and empower people to this day.

Adaptation

Resilient leaders adapt in the face of adversity and focus their efforts on ensuring their teams can do the same. They improvise with intention, make the most of what they have, and acclimate to the needs and priorities at hand.

Sylvia Metayer (**17**), the former CEO of Sodexo Corporate Services Worldwide, is an excellent example of adaptation. She defined her former role as a servant, focused on supporting her employees and preparing them to adopt: "I think the most important thing is how you make people's work easier? (...) It's also very much about making them ready. The world is changing very fast, so we have to create career paths, and we have to support the training of our people so that they're ready for change."

Takeaway bits: Exercises to boost resilience

Now that you have a deep understanding of mindful and resilient leadership, you can start cultivating resilience within yourself and your organization with the resources below:

Affirmations for resilience

Repeat the following affirmations to yourself or out loud. Share them with your peers and teams as desired:

- *I will thrive in the face of adversity.*

- *I navigate change with ease.*

- *I have the power to adapt and transform.*

- *I see failure as an opportunity for a breakthrough.*

- *I accept the things I cannot control.*

- *I let go of what doesn't serve me.*

- *I embrace curiosity.*

- *I can manage my emotions.*

- *I have a support system.*

- *I can move in stillness.*

A guide to leading by your values

STEP 1: Start with some questions

Grab pen and paper and answer the following questions:

- *What makes you happy, proud, and accomplished?*

- *What do you dream about?*

- *What are your goals in life?*

- *What drives you or guides your decisions?*

- *What matters most to you?*

STEP 2: Look out for patterns

Check your answers and find some common ground. What's standing out? Is it family, taking care of others, or working with teams?

Whatever it is, sit with it for a moment.

STEP 3: Make a preliminary list

Look at those common areas and give them a keyword. Then, make a list with those keywords and reflect.

Are these your core values?

STEP 4: Review, revise, and organize

Review your list with caution. Make adjustments and go back to the questions if necessary. Once you are happy with your list, organize and group your values as desired.

Perhaps some of them are at the top of your list (e.g., family). Maybe others are too similar and can be consolidated in one value. Or perhaps some could be split up into more than one.

STEP 5: Finalize and display your values

Give your list of values another look to finalize it.

When ready, display your values in your home, office, or anywhere you can look at them daily. Perhaps you can create a mood board, a desktop background, or a handwritten list to hang on your wall. Find what works for you.

STEP 6: Live by these values

Lastly, make a conscious effort to think, act, and lead according to these principles. Remember, you can revisit these values over time as you progress in your journey.

And when a problem comes your way, use this list to remind you of what's truly important to you.

Guided meditation: Aligning your inner leadership with outer manifestation

Contact me to listen to the full guided meditation or read on to follow along.

1. Take a moment to settle. Breathe in three deep breaths. In your own time, close your eyes or soften your gaze.

2. Release any preconceived thoughts and ideas about leadership with each exhalation. On the next in-breath, direct attention to how you typically lead. Notice what you hear internally and externally. What is calling you to listen from a place of deep meaning?

3. Upon the next out-breath, let go of ways of being that are not serving you to step into being vulnerable, real, and present.

4. Inhale a state of authenticity and genuineness that reflects the real leader in you. Expand your awareness of your people's needs beyond the workplace. Draw a mental boundary or a picture frame around your work, your life, and the people around you. Breathe into the clarity and perspective you create relative to communicating your needs, listening, and honoring the needs of others. Use this as a starting point for exploration.

5. With the next out-breath, release any limiting beliefs, ways of communicating, or garnering feedback that creates barriers to healthy expression and authentic being. Notice what is working and what is not.

6. On the next in-breath, invite an open awareness of other ways of seeing and perceiving. What are you noticing or not noticing?

7. Continue investigating your inner leadership landscape, checking in with yourself, a coach, a mindfulness buddy, a consultant, or a trusted peer. Envision a plan in your mind's eye: a roadmap to reinvent **how you are** as a leader in a meaningful and authentic manner, as well as **what you are doing** as a leader—how you are talking, walking, acting, influencing, learning, and listening.

8. Move out of this way of knowing into sensing with your eyes, ears, body, and instincts. Honor your lived experiences and the collective experience. What are the invisible and visible ways that leaders benefit from the workplace and the organizational systems they are emerged? What are your blind spots and areas of unconscious awareness? Let go of these blindfolds and open your eyes to the truth of the present state in your workplace. Honor who you are and all other beings regardless of their label, identity, or title.

9. Become aware of states of separation, division, and exclusion. Breathe in states of diversity, inclusion, acceptance, and gratitude into your leadership state and the space where you lead.

10. Breathe expansion into your circle of friends, family, and colleagues. View the world and your workplace from a place of curiosity and wonder. Embrace discomfort, change, mistakes, and uncertainty. Open your mind's eye and actions to accept human error. Be the captain of your ship of life and lead with the moral compass of the heart and soul of your organization.

11. As you envision this state of being and way of forwarding the action, begin to bring your attention back to the breath. Take three deep, cleansing, and soothing breaths. Notice the weight of your body as it's grounded into the surface beneath you, as well as your feet as they sink into the ground. Become present and aware, slowly opening your eyes. At the sound of the bell, bring this state of being into the rest of your day.

***

To contact Bonnie:Bonnie Kowaliuk

Phone: 403-519-1959

Email: Info@sensesmindfulness.com

Website: www.sensesmindfulness.com

\References:

1. *COVID at Two: Vast majorities say the pandemic has pulled Canadians apart, brought out the worst in people.* Angus Reid Institute.
https://angusreid.org/covid-19-two-year-anniversary/
2. (2017, January 11). *Jon Kabat – Zinn: Defining Mindfulness.* Mindful
https://www.mindful.org/jon-kabat-zinn-defining-mindfulness/
3. (2019, May 15). Mindful Leader Development: How Leaders Experience the Effects of Mindfulness Training on Leader Capabilities. Frontiers
https://www.frontiersin.org/articles/10.3389/fpsyg.2019.01081/full

4. Patrick K. Hyland, R. Andrew Lee and Maura J. Mills. (2015, July 15). *Mindfulness at Work: A New Approach to Improving Individual and Organizational Performance.* Industrial and Organizational Psychology, 8, pp 576-602 doi:10.1017/iop.2015.41 https://www.researchgate.net/publication/282628776_Mindfulness_at_Work_A_New_A pproach_to_Improving_Individual_and_Organizational_Performance

5. Daphne M. Davis and Jeffrey A. Hayes.(2011). *What Are the Benefits of Mindfulness? A Practice Review of Psychotherapy-Related Research.* American Psychological Association 2011, Vol. 48, No. 2, 198 –208 0033-3204/11/$12.00 DOI: 10.1037/a0022062. https://www.apa.org/pubs/journals/features/pst-48-2-198.pdf

6. Emily k. Lindsay, Joshua M. Smyth.(2018, January). *Acceptance lowers stress reactivity: Dismantling mindfulness training in a randomized controlled trial.* Science Direct. https://www.sciencedirect.com/science/article/abs/pii/S0306453017304109

7. Joyce S, Shand F and Laurent J. Steven. *Road to resilience: a systematic review and meta-analysis of resilience training programmes and interventions.* BMJ Journals. https://bmjopen.bmj.com/content/8/6/e017858

8. Hanna A, Pidgeon A. *Leveraging Mindfulness to Build Resilience and Professional Quality of Life in Human Service Professionals.* OBM Integrative and Complementary Medicine 2018;3(2):007; doi:10.21926/obm.icm.1802007. http://www.lidsen.com/journals/icm/icm-03-02-007

9. (2020, February 1). *Building your resilience.* American Psychological Association. https://www.apa.org/topics/resilience

10. *Resilient.* Macmillan Dictionary Blog. https://www.macmillandictionaryblog.com/resilient

11. Southwick, S. M., Bonanno, G. A., Masten, A. S., Panter-Brick, C., & Yehuda, R. (2014). *Resilience definitions, theory, and challenges: interdisciplinary perspectives.* European journal of psychotraumatology, 5, 10.3402/ejpt.v5.25338. https://doi.org/10.3402/ejpt.v5.25338

12. Ovans A.(2015, January 05). *What Resilience Means, and Why It Matters.* Harvard Business Review.

https://hbr.org/2015/01/what-resilience-means-and-why-it-matters

13. Gleeson B.(2021, April 13). *Resilience In Leadership: How To Lead And Win Despite Change And Obstacles.* Forbes. https://www.forbes.com/sites/brentgleeson/2021/04/13/resilience-in-leadership-how-to-lead-and-win-despite-change-and-obstacles/?sh=782079633c5d

14. Karen Kimsey-House and Henry Kimsey-House. (2011, September 16).*CO-ACTIVE COACHING: CHANGING BUSINESS, TRANSFORMING LIVES.* Mobius. https://www.chapters.indigo.ca/en-ca/books/co-active-coaching-changing-business/9781857885675-item.html

15. (2012, March 27). *Women Poised to Effectively Lead in Matrix Work Environments, Hay Group Research Finds.* Business Wire. https://www.businesswire.com/news/home/20120327005180/en

16. WEINZWEIG. A. Ari Weinzweig. ZingTrain. https://www.zingtrain.com/trainer/ari-weinzweig/

17. Metayer. S. Sodexo Quality Of Life Services. https://tracks.sodexonet.com/files/live/sites/sdxcom-global/files/PDF/Group/Biographies/Sylvia_Metayer_EN.pdf

18. Sinek. S. Simon Sinek. https://simonsinek.com/

Donna Connor

Donna Connor is a proud mom and wife, serial entrepreneur, CEO of a multi-7-figure consulting firm, NuQuo Group, and the founder of Life on Purpose Academy, where she helps people heal their relationship with money and live a life of purpose. After growing up where there was never enough, she developed an unhealthy relationship with money at a young age that led to two bankruptcies before the age of 40. Since then, she has been able to recover from bankruptcy in record time, set herself and her husband up for retirement, become a financial advisor, travel multiple times per year, start 3 highly successful businesses, and create a money legacy for her family.

Donna has an empowering story of how she went from being bankrupt twice before the age of 40 to CEO of a multi-7-figure business and helping people heal their relationship with money. Because of her experiences, she is passionate about helping young adults create healthy relationships with money and to help them begin adulthood with more skills and tools than she had at their age.

Two Powerful Secrets to Reach Your Goals *FASTER*

By Donna Connor

"Quality questions create a quality life. Successful people ask better questions, and as a result, they get better answers"

– Tony Robbins

ASK BETTER QUESTIONS TO GET BETTER ANSWERS

This topic is one of my favorites. I've been helping couples get out of debt and create a plan to realize their dreams for almost 17 years. I worked with one couple three separate times to get out debt! I initially spent nine months working with them. They were THRILLED with the results! Tears accompanied their expressions of gratitude and disbelief when their debt-free day had finally come. About six months later, they called me in total shame because they were back in debt. So, we started working together again and they were able to pull themselves out of debt a second time. This time, they went forward with a strong determination to stay out of debt. They reached out to me about nine months later. Again, they were in debt. I was perplexed to say the least. I thought, "What is wrong? They have the needed tools and skillset. I've taught them everything, TWICE!" It was then that I realized that 90 percent of life is about mindset, not skillset. Mindset is the game changer. Mindset is what helps us win or lose in life, love, and business. It's the six inches between our ears that continually tries to stop us from going after our dreams. Our mindset is what helps us get over the hurdles when everything seems to be crashing down on us. Our mindset is what helps us get past that wall that we keep hitting repeatedly. Our brain is meant to protect us, and it will try to do so at any cost...even when it comes to going after our dreams.

If you can master your mindset, you can master ANYTHING! Why do you think there are so many books written about mindset, habits, etc.?

Life is the ultimate "Choose Your Own Adventure!" When you're on the road to creating your dream life, it doesn't matter that you have a full tank of gas if your engine needs work. Your mindset is the engine for your journey to design your dream life. We need to make sure our engines are always working.

Our brains were designed to solve problems. We need to get out of the way and allow them to do their job. When we find ourselves stuck, we need to ask ourselves the right questions, in the right order, to solve the problems we are facing. Once we learn to ask better questions, we will get better answers.

When we start dreaming of what we want to DO, HAVE, and BECOME, our brain immediately asks, "How?" How are we going to do that? How are we going to get that? How are we going to become that? And the minute we ask ourselves "how?", our brains shut down. They go into protective mode and will start to tell you all the reasons why you can't do, have, and become. They recite all the lies we've been fed about not being good enough, smart enough, or educated enough. These lies are a metaphoric tire boot that prevents you from moving forward on your journey. They hold you in place - fearful, discouraged, and hopeless.

There is a formula though, that if mastered, will allow you to reach all your dreams FASTER than you ever thought possible. This shortcut will get your brain working *for* you instead of *against* you. It will become your greatest advocate and problem solver instead of trying to stop you at every turn. So, let's get your brain doing what it's meant to do to help you on your journey. This is where you learn to start asking better questions!

You need to stop your brain from first asking "how?" and implement this formula to get better answers and results.

Question 1:   WHAT do I want?

Question 2:   WHY do I (and my family) want it?

Question 3:   WHO benefits from this?

Question 4:   WHEN can I get this done?

Question 5:   WHERE can I do this?

Question 6:   WHAT am I willing to sacrifice to accomplish this?

Question 7:   HOW can I do this?

Can you see how changing the order of the questions allows your brain to go into hyperdrive to help you figure things out? With asking these questions in this order, you've already eliminated your brain's natural objections! You've taken your brain out of protection mode. It can now see the value of your dreams and will start problem solving for you! How awesome is that?!

Let's go through this process with a real-life example. Let's say you want to save $20,000 to start a business. Normally, your brain would naturally ask itself "how?" and come up with 20 reasons you can't do it. You don't make enough. You've never had that much money before. You need the money for other things. You're not smart enough. And the list goes on and on.

Now let's change the order of the questions and see where it gets us. Let's say you want to save $20,000 to start a consulting firm. Let's see how changing the order of the questions you ask changes your outcome.

Q. WHAT do you want?

A. I want to start a consulting firm that will save companies money on their copiers and printers and put contracts in their favor instead of the vendor's favor. My consulting firm will allow companies to save a lot of time and money. It will add to the company's overall bottom line and create a more financially sound company for its owners and employees.

Q. WHY do I (and my family) want this?

A. My consulting firm will make a difference to businesses and individual lives. Knowing that I am making a difference to stabilize companies legally and financially, makes me proud and will allow me to feel good about what I do. Knowing that my company only takes a percentage of the cost savings we create, makes good financial sense that will provide a good living for my employees as well as my family. Knowing that I can run my business from anywhere thanks to great technology, affords my family the opportunity to enjoy a lifestyle we only dreamt possible.

Q. WHO benefits from this?

A. Our clients that we help by contributing to their bottom line and putting contracts into their favor.

Our client's employees who are now working for a financially stronger company.

Our employees who can make a difference with what they do and the money they earn.

My family who gets to see me more and has a great life with what I earn from this business.

My friends whom I can serve more and help more with money my business generates.

My community who I can support and give back to on a regular basis.

Phew! That's a lot of positive reinforcement for our brains to consider!

Q. WHEN can I get this done?

A. If I want to boot strap this venture, we can take $500 per paycheck and put it into savings. This process will take 20 months. If I also throw extra money at the dream, I can get there faster. If I take our tax returns for both years and add them to the savings account, that will save me another six months, so now I can have this done in 14 months! I can also look for investors or consider a business loan, if it makes financial sense.

Once I have the money, I can start working on this part-time until the business has a couple of clients. Then I can quit my job and go full-time in this new business.

Q. WHERE can I do this?

A. I can continue to work full-time while we are in saving mode. I can run the business from home or on the road. All I need is good internet connection and a quiet place to hold calls. Using a virtual office model, my employees can do their job from home, keeps overhead low, and offers a great benefit to my employees. It allows me to travel with my family and work from anywhere.

A. WHAT am I willing to sacrifice to accomplish this?

Q. I deeply believe in this dream and recognize the opportunity to create a needed business that will make a true difference to our clients and many individuals as well. I am willing to sacrifice the extra money from our budget, for a time, to build this dream. I'm willing to cut back eating out so we can throw everything at it. I'm willing to sacrifice my sleep while we get the business off the ground. I'll work full-time during the day and launch the new company in the evenings. I'm grateful my family is willing to make some sacrifices as well to help me realize my dream.

WOW!!! Now, we get to ask ourselves the BIG question: How can I do this? We've taken all the objections out and allowed our brains to start working on more answers for us! Now is the time to be patient and have faith. Your brain will surprise you as ideas come to you on how to accomplish this worthwhile goal. Pay close attention to the thoughts and promptings that come to you after this exercise!

"Good Coaches share lessons from their experience. Great coaches help you crystalize lessons from your experience. Good Coaches give us useful answers. Great coaches help you ask better questions. Good coaches walk you through their path. Great coaches help you identify your path." – Adam Grant

HIRE GREAT COACHES

Hiring a great coach is the number one success tool in my toolkit. Coaches have defined me, changed my trajectory, and improved my life in ways I can't even put into words. They have impacted my life forever.

Coaches assist their clients in improving their relationships, careers, and day-to-day lives. Coaches can help you clarify your goals, identify the obstacles holding you back, and then come up with strategies for overcoming each obstacle.

One of the main benefits of working with a coach is the fresh, informed perspective they can offer on problems that you face. In addition to offering new insights into challenges, a coach can help you zero in on negative patterns that could be standing in the way of your success. Many people view working with a coach as a means of bridging the gap between your current circumstances and the life you'd like to lead.

I've worked with some great coaches, as well as some mediocre coaches. I learned something from each of them, but the great ones truly skyrocketed me to the next level, and I am eternally grateful for them. Mediocre coaches may provide some great information, but great coaches give you opportunities to make a transformation.

My coaching career actually began by accident. A friend knew my accounting background and that my husband and I were in a good place financially. She reached out to see if I could help her and her husband get their finances in order and get out of debt. I met with them, created a game plan and sent them on their way. I checked on them each month and discovered that they weren't doing the work we had planned. We discussed why they were struggling and then revamped the game plan. This time, it worked better for them. As they worked the plan, the plan worked, and they saw great success. They were very happy and enthusiastically recommended that a family member reach out to me for help, and they did. And the rest, as they say, is history. Word-of-mouth referrals have kept me busy helping couples with their finances for almost 17 years. It has been very rewarding. I have literally saved marriages by helping them get their finances in order! I love what I do and want to continue to grow and serve more people.

The example set by my great coaches has created a strong desire for me to hone my skills and become a better coach. My journey has taken years and has covered a lot of ground. Along the way, I've become a Certified Personal Empowerment Coach as well as a Timeline Therapy® practitioner. I've also earned certifications in Neuro-Linguistic Programming (NLP) and hypnosis, become a financial advisor, and a licensed insurance agent. I now have more tools in my toolbelt to help more people. I love helping someone who is stuck and providing them with the tools and skills they need to see massive results. I am grateful for the coaches I have worked with and for the time they took to hone their skills. I have taken what I have learned from each and incorporated that knowledge into my personal life, the life of each member of my family, and my businesses. I have made a difference in my clients' lives because great coaches have made a difference in mine.

I have learned the importance of finding people who have accomplished what I want to accomplish and to learn from their experiences. I have also learned the importance of coaching and will always have a coach to help me on my journey. Coaches are the ultimate pit crew on your journey to creating your dream life.

I'd like to share with you some of the GREAT coaches I have personally worked with, what I learned from them, what they helped me accomplish, and how you can start learning from them immediately.

Richie Norton

Known for: Bestselling author of the book The Power of Starting Something Stupid

Short Bio: Richie Norton is the award-winning, bestselling author of the book *The Power of Starting Something Stupid* (in 10+ languages) and *Résumés Are Dead & What to Do About It*. In 2019, Richie was named one of the world's top 100 business coaches by Dr. Marshall Goldsmith. He is an international speaker (including TEDx & Google Startup Grind) & serial entrepreneur.

What I learned: Richie was my first coach, and you never forget your first. He set the bar high for every coach in my future.

He taught me how to determine what my true passion in life was and how to have the courage to go after my dreams. He taught my business partner and me some great business acumen that helped launch our first business. He was a great cheerleader when we really needed it. He made personal introductions to some very strong partnerships to help our business grow and scale.

Introduction: Read the book, The Power of Starting Something Stupid

Sign up for this 76-Day Challenge to make your STUPID idea Your SMART Reality at http://richienorton.com/76daychallenge/

Kirk Duncan

Known for: His *Master Your Influence* program

Short Bio: President & Founder of 3 Key Elements and member of The National Speakers Association, Kirk has developed his company from a card table in the garage into a multi-million-dollar, award-winning company. 3 Key Elements has been recognized 4 consecutive years by Inc. 5000 as one of the fastest-growing companies in America. Kirk Duncan has given over 5,800 presentations, appeared on television 75 times, and regularly trains audiences of 200—900 students.

What I learned: It's not an exaggeration when I say that Kirk saved my life, my marriage, and put me on a trajectory I never could have imagined. His mindset training pulled me out of a deep dark place I didn't even recognize I had fallen into until he showed me the light. I was in a room with over 1,000 people and was profoundly and irrevocably changed. I attended every class he put on in 2017 and 2018. These three-day classes taught me so much! To this day, the tools I learned from Kirk sparked unimaginable levels of personal and profession growth, and I couldn't be more grateful. Kirk taught me how to go after what I want and how to get it using shortcuts.

Introduction: Check out his Master Your Influence group coaching at https://3keyelements.com/master-your-influence-join-today/

Listen to any of his audiobook trainings at

https://3keyelements.com/audiobook-library/

Natasha Hazlett

Known for: Bestselling Author of *Unstoppable Influence: Be You. Be Fearless. Transform Lives.*

Short Bio: Natasha empowers solopreneurs and aspiring solopreneurs with the clarity, confidence, training, and resources they need to BOOST their income and influence in the marketplace by monetizing their message online.

In addition to being an inspirational speaker, author, coach, and life changer, she's an award-winning internet marketer, attorney and co-founder of Fast Forward Marketing, LLC. The Idaho Business Review honored her with the 2013 Idaho Women of the Year Award.

What I learned: Like Kirk, Natasha has irrevocably changed my life. From her 21-day Unstoppable Influencer Challenge, I discovered the lies I was telling myself that kept me stuck and no longer moving forward on my journey. It was like I had that darn tire boot on me! I was struggling in my business. I wanted to take it to the next level but couldn't gain any traction. I was spinning out and stuck.

Natasha taught me the power of divine timing. For me, everything happened for a reason at the time I needed it to happen. Natasha has elevated my work and mindset to a level that meets my life's current demands. I'm in my second year of her Inner Circle coaching program which has skyrocketed my mindset and my skillset. She has given me power tools for my tool collection. I credit her coaching for the *two* book deals I was offered this year as well as the invitation to guest write in three other books! She made introductions to influential people I would never have had access to and provided me with an opportunity to grow personally and professionally.

Introduction: Join her next 21-day Unstoppable Influence Challenge at https://natashahazlett.com

Michael Yeung

Known For: Creator of Productivity and Performance Coaching

Short Bio: Michael Yeung is a high-performance coach and business consultant who specializes in helping entrepreneurs to achieve more with less.

With the help of his mentors as well as lessons learnt from countless trial and errors, he managed to unlock the secrets to maximizing one's Return-On-Time-Invested in the world of business. Leading him to evolve from a struggling entrepreneur trapped in constant overwhelm and anxiety, to building a thriving business within a year.

What I learned: The biggest lesson Michael has taught me is to focus on tasks that move the needle instead of tasks that make me feel important but are wasting my time, wearing me out, and not moving my business forward. I took great pride in being busy even though I wasn't accomplishing anything. Michael helps me distinguish the forest from the trees. I have spent years chasing shiny things. I've dabbled. I've pivoted thinking I'm making smart decisions. I've gotten in my own way too many times to count. Michael has help me see why those decisions won't ultimately help me reach my destination. He is a master at seeing how I'm getting in my own way again and again and getting me back on the path to success.

Introduction: Join his free Facebook group at www.facebook.com/groups/teamppe

I hope you can see the value of these two simple, yet powerful tools, to take you to the next level. Asking the better questions gets you better answers and working with people that are where you want to be will help you get there faster. Why reinvent the wheel, when you can learn exactly what it takes by those that have done it?

To contact Donna:

Life on Purpose Academy

801.337.9933

https://lifeonpurposeacademy.com

info@lifeonpurposeacademy.com

Nicole Weyer

Nicole Weyer is the founder of *Root to Rise Coaching*, and co-host of *Midlife Calling*, a podcast empowering women as they celebrate, approach, and navigate midlife. She is a curious global citizen who has lived, learned, and explored Southeast Asia, Scandinavia, Europe, Turkey, Canada, and Central America. This adventuresome spirit can be attributed in part to being raised by Peace Corp volunteers who had a strong commitment to service.

Gratitude is the word Nicole uses for the experience she gained in 20+ years of school leadership where organizational cultures sometimes fostered wellness and sometimes encouraged self-sacrifice. Those lesson-filled years lead her to work as a burnout prevention coach and to partner with educators and school leaders to learn ways to nourish and sustain themselves. "Our most powerful blind spot is ourselves, and we often are last on our priority list if we show up on it at all." We must be the best version of "me" before we can be effective for the communities we lead, teach and serve.

Nicole volunteers with *Safe House Project* to support survivors of child sex trafficking and organizations dedicated to HIV and suicide prevention. This busy cat-lover rejuvenates herself by hiking, practicing yoga, reading, cooking, or planning her next excursion. She lives in Eugene, Oregon, and finds the Pacific Northwest the ideal place for energetic alignment, nourishment, and restoration.

Escaping the Leadership Trap: My Journey to and Through Burnout

By Nicole Weyer

Imagine! Landing your dream job days before your 30th birthday.

Eager to learn.

Ready to jump in.

Overjoyed to begin your career in educational administration.

How will it unfold? Are you up to the challenge?

These are the questions as you drive across the country to a place that you love.

To say I was thrilled to immerse myself in this school community, be mentored by those who had walked this leadership path, and who knew the culture was an understatement. I was going to make a difference!

I had youth on my side, a strong work ethic, an abundance of energy, and crazy good time management skills.

I was going to absorb every experience, build on what had been created, and take the program to the next level! I listened to their wisdom and followed the lead of my more experienced colleagues. Unknowingly, I also bought into the unspoken core values of prioritizing work over self, regularly adding things to an already overflowing plate, and feeling guilty saying no to the next "mission-critical" project.

My learning curve was steep, akin to deciding to run a marathon on race day without any training- in my mind, I could do it. In reality, I had a lot to learn. I possessed the tools and core abilities for my new role. I just hadn't gained the confidence to use my voice or be discerning with my 'yes' and my 'no.' Along with this learning process came eye-opening lessons in self-worth, self-advocacy, and resilience.

The conversations about how "busy, busy, busy," we were increased, the workdays extended, and those whom we acknowledged for contributions were openly and dare I say, willingly running themselves into the ground. My inner voice kept screaming at me to say something, begging me not to go all-in on living to work, all the while knowing, pleading that this wasn't sustainable.

What puzzled me was that as a leadership team, we could talk about how "crazy busy" we were, yet none of us could speak the words of the toll it was taking on us physically and emotionally. Those words were reserved for offline chats. As a team, we could not bring ourselves to step into that level of vulnerability. This was the leadership trap. The fear of sharing our struggle, of exposing our humanity, and of being seen as not up to the task was too great. We were highly skilled at condoning the process of burnout and/or breakdown. Sadly, this pattern is more present than absent around leadership tables - academia is not alone. Friends and colleagues in corporations, nonprofits, and healthcare concur.

Personally, I had to flip the script in order to maintain some sanity and avoid burnout! For me, it was akin to solving a puzzle one piece and one 'aha' moment at a time. My first step to change was removing myself from the "crazy busy" chats, I could no longer validate them, this required changing the subject or stepping away from the conversations. I ate lunch with other colleagues to surround myself with a healthier perspective. I spent solo time outside of work to stay present and find joy. These small actions made a huge impact.

In reflection, the process of burnout doesn't happen overnight, it happens over time. Similar to a bank account compounding interest. We don't recognize the symptoms, because we don't slow down long enough to listen to the messages coming from our mind, body, and spirit. It is easier to ignore and accept the status quo - until it is no longer sustainable. Just as it took time to put myself in this position, it would take time to clear a path and walk through it.

It became my mission to help others understand that burnout is a multi-step process. At each institution I served, I would untangle it, dive into trying to understand its 'why' and 'how' then integrate the learning. Thankfully, I carried those lessons forward to each role because there was always another one waiting.

Doing nothing wasn't an option, I had to apply my learning to new situations, so my train didn't travel down the same track I had embraced. Schools cannot effectively deliver on their mission with a team of adults who are running on empty. Schools help shape the hearts, minds, and spirits of students and need healthy staff able to bring their best selves into play.

Balls Bounce and Most People Can Catch

Are you driven to get things done? Do you feel compelled to volunteer and throw yourself into the mix to make things happen? Do you believe that being a team player means always raising your hand and taking on more?

If this is a belief that you hold, you are not alone. The drive to finish things can produce many positive results. Deadlines are met. Orders placed. Phone calls returned. Emails sent. Goals achieved. Boxes checked.

This hyper-vigilance can also be a trap. In excess, our compulsion to get things done can become the ripe fertilizer to the weeds of overcommitment, overflowing plates, and volunteering too much. Often these springs from our need to feel useful and valued. After all, who doesn't want to be seen and appreciated? Could this be about control rather than quality, filling a void within ourselves rather than a true desire and capacity to take on more?

I learned at an early age to take care of others. Putting others' needs before my own became second nature. I took pride in getting things done. A colleague once shared that I was "the go-to person because I always got shit done." What a compliment?!

In my mind, raising a hand, consistently saying yes, and pitching in early or at the last minute, were 'helping' behaviors. Or were they enabling behaviors? What I considered helpful made me miserable and kept others comfortable. I wanted to be known as hard-working, dependable, and available, a real team player. In reality, my consistent 'yes' filled a void within me or at least quieted the self-doubt I was experiencing; replacing it with seeds of resentment. I set myself up for the stress, the struggle, and the irritation. This wasn't happening to me. I was doing it to myself. Here was a tremendous light bulb moment!

"No is a complete sentence." Anne Lamott's words are a powerful reminder for me.

Learning to say "no" when it is second nature to say "yes" – regardless if you have the capacity to take it on. I could have sat quietly and waited for others to volunteer. I could have been more comfortable in the silence while everyone glanced around the table to see who was going to step up. I could have but didn't. I was sacrificing myself and didn't realize it. I fully embraced the notion of being a good colleague and good leader by always volunteering and taking on more.

Each time I jumped in to help or pick up a ball that was dropped, I stole an opportunity for others to grow and usurped an opportunity for them to take responsibility. For me, that meant taking an inventory of how I was living and leading. Once I learned to step back and sit in the pause, those around me had an opportunity to lean in, stretch and grow.

'No' doesn't have to lead to confrontation. 'No' doesn't have to shut down a conversation. 'No' can exemplify how we honor ourselves and demonstrate how much faith we have in others.

Balls bounce and most people can catch them. All roads don't have to lead to me.

Old Habits Die Hard

Am I good enough?

Am I capable?

Am I worthy?

These big questions rented space within me for far too long. Each earned its respective eviction notice because each found ways to overstay its welcome.

We overlook the powerful messages absorbed at an early age and how they shape our habits and beliefs as adults. Growing up, I knew I was loved, yet was not sure where I fit or how I stacked up to others. At times I felt invisible. In time, I found ways to shine, build confidence, and quiet my inner critic who was all too happy creating stories about not being enough.

Those whispered questions about being enough, capable and worthy followed me. I tried to silence them by throwing myself into my work. Surely success in my professional life would put those questions to rest, right?

Do you play the overcompensation game? Trying to fill yourself up in one way to compensate for some emptiness in another place? It's a game many of us play and have MASTERED. The cost is high - an obsession with our performance, seeking recognition, working ourselves into the ground to demonstrate our worth to the organization we serve; all the while exhaustion compounds, resentment grows, patience wanes, and we burn out.

For me, it translated to COUNTLESS unused hours of vacation time and WEEKS of sick time in the bank. The work lost its joy, I lost my center and struggled to comprehend how anyone could be in school administration for their entire career.

The old answers to the big questions made it easy to buy into the idea of living to work as the path to feeling complete. In my mind it made sense, there's a void in place and you fill it with work, then magically it all balances out. That's not how it works!

We are not balancing a Chemistry equation; this is about how we honor ourselves and how that shapes the way we are living. Getting truly, deeply honest with myself about where the stories of worthiness originated was the first step. Identifying how those stories served me at a specific time in my life came next. Deciding that the stories were untrue followed. Releasing the stories because I had outgrown them, and they no longer served me came last.

Our voice around a leadership table is a reflection of how we see ourselves and our abilities. When we question our self-worth and wonder if we are enough, our tendency is to stay quiet. We bite our tongue, censor ourselves, and leave SO much unspoken. Leading confidently from that place is incredibly difficult. When we trust ourselves and our instincts, we show up boldly. We are far more inclined to entertain ideas different from our own, work to find a middle path, and get creative in our solutions. Thinking outside of the box is how we function.

When we know our worth and understand our value, feedback is welcome rather than threatening. We seek the best solutions and tap the expertise of others without fear of losing power or control. Sharing ideas, acknowledging the contributions of others, holding ourselves and others accountable, and celebrating the accomplishments of others come naturally because it makes us better.

What's Easy and What's Important

My first year as a dean was learning-filled in every possible way. I knew how to build a team, I needed to figure out how to *lead* a team. Year One was sprinkled with successes, stumbles, and outright struggle, all of which laid the foundation for a leadership journey that continues today.

As I discovered new opportunities to grow and new institutions to serve, I carried with me the commitment to being always in motion. The compounding exhaustion from trying to lead in a way similar to my colleagues, and an inner struggle of knowing something needed to change. With each lesson learned and new habits created, there was space for another lesson to manifest.

What I have come to realize is that leadership is a daily practice and an evolutionary process. It meant figuring out who I was on the team, finding my voice, and creating my own way of leading.

How candidly could I speak? How boldly could I lead? What did I bring to the table? What did I need to learn? What type of support could I seek?

These became my guiding questions and ones I posed to myself as I joined different leadership tables at each institution, I had the privilege to serve.

The important work of leading has courage at its core. It is more than filling a role. It requires bringing our *full selves* and living authentically. It means giving ourselves time to find our footing, learn the landscape, and get to know colleagues, clients, and constituents. It involves listening to the inner voice and knowing that we can do it. We can be bold, take our leadership to the next level, and inspire those around us. We should trust ourselves implicitly, so we live and lead from that place instead of from a place that over-values the external noise that surrounds us.

It would have been easy to walk the path of "go along to get along." To get comfortable in my office, rest on my laurels, fill a role and stay in my lane. This is the Ego mind at work because it seeks to keep us safe, comfortable, and away from conflict. Our Ego mind convinces us that wisdom comes from external sources and experts, not from trusting ourselves. Ego skillfully nurtures within us a fear of losing what we have as a way to stay in control. So we stay comfortable and stay the course. This approach, this way of 'being' felt stifling. It wasn't authentic and was steeped in "that's the way we've always done it."

The disconnect between who I was outside of work and who I was at work grew. As the gap widened, my stress increased, joy in my work decreased, resentment sprouted, and it was clear something had to give. I didn't like the version of myself that I was becoming, a deep-fried, extra crispy version. I was tired, a bit lackluster, and annoyed with a harsh inner dialogue increasing in volume.

I knew that change started with me. I had no idea how to go about it. I had to take responsibility for my choices, how I felt, functioned, and how I was, and was not, showing up for myself. Nobody had put me in this position. When the outside of work and at work sides of me got into alignment, I was bolder, a better listener, more in tune with, and responsive to my team. I focused on what was right and didn't concern myself with what was popular. Now, I could forge my own path and define what leadership meant to me.

Did I find myself outside of the "loop"?   Sometimes.

Did I feel isolated?   Sometimes.

Did I reignite my passion for my work?   Yes.

Did I rediscover the joys of leading, supporting, and empowering my team?   Yes.

Did this go over well?   Sometimes.

Did the stress fade and the joy jump?   Yes.

Was it worth it?   Absolutely.

Was it easy?   No.

Was it important?   Yes.

Go Through or Grow Through

The more I transformed my inner dialogue from hyper-critical to compassionate, the easier it became to write a new story about my worthiness. Standing time and time again at the crossroads of success & failure, ease & struggle, self-doubt & self-worth. These crossroads I suspect are familiar to many and the knowledge in those quiet moments was that a better version of me started showing up for myself and for everyone else.

Would it have been "click your heels in the air delightful" to learn these lessons as part of my graduate school curriculum? Absolutely.

And yet, I am ever grateful for my path because it allowed me to be a participant working on the problem rather than an example in a book or a tabletop exercise. I needed to consistently be at my growing edge - put myself in uncomfortable positions- in order to figure out who I was, who I wanted to be, and what I wanted to represent. This wisdom was cultivated from being on the front line of my life, not a concept I heard about in a lecture. I needed to grow through the process, not go through the process.

Going through is an end game, finish line, goal reached, check the box type of focus. It is a commitment to always be in action, push, put our heads down and work hard. Ego leads this process and drives us to always do more.

Growing through is an inquisitive and curious process. At its foundation is a commitment to creating choice, cultivating presence, and joining the dots between action, outcome, and experience. Soul leads the way by allowing us to inventory who we are being, and how we show up for ourselves, and for others. Growing through supports our process of becoming.

All of this learning meant launching a new venture. It created opportunities to engage with educators and leaders in new and very different ways; as a person who has been in their shoes and worked through the leadership trap. We can arrive on the other side stronger, more aware, more thoughtful, and able to extend grace inward.

Why didn't I leave education and take this wisdom to another sector? It was simple, yet complicated because I kept learning and rediscovering my love for the work. In time, it became clear my mission was to start a new conversation with educators and leaders about how we are living, leading, and learning, so we can avoid the leadership trap and bring our best to our students, families, and colleagues.

We can position ourselves for success or struggle. It means **knowing** we are gloriously, beautifully, and perfectly imperfect. This requires us to embrace ALL parts of ourselves, the ones we adore, the ones we accept, the ones we are still working to befriend.

To contact Nicole:

LinkedIn www.linkedin.com/in/burnoutpreventioncoach

Facebook https://www.facebook.com/CoachNicoleWeyer

Website roottorisecoaching.com

Anchor https://anchor.fm/midlife-calling

Email: nicole@roottorisecoaching.com

P. Nathan Thornberry

P. Nathan Thornberry ("Nathan") is a business owner, investor, author, and speaker focused largely on the Real Estate industry. His specialties include Risk Management and Marketing with most of his experience coming from owning and operating one of the largest Service Contract companies in the world along with Environmental Laboratories and Manufacturing operations. Nathan currently serves as the CEO of PriorityLab and Breeze Products and as an active investor in holdings within and outside of Real Estate within which he has been involved in over 7 million unique transactions over the last 22 years providing Service Contracts, Environmental Testing Laboratory Services & Equipment, a variety of home services, and digital services including software for professionals largely in the home service space. Nathan has written four books, filed for and received several patents, and designed some of the most utilized equipment in the mold and radon testing space.

When not busy serving hundreds of thousands of clients, Nathan enjoys time with his family and two of his favorite hobbies – playing music and flying planes. You can learn more about Nathan and contact him at www.Nathan.tv .

The 3 Key Components to a Successful Career: Availability, Knowledge, and Commitment.

By P. Nathan Thornberry

My apologies in advance for being so direct! Sometimes I find myself unintentionally offending my readers. If this includes you, please keep in mind that my intentions are most certainly good.

It is my firm belief developed over many decades of keen observation that there are two basic methods by which someone becomes incredibly successful and rich in financial terms. Those two methods are Luck or Deliberation (a diligent, consistent approach to improving one's position in the world daily).

Having personally not had the good fortune of being the recipient of a massive inheritance, nor having the physical capabilities of a world-class athlete, nor having any of the luck that comes with being a part of the next popular gadget or magical mobile app startup or lottery winning, I had to travel the severely more difficult path to prosperity of making it happen through very hard work. If you're anything like me, your respect for those that did not earn it pales in comparison to those that did making you glad for your own unlucky circumstances. It is good to accomplish something and to be proud of it!

Without a college education nor any substantial resources, I found myself jobless and in the position of running a small business at 18 years old. By 40 years old, I would become one of the wealthiest individuals in the world, with wealth in the 10-figures. Quite uniquely, this was accomplished with no debt, little to no bank financing, and no partnership nor client relationship ever exceeding 1% of the businesses I built, bought, and sold outside of investments I made in other companies where the intention was to be the minority shareholder. It was all also accomplished "clean," as they say, which means I didn't break any laws or violate my strict moral compass in the process. I didn't have to murder anyone or screw over a partner. With minimal exceptions, deals were closed while oftentimes improving the friendships and relationships that surrounded them. I would humbly suggest that both the intention and result of my business dealings were "win-win" from start to finish.

In order to accomplish the above, I have been, for more than two decades, running circles around my competitors while grabbing dominant market share positions in multiple industries and turning somewhere between 7-10 million people into clients in the process and creating hundreds of millions in revenue... and growing. I have been incredibly fortunate to have met, befriended, and even done deals with the leaders at some of the world's largest corporations while simultaneously enjoying the majority of my connections in the small business space on an equal level. I get the same level of excitement out of closing a deal worth thousands as I do one worth tens of millions, and I hope you feel the same! If you are so lucky as to transact most of your business with local service companies and sole proprietors as I have, you've definitely experienced the best of people.

There is a lot that goes into success on a stellar level (millions, tens of millions, and beyond) that we couldn't possibly touch on together in a single book so let's stick to the 3 Components of Success that are most crucial and universal. Without all three of them in place and utilized daily, your success becomes largely a matter of chance rather than a deliberate course of action, and wealth becomes an incredibly unlikely outcome.

Key Success Component #1: Availability.

Have you ever heard a consultant/coach/author suggest you should "Work Smarter, not Harder"? "Charge what you are Worth"? "Work 4 hours per week"? "Have a Good Work/Life Balance"? "Focus on profit"?

These are all phrases that can be interpreted to mean, with only minor semantic differences, that you should be making more while working less (if only you weren't so dumb for not listening to the unqualified, oversimplified logic of the "guru" with the advice to sell you).

Why are these concepts so commonplace despite their demonstrable history of futility? The first reason is that fools are most easily fooled into parting ways with their money for information they find most agreeable, and "working less while making more" sounds incredible to the large majority of the majority destined for mediocre success or worse.

The second reason is that those destined for deliberately high levels of success don't need to be told that working 60-80 hours a week or more is par for the course and 24/7 availability is necessary to accomplish exceptional things. This sort of advice is also seen as "one time only" advice that is hard to build onto and creates waves of profitable info-marketing media to sell. "Work hard and be very available to your clients" doesn't exactly, as a concept, have a sexy ring to it, and any book on the topic would be too short to be taken seriously.

If you want to impress the masses into paying you well, paying you consistently, and doing so for any lengthy period of time, you (and your teams, if applicable, but especially and always you!) need to be nearly immediately available to clients (and staff) all the time without exception. For clarity, I am not suggesting this is the best or happiest way to operate as a human being. Still, it is the best way to ensure the highest chance possible at achieving enormous levels of personal wealth.

Here's how to know if you are *failing* to be as available as a truly successful individual:

- You take vacations (especially noticeable ones)
- You have told a client/staff that you were unavailable because of a personal/family/kid(s) issue

- You have temporary or permanent email autoreplies making excuses for your lack of a timely response (or text messages that accomplish the same)

- Your voicemail suggests you will return the call "during normal business hours"

- You turn off your phone/phone notifications for any reason.

- You have a specific time to arrive and depart from your place of business

- You have social functions scheduled more than once per month.

- You watch sports

- You meditate or participate in other activities requiring disconnection from professional communication methods and designed to reduce your levels of tension/anxiety/pace

- You attend organized religious gatherings regularly (Sundays or even as little as once per month will diminish your success capacity greatly)

- You golf or have created other "professional" methods of burning substantial periods of time

- You have more than 20 minutes' worth of meetings per week

- You allow personal life, personal issues, drugs, or annoying/unlucky persons in your life to take time away from your work missions/consistent availability.

The above certainly isn't an exhaustive list but rather very common examples of how people become unavailable to their clients and staff to their own detriment. Making an effort to be ridiculously available will contribute to success, while any lack of effort in the opposite direction will lead to mediocrity, and there is very little one can do to offset such, statistically speaking. It is simply an inconvenient fact that difficult and challenging tasks (like accomplishing more than 99.99% of other humans) is, in fact, difficult and challenging.

To this day, even after substantial liquidity events affording me the ability to retire with much of my hair color intact and the rest provided in a very fashionably plausible way by my favorite stylist around every other month or so, I find myself on 3-4 occasions per week working obsessively on projects until 3 am while my competition is asleep falling even further behind or out enjoying the immemorable. Everyone I know in the $100 million+ net worth range category of businessmen and businesswomen operate precisely the same way, and it is no coincidence. I know similarly situated individuals who have surpassed the incredible $1 billion mark that still work 20+ hours a day. It's seemingly so core to who they are that one might surmise it is "in our blood."

Another form of availability comes from being ahead of the game in so many ways that you are prepared for virtually anything that might come up - particularly opportunities and disasters. Be so far ahead in your work at all times that you can take the next 24-36 hours working on a new project if need be, and be so effective and efficient in your regular workflow that you accomplish a multiple of what anyone around you does.

Here are some more rules for you to follow if you are serious about being uber-successful;

Make every lunch a working lunch.

Make every dinner a working dinner.

Skip every breakfast.

Be "too busy" for every destination wedding invite.

Avoid funerals.

Hire out every single medial task (yard upkeep, laundry, dishes, etc.) and never wait in a line for anything.

As soon as you can afford it, get a driver and work in the back of the car on any and all occasions where driving is appropriate.

Always take the midnight flights until you can afford your own planes.

If any of the above sounds crazy to you, it is indeed both crazy and exceptional. If it makes you uncomfortable or miserable to think about, you might consider not aiming for ultra-rich. You might be someone, a better person than I almost certainly, who strives to spend time with friends and family as your main prerogative and has a healthy grasp on the "important things" in your view. There is absolutely nothing wrong with being less than extreme, but if your life seems destined for greatness in business and you go down this path of workaholism with me you can be somewhat relieved by something we all do at this level – we may have less time for personal matters in our lives but when we have the time we make sure it counts and your kids will still love you! From what I have experienced personally, the views of a "Scrooge" like character are almost entirely a mix of myth and misunderstanding. Further, your ability to help those in your life with issues becomes exponentially more significant when your financial means are great.

Key Success Component #2: Knowledge!

The absolute best kind of knowledge for deliberately accomplishing wealth is the vast, nearly instantly recallable knowledge that Dustin Hoffman's character in the movie Rainman had on topics he was familiar with. While it might seem less than PC to allude to the Hollywood moment that introduced many of us to the now prevalently known condition known Autism, I am largely complimenting what can be in some cases a nearly superhuman ability to recall facts. I have often wondered, just based on my personal ability to recall facts and compute equations instantly (along with a slight social awkwardness I tend to utilize in jovial, unusually charming ways) if I may have just a little bit in common with some of our special friends on the spectrum. Perhaps we all have a bit of a malfunction in our minds we all cope within our own ways.

Nevertheless, when it comes to your career and the topics you should know even a little about… become an expert!

Learn everything there is to know and then some, delving into related topics as well. Ensure that 99% of the time, you have an accurate and thorough answer to every possible question. Then, diligently follow through on the other 1% when the opportunity arises. Always seek industry-specific information and avoid generic sources of advice/self-help, as your ability to change your processes based on concepts has very likely long been departed along with the puberty that killed your ability to function with such flexibility, and instead laser-focused your instincts on procreation.

If you don't know more than everyone around you regarding your chosen vocation, your chances at anything resembling massive success drop to virtually zero. Do not consider the "bar" here to be outdoing those around you, as most people remain entirely oblivious to even the basics of their jobs and watch the clock all day awaiting their next beer or video game to help numb the pain and pass the time away. Be exceptional in every way regardless of your position, and you will be rewarded. So long your achievements do not go unnoticed (something I address in other writings and on my YouTube channel).

Use your knowledge base and your ability to seek out answers to avoid answering to clients/associates in ways that diminish your worth. Using phrases like "Not to my knowledge" or "Not that I am unaware of..." are the best ways to demonstrate that you are lazy and worthless while likely harming the success levels of yourself and everyone around you.

Let's put these concepts into practice and create a scenario in the retail world with an entry-level position to emphasize the points made about knowledge. Let's say, for this example, that you work in customer service in a Target store, and that a customer asked a question of you about inventory and whether you still carry DVD's.

Customer: *"Excuse me, do you know if this store carries any DVD's?"*

You: *"Not that I am aware of."*

Let's over-analyze this customer interaction for all the ways in which being "unaware" (aka dumb as a rock) is harmful to the careers of you and everyone around you.

First, no one asked you if you were "aware". You were asked a simple factual question of whether, within the hundreds of thousands of square feet of retail space a typical Target occupies, there were any DVD's. By stating your ignorance in the matter, you answer a different question altogether and demonstrate your stupidity.

Second, there is an implied statement here of how badly you are willing to fail in delivering for the client. That is to say, "I am so terrible at my job that I am unwilling to even ask whether such an item exists for you, so you should probably shop somewhere else."

Third, you've now taken a valuable customer request (and indication by the informal survey, you might say) that there is interest in physical video media and made certain it went nowhere but your lazy face, rather than to someone with a brain that might be able to act upon such information.

There's nothing cool, sexy, or productive about being uneducated in what you do. It makes you look bad. It costs you in your career, and it hurts the business you work in (noticeably). Educating yourself just enough to get by makes you dull and nearly useless. Always be in the know, seek knowledge when called upon to do so, and continue learning every single day.

If you want to make yourself even more valuable to the business you work in, learn to convey some of your knowledge to those around you in ways that create a better client experience!

Key Success Component #3: Commitment.

Play through in your head the last half a dozen conversations you had in your professional life but put yourself in the other party's position. Close your eyes, start from the beginning of each conversation and visualize each all the way through to the end.

Once complete, ask yourself the following;

- When, down to the day and hour, is follow-up expected?
- What obligations do you have to the other party following the call?
- What obligations does the other party have to you following the call?
- What were the top 3 items accomplished through the conversation?
- How long was the last communication?

If the first four questions above do not have indisputably great answers and the fourth isn't an approximation of minutes under 10, your ability to communicate true levels of commitment to important people in your career needs some help!

The absolute best resource to help you with this problem is every party on every call/communication. If you do not have a great answer to each of the above in the future, convert the first three into closing conversation points as follows…

- *"I think it would be great to schedule a follow-up right now. How does (day in near future) workaround (time you can commit to)?"*
- *"To sum up, I owe you (list of follow-up items). Can you think of anything I missed?"*
- *"I believe you have a few items on your list, including (name 2). What else was I missing so I can add them to my notes from this call?"*
- *"I feel like we accomplished something here today. I am especially pleased we seem to be in agreement on (issue/resolution)."*

If you are still having trouble, my strong recommendation is that you watch the first 4 seasons of *The West Wing* until you learn how to communicate like the characters on the show do – concise, to the point, and timed as if the building were on fire!

Whether you are the CEO of a multi-national large-scale business or starting in the very first position of your career, abide by the above to ensure your success. Don't be afraid to seek out what you need to get back to someone with a helpful response.

Share your stories of true hard work, commitment, and knowledge at www.Nathan.tv and join me in sharing with other similarly situated business owners what it truly takes to strive and thrive in a world where the word "value" has been so perverted in its meaning that it no longer includes a monetary sum.

To the enormity of your success!

***

To contact Nathan:

www.Nathan.tv

Adam Ringham

Adam Ringham is a prior Military Veteran, Wellness Educator, Author, Activist, Minister, Speaker, Father, Husband, Inspirer, and currently resides in Florida. He studies ancient linguistics, genetics, astrology, astronomy, Newtonian and Quantum physics, anatomy, physiology, essential oils, neurohacking, biohacking, music, cosmology, crystallography, metallurgy, and is proficient in photography and videography, graphic design, marketing, technology as a whole, and speaks/reads/writes Biblical Hebrew, Aramaic, Greek, and some Ancient Sumerian, as well as has played piano for over 35 years. His passions include research and implementation of alchemical practices from ancient Egypt and beyond and incorporating them into 21st century living.

As a 7-figure earner in multiple MLM's – Adam's passions are about rising above your current situation and becoming someone of value, so that you can provide value to the world. As a prior 300-pound alcoholic for a decade, he understands the importance of personal and internal change before the external reflection is materialized in your daily life.

Currently he is focusing more on the release of a number of his own products and companies to provide more value than before to the world and help go guide people through the process of "Ascension" and remembering who you truly are, before the world told you who to be.

Think and Grow Rich

By Adam Ringham

The title of the book is "Think and Grow Rich".

But I'd like people to stop for a moment and ask themselves what "Rich" really means.

Does it mean monetary accumulation?

Does it mean fame and recognition?

Or does it mean you have provided VALUE the lives of yourself and others?

I'd like you to examine the word "Earn" for just a moment with me. When you "Earn" a paycheck, you're "URN'ing" a paycheck.

What is an "Urn"?

Something you put dead people in.

If you make a sale, you'll earn a paycheck.

If you change a life – you'll BE a LIVING.

This is what will separate those who seek to provide value to people, vs those who are simply seeking to "urn" a paycheck.

When you think of growing rich – it should be about the VALUE that you provide to people in their lives.

How do you provide value?

By becoming someone of value YOURSELF.

The world is filled with "Get Rich Quick" programs and "Fix your mindset" gurus – that arguably so do provide value to an extent. Heck, many people including myself have benefitted greatly from such perspectives…

But one must be careful to examine at what COST does one become "rich" – and what does this actually mean to you?

Are you becoming "rich" in experiences? In family? In friends? In LIFE in general?

Or have you simply accumulated yet another comma in your bank account – little electrons whirling around that will not follow you into the life beyond this.

True riches come from the value that you provide other people – without the expense of yourself.

People love to say, "money can buy happiness". Sure, for a few fleeting moments you can run away from your internal reality and say "look how much money I made, and look at the vacations I went on, and look at my house and all the stuff I have to have fun with!"

Yes, money can buy temporary happiness...

At the expense of your soul.

If your "soul" purpose in life is to become rich – then buy all means, please do so. That is your choice, and you are free to do so.

The only thing that I can ask you, is that in the long term – how much of this can you bring with you?

Jesus spoke of "The Forgiveness of Sin, The Resurrection of The Body, and The Life Everlasting".

Now, I'm not here to sell you Jesus or any kind of religion – I'm only here to sell you and IDEA (for free too).

How many people do you know have toiled their whole life to accumulate commas in their bank accounts, personal fame and recognition, and "stuff and things" in order to fill a void within them that just keeps getting bigger and bigger.

They've traded their entire lives for those little electrons in a bank account – at the expense of their soul, and the lives of those around them.

For a long number of years – I spent my time glued to my phone.

I've accumulated vast amounts of wealth, was a 6 and 7 figure earner multiple times with two different businesses in a matter of only a few months.

The problem became however – when God decided to take it all away in which to teach me a valuable lesson.

God/He/She asked me:

"At what cost – did your 6 and 7 figure earnings come at?"

I had difficulty writing this chapter, because while I was both a 6 and 7 figure earner at the same time -unexpectedly I had both businesses collapse within only a few months of each other. Regrettably so, a few months down the road, while I had built another successful business – it wasn't enough to cover the bills of everything I had committed myself to and was forced to sell my house in order to ensure that all the bills were met.

This is kind of a "counter-productive" story at first to the idea of "Think and Grow Rich" – and I barely made an graciously extended deadline in which to authentically write a chapter that was of value to people.

Now fortunately, as God would have it – the house was worth over a million dollars more than I had paid for it only 12 months previously.

While I initially fought the change and cursed my luck and failure to plan ahead more properly, in the end the lesson that was delivered was one that I desperately needed.

For the past 7 to 8 years while building my businesses, I sadly had succumbed to the dopaminergic pitfalls of being glued to my phone and needed to respond to comments and messages on social media pretty much 24/7.

While this brought me financial success, it took me slowing down enough and humbling myself enough to see that I had lost all joy and passion for the work I was doing, and it cost not only myself, my hobbies, and my passions – but also had robbed my family of my attention and time most of the day and night.

I was constantly distracted with the next business post, replies, messages, and marketing strategy so much so that I had lost the desire to do basically anything anymore. Getting out of bed due to drama and the level of attention it sapped from me, had made getting out of bed more of a chore – more than something I actually WANTED to do and ENJOYED.

In life there will be seasons of feast and famine, expansion and contraction.

The KEY to getting through it is the most important lesson of all – learning to multiply or divide by the golden ration of 1.618 or 0.618. Christians would says this "In Jesus Name" – or doing everything that survives to eternity, and instills a PASSION into your life.

It's an old saying that you hear a million times in your life:

"You can't take it with you."

But...

What if that's not ENTIRELY a True Statement?

What if you CAN bring things with you after death?

This is where "In Jesus Name" or 1.618 or 0.618 comes in.

That which was done out of unconditional love and compassion – is able to survive fractal compression and survive death to eternity.

What does this mean?

Space and matter are infinitely compactable.

An atom is 99.999999999999999999% empty space.

However, only that which has coherence and is self-similar and phase conjugate fractally compressible will survive to eternity, because only those intentions can survive death and continue on without limit.

You're not doubt familiar with people who have "gifts" and "skills" that seemly are just "there" without effort of any kind. They just naturally know how to do different things, and learning different skillsets or information is effortless to them.

Yes, nurture has an aspect to play in this – and a person's family and home life will dictate much of their future reality...

However, this doesn't explain away someone who is just "gifted" with the ability to learn and play musical instruments with ease – yet has no musicians in the family.

There are genetic memories that can be passed down through family lines and allow family subsequent offspring to inherit both genetic traumas and gifts both, but there is also the ability to "remember" throughout all of time and space that is dependent upon the person's actions of how they SHARED those gifts and the intention in which they brought VALUE to people's lives through their gifts.

Let me tell you an old story that will provide perspective:

There once was a King who needed to go on a long journey and couldn't bring with him more than a few things from his Kingdom. He had to travel light and didn't want to be recognized and robbed – so he had to leave pretty much everything behind.

Upon his departure, he entrusted 3 of his most trusted servants with his "gifts".

To the first servant he said:

"I must go on a journey, and I have 10 gifts I want to give to you while I'm away. Take care of them for me please"

To the second servant he said:

"I must go on a journey, and I have 5 gifts I want to give you while I'm away. Take care of them for me please."

Finally, to the third servant he said:

"I must go on a journey; I have 3 gifts I want to give you while I'm away. Take care of them for me please."

A year went by, and the King returned from his journey and sent word to his servants to have them come before them. He said, "My servants whom which I have entrusted much, I have returned from my journey, and I ask to see what you did with the gifts that I gave you."

The first servant presented himself before the King and said:

"You entrusted me with 10 gifts that you had asked me to care for, and I found it that the best way to care for them was to give them away. Now instead of 10 gifts – your gifts have been multiplied and I instead now have 20 gifts, because through giving them away I have been blessed with more."

The King told the servant "Well done, my faithful servant. You have done what you were supposed to do, and I want you to keep all 20 gifts for yourself, as I know I can trust you with them and to do the right thing."

The second servant presented himself to the king and said:

"My Lord, you entrusted me with 5 of your most precious gifts, and as time went on I searched and searched my soul in what to do with them – but was only able to give away 3 of the 5 gifts, for it was all the capacity I had within myself to share appropriately. In return I now have 8 gifts instead of 5 through sharing them with others."

The King said in return,

"Well done my faithful servant. You shared the gifts you could, and you had the mental capacity to know your limits of what you could share appropriately and yield even more blessings than before. Keep all 8 gifts as a token of my appreciation of knowing I can full well trust you, even if you don't yet know what to do with all the gifts at one time."

The last servant presented himself before the King and said,

"My Lord, I took the gifts you gave me, and I did my very best to keep them safe. I buried them and hid them from the prying eyes and minds of others, that they might be here in the same condition in which you had left them. During your travels, a flood came and washed away one of the gifts, so in return I have only 2 gifts to give you back of the 3 you gave me."

The King replied,

"I knew I could trust you to do your best with them, but your best was to squander away the gifts I had given you and sequester them from the minds, eyes, hands, and hearts of those who would need them most. In return you have not only kept them from others, but in attempting to keep them for yourself – you have lost one of the only 3 gifts I have given you.

In return, since you have not learned the lessons of what it means to be given a gift, I'm taking back the two you have left and you will have none."

Our lives are really no different than the story of the King and the 3 servants – in which we all are allotted a certain number of gifts upon our birth, and others are developed along the way. The more we share our gifts with others, they more they are multiplied and returned to us in greater numbers and greater magnitude.

Those who squander their gifts away and turn a blind eye to those in need – will in turn lose the very gifts they have been given and have future gifts removed from their soul as well. Those who share their gifts out of love and desire to help others and provide value, will be given riches that cannot be measured in bank account commas and whirling electrons.

You become able to provide value, by becoming someone of value yourself.

As Jim Rohn said:

"You must work harder on yourself, than you do at your job."

Myself it took me nearly 10 years in Network Marketing in order to become someone of enough value that I could then provide that value back to the world. I worked an overnight job at a group home with individuals with special needs for 10 years, while simultaneously working as a photographer and various jobs during the day.

There would be weekends where I would shoot a wedding all day Friday, head to my overnight job Friday night, back to shooting a wedding all day Saturday, and back to work at my overnight job from Saturday night until Sunday at noon. I would also work a network marketing "job" all week long as I attempted to find my "groove" and make that successful. This was also the period of time that I was a hardcore alcoholic, and somehow managed to accomplish all this – while also spending hours per day researching natural health in order to become someone of enough value to make the shift.

Eventually however, the skills I had learned through working so many different jobs, and eventually deciding to apply myself and do something besides get drunk on my time off – I was blessed not only with my first child, but shortly afterward I was given the gift of a second child and the ability to make Network Marketing my full time "job".

This all could have happened faster had I applied myself better and decided to quit drinking sooner, but everything has its seasons and lessons in life that are part of the Grander Orchestration that plays out through your souls experiences and lessons.

As I did the network marketing for a number of years, God finally got my attention and the message came through loud enough that it was time for yet another shift – as the skills and developments and stages I went through were to come to enough of a spearhead accompanied by a period of pressure before the transition into the next phase of my life yet again (which oddly enough was right around 40 Earth years).

The larger points to make, is there are seasons in life that you'll go through, in which you learn different lessons and expand upon your capabilities, and new lessons will be learned through those experiences and present new opportunities for growth.

The highlight of it all however, is making sure anything you're doing – that you're actually passionate about what you're doing, and that you're working for the things that can survive the phase conjugate fractal compassion at death.

Imagine if you were able to carry over all the gifts, skills, experience, and abilities onto the next world and beyond – because you had shared your gifts like the first servant in this lifetime. Imagine how much more you could accomplish if your future self was to reap the rewards of sharing your gifts today out of a desire to better the lives of another person?

This kind of value and intention builds eternal riches in which you can never put a monetary value on, and it also keeps you mindful of the expenses of your "riches".

Being rich, and being successful - are two different things.

Everyone runs around asking each other what they do for a living (or for "death/urning") – but so few people ask ARE YOU HAPPY?

Learn to plan ahead not only for this life, but for the lives beyond this – and recognize the warning signs when you have fallen out of alignment with what your purpose for even being on this planet is before all joy and passion (and your gifts) fall away.

Most importantly, learn how to become someone of value – that the value you've accumulated is shared with the intention of making someone else's life better than it was before they met you.

There's 2 ways to fail:

1.) Quit

2.) Keep your gifts and your success for yourself and hide them away from others.

There is no shame in being successful – the shame only lies in not using that success to help others become successful for themselves and helping those who are unable to help themselves – for the sake of making the world a better place.

It might sound corny – but the acronym of "WWJD" (What Would Jesus Do) is an excellent, simple reminder to help keep you sharing your gifts and your success for this world and beyond and assure that your soul continues to have even more successful and expansive journeys in the future.

Make sure when the King returns to ask what you've done with the gifts you've been given – you're able to proudly say that you shared them with everyone you could.

Simply put – if you haven't wrapped Eternity into the equation, you're missing the point of life.

***

To contact Adam:

www.stayhealthymyfriends.win

adam@stayhealthymyfriends.win

https://www.facebook.com/iamonethirtyseven/

https://www.instagram.com/adamringham/

Ministries: www.iam137.com

https://www.tiktok.com/@iamonethirtyseven

Karen Louise Floyd

Karen Floyd is an entrepreneur, writer, coach, communication, public speaking, leadership, and energy work specialist with a passion for helping entrepreneurs and business executives be better and do better in their personal and professional lives. From her humble beginnings in England, Karen Floyd dreamed of travelling the world from an early age, but as one of the poorest people she knew, she had no idea how she would escape her environment and explore the world. So, she tapped into ancient spiritual practices and modern-day techniques to realise her dream and create a rich life, and by her mid-20s, she had visited many countries travelling first-class. Karen has studied, worked, and lived worldwide, building her PR and marketing business and coaching entrepreneurs and business executives. She speaks Spanish, French and Russian and has attained the highest accolade possible in Public Relations. Karen coaches executives from startups and SMEs and directors and CEOs from well-known multibillion-dollar tech companies. She delivers talks about entrepreneurship, public relations, presenting and how to use energy work using her Ivaar model to create and sustain a thriving business. She loves to help people develop intuitive intelligence for greater clarity, confidence, creativity and better decision-making. For future-thinking leaders who are ready for it, Karen likes to approach coaching and business holistically, aligning a company's energy with its leaders for purpose-driven success that creates a rich experience in all areas of life. Karen enjoys teaching people how to change their brainwaves to boost physical, emotional, mental and spiritual wellbeing. She coaches online and in person. Karen loves to spend time in nature and be with animals.

Cracking the Rich Code with Ivaar

By Karen Louise Floyd

"Whether you think you can, or you think you can't, you are right."
Henry Ford

Being rich means different things to different people. So before writing this chapter, I asked friends and acquaintances what being rich and cracking the rich code meant to them. My network is diverse, and I spoke to dozens of contacts, from millionaires to schoolteachers. Most said that cracking the rich code meant finding a holistic approach to achieving richness in all life areas. I agree. Richness in all areas of life included feeling fulfilled, living a life with purpose, robust physical, mental, emotional and spiritual health, thriving relationships, and peace of mind. For many, it also involves above-average financial wealth, but not necessarily. So, whether you want more financial wealth or better relationships, this chapter is for you.

I will share an approach to cracking the rich code using a technique I call Ivaar, which is Intention, Visualisation, Action, Alignment, and Results. I began regularly using Ivaar as a young child without knowing it. The method combines ancient spiritual practices and modern-day techniques. All you need is yourself, and I am convinced that anyone can do it.

I come from a disadvantaged childhood. I was one of the poorest kids in my school, and by my mid-20s, I was living a life of luxury on a multimillion-dollar country estate, travelling the world first-class, riding and living with horses and driving sports cars. Since then, my life has had its ups and downs, gains and losses. However, I believe that the more I am in flow with Ivaar, the richer my life is, in all ways. And the more richness I can include in my life in the form of 'delights', the richer I feel.

How often do you hear someone tell you to give it time, that it will happen in time, that it is not the right time, and that all good things come to those who wait? We tend to think and believe that things take time, but that is not true. Rather than time, there must be an alignment of the energies at play for anything to happen. It is about frequency and vibration, and once we learn how to harmonise frequency and vibration, we can learn how to bring about alignment in quantum leaps in a smooth, joyous and fulfilling way.

I was born in the early 1970s in England. My parents divorced when I was four, and I was one of the poorest kids through school. Statistically, I was far more likely to become an unmarried mother at the age of 16, living off government benefits for the rest of my life, like many people around me, rather than living an international life of luxury from an early age. I am very grateful for my humble beginnings. I may never have discovered Ivaar if my life had been easy. I had a rich inner life as an only child, and I began consciously using Ivaar from about age 11 when I changed schools, and my new school had a high proportion of people who were far wealthier than me.

My new school was an hour away from where I lived and attracted children from more affluent families, thanks to its excellent curriculum. Many of my new friends lived in lovely houses in desirable neighbourhoods and enjoyed foreign holidays. In addition, my friends enjoyed trips abroad during the long summer holidays at the end of the school year. Meanwhile, I felt a strong desire to escape my poor life and environment and intended to travel the world one day.

Rather than mope around bored, I chose to have my own adventures. I was determined not to feel sorry for myself, and I intended to have fun somehow. So, I decided to take brochures from travel agents and then plan and daydream about my imaginary holidays. I cut out pictures of beautiful beaches, hotels, quaint towns, and villages and put them in my scrapbook. I focused so intently on the images that I could recreate them in my imagination and step into them for an adventure. I have no idea how, but after doing this for a while, the experiences grew richer, and I felt I could engage all of my senses.

Call it coincidence, call it Ivaar, but I went on my first foreign trip at the age of 14, and I have gone on to live, work, and study worldwide. I am writing this from a sub-tropical paradise island overlooking the mountains and ocean, and next month I will be in the U.K.

About Ivaar

We are in a period of significant transition and rapid change. We are experiencing a paradigm shift—a collapse of the old and the birth of something new. Now, more than ever, we must harness the power and potential of Ivaar to create that which we choose to have, be and do.

The Ivaar method combines ancient spiritual practices and modern-day techniques, but you do not need to consider yourself religious or spiritual to practise it. You can apply this method to any aspect of your life, whether business, health, family, etc. However, you do need to leave your inner sceptic to one side (to be recovered later if you choose), forget your current reality, and give your all to the practice. Practising from the heart with love amplifies the energy.

The cleaner you can keep your energy, the better. Think of yourself as a vessel through which Universal energy flows and through which you send out all your thoughts and feelings. Negativity, doubt, procrastination, complaining, criticising, comparison, guilt, shame, blame, jealousy, bitterness, resentment, anger, frustration, disappointment, and fear only block the healthy flow of energy. Conversely, optimism, trust, action, praise, gratitude, joy, enthusiasm, commitment, pleasure, joy and love help the energy, and life, flow more smoothly and gracefully. Good ways to take care of our energy include sleep, bathing, clean food and drink, movement, and laughter. Other methods include meditation and smudging, for example. But, of course, it depends on how far you want to go. I like to cleanse, strengthen and protect my energy regularly. I use several short meditations daily, and I pick a more extended, more elaborate mediation for a weekly boost.

We form an energetic connection with everyone and everything we come into contact with by touch, thought, sight, sound or sense.

Imagine how many energetic connections we form during the course of a week, a month, a year, a decade, a lifetime. We must ensure these connections are healthy and beneficial; otherwise, they become baggage, which blocks the flow of divine, Universal energy, making it harder to crack the rich code and reach our potential.

At the end of the chapter, I share a few short meditations I use to cleanse, strengthen and protect my energy and realise any unhelpful energetic connections.

Be conscious that everything - what you see, observe, think, say, do, feel, choose, consume, watch, read, listen to, dream, imagine and believe - influences your energy and how you experience life. Whatever frequency we put out, the Universe will match, so we receive what we believe. As Henry Ford famously said, "Whether you think you can, or you think you can't, you are right."

Therefore, when you start working with Ivaar, you must do so with the right mindset. Being negative and having doubts is counterproductive for this work. Your attitude is everything. And it travels before you. The messages in this chapter will not reach you if you read with a closed mind and critical attitude. It is vital that you do not focus on the how or when of whatever you want to bring into your life. Forget about how and when, that is the job of the Universe. Just keep on with Ivaar, and remember your 'why', the reason why you want to attract or achieve something.

I is for Intention or Idea

Everything starts with an idea or a strong and focused intention, which creates the foundation of all that follows. Once we have an idea, we can set the intent to execute. Intention setting can be a simple or an elaborate process. Sometimes, it might look like sitting in quiet contemplation to focus on the intent. On other occasions, it could involve a beautiful, day-long ceremony. The intention must be clear and strong and worded very carefully. Remember that words are also energy. The word and concept of 'spells' exist for a reason. To keep it simple, work with statements like I am, I invite, I attract, I choose, I love, and I have.

V is for Visualisation

Once you are clear about your intent, visualise it. Sit and daydream about it. Engage all of your senses. How does the attainment of your goal, idea, or dream feel? Use emotion to add fuel to the visualisation. Hold the vision as though it is happening. Do this as often as you can. What you imagine, dream and visualise pre-exists out there in the ether. Now you need to bring it closer with action.

A is for Action

First, you need to take practical action, such as creating a presentation for investors, reaching out to your network, researching, studying, or whatever. Second, you need to embody the visualisation or the dream. So, if you intend to be a number one best-selling author, and you visualise yourself signing books, your follow up action could be to get in touch with other writers and start writing. Another way to embody the energy is to repeat your intentions aloud with passion. "I love signing my books. I am a magnet for book sales. I attract lucrative publishing deals easily."

Earlier, I mentioned that I like to incorporate many 'delights' in my life. In doing so, I am embodying being and feeling rich. For me, sometimes, feeling rich is found in simple things. For example, it means making sure that my environment is clean, organised and vibrating high with flowers, plants and delightful aromas. It is how I prepare and take my coffee. It is how I light my candles. It is the glass I love to use for my wine. It is how I connect energetically with my clients before coaching sessions. It is taking time to sit in silent contemplation. It is consuming the best products I can. Small but important details.

A is for Alignment

In some cases, alignment is immediate, and we experience quantum breakthroughs. Other times, it can take years, even decades. The more we work to master our energy and ensure we are clear vessels through which the energy can flow, the more rapid the alignments. Find ways to harness your power and master your energy. There are many options. Meditation is one way, and it can be done anytime, anywhere, for free. However, we can encounter setbacks, self-doubt, and other challenges throughout the alignment period. It is essential to maintain the intent, visualisations, and actions, ensuring that they align with the heart. For example, if you can say, hand on heart, that you love signing your books and it feels good, rich and joyous, that is alignment. However, if it feels off or wrong somehow, it is not in alignment with your heart and soul, which could be why alignment seems elusive.

R is for Results and Reassess

You will know that Ivaar is working from the results and how you feel. So be patient, make a note, and celebrate and show gratitude for all results, no matter how insignificant they seem. For example, if you intend to be a number one best-selling author and have a great writing session, celebrate that and express gratitude from the heart. The Universe will pick up on this frequency and match it, making it easier for you to repeat the experience, and several great writing sessions can result in a number one best-selling book. If you are not getting the intended results, reassess your intentions, ensuring they align with your heart.

By the Law of One, if Ivaar can work for me, it can work for you. It is a muscle, and practice is vital.

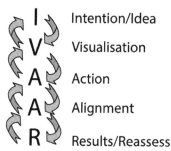

I   Intention/Idea

V   Visualisation

A   Action

A   Alignment

R   Results/Reassess

Ivaar in Action

A few words about taking action. I am not saying that any of this is easy. To be successful working and living worldwide, I studied Latin, French, Spanish and Russian to an advanced level. I take the initiative on many occasions. I am not afraid to ask for what I need. I continuously invest in my development.

Life is an adventure, and sometimes the highs are high, and the lows are low. In 2007, I reached a real low point in my life, and I felt trapped. It was time to put Ivaar into action and reassess my life. I intended to work from anywhere running my own business, but we were in a deep recession. I had to overcome some insecurities before fully activating Ivaar.

A year later, I founded a U.K.-based marketing and public relations agency. I earned more during my first two years of business than I had in my whole life up until that point. I worked globally with some industry leaders, particularly in technology and travel. I can run the business from anywhere.

After running the business for years, at the beginning of 2017, I activated Ivaar to work more in an advisory and coaching capacity. After being tested on ethics, strategy, and leadership, the same year, I achieved Chartered Practitioner status, the profession's highest accolade in Europe. The award placed me in the top one per cent of PR professionals. As a result, the Chartered Institute of Public Relations invited me to be a Client Advisor. Result.

Then, my next goal was to attract more coaching clients. I focus on communication, public speaking and leadership. I went through the Ivaar, process, and soon, I had 20 clients each week for several months. However, I started to feel misaligned because I was overdelivering and undercharging. So I reassessed my intention and set a new one to work less and earn more, attracting clients who were open to becoming more self-aware and keen to develop their intuitive intelligence. I received what I intended pretty rapidly. Now, I work less and earn more, and my clients align with me more often than not.

One client recently landed her dream job as a global multibillion-dollar tech company director after working with me for 18 months. Another, the CEO for Europe of another global multibillion-dollar tech company, shares what he learns during our sessions with his leadership team and is about to send some of them to me for more in-depth coaching. Another I have been coaching for almost two years is a famous South Korean media personality with a PhD. Since we met, she has accepted more speaking engagements in English than previously, including events involving her liaising with The Vatican.

I love my work, and I know - and I mean that inner knowing, not the knowing of the brain - that I attract clients whom I love and who reach their goals. Our relationship is a mutually beneficial energy exchange. I know that no matter what is happening for them, my clients feel better after a coaching session with me. And no matter what is happening in my Universe, I feel better after a coaching session with them. So if I feel great, I feel even better. It is beautiful, and I am deeply grateful.

I would love for you to benefit from reading my words. I would love for you to give Ivaar a try. I invite you to reach out to me and tell me what works for you, how you crack the rich code and how that looks.

Wishing you well in all endeavours,

Karen

Three meditations to cleanse, strengthen and protect your energy

Imagine standing in a sparkly, white Universal energy column covering you entirely, from above your head to below your feet. This simple meditation is an excellent exercise for a quick energy boost when you feel tired.

Before you have a meeting, go on stage to present, or attend an event, spend a few moments with your hand on your heart and your eyes closed. Imagine someone or something you love. Feel this love and smile. Send this love out from your heart as far as possible and visualise yourself having a successful meeting, presentation, speech or event.

For deep energy cleansing, imagine you are standing inside an egg. The egg is your energetic field. Imagine you have roots from the soles of your feet that travel down deep into the earth until they make contact with the centre of the planet, which could be a rock or a crystal. The earth energy travels up the roots and into your body as you breathe in, travelling through each chakra, leaving them clean and sparkly. The energy comes out of your crown chakra and is absorbed by the Universe on the out-breath. Then, call in Universal energy from high above, and invite it to enter you through the crown chakra to fill your entire body and the egg with love and light. Smooth the energy, so there are no gaps or cracks in your egg. Then, invite more energy from high above to pour down through the crown chakra and cover the egg with liquid glass for protection. Hold the intention that only love can reach you through the egg.

Always give thanks.

Thank you!

To contact Karen:

https://karenlouisefloyd

karenlouisefloyd@gmail.com

+44 7907 293 493

+34 692 336 787

Jessica Brothers

Jessica Brothers is a mom, a wife, yes. She also started her first profitable business at age 12. Was born an artist and earned her art degree. Has traveled the world. She's unrelentless about studying human biology and has been for over half her life. She's also accomplished multiple certifications and won awards in the health and fitness industry. Today she belongs to elite entrepreneur communities, speaks on stages, podcasts, and can be found on many social media platforms. At this moment selling two of her businesses for well into the 6 and 7 digits that she started with a mere $3500.

Founder of the FitClub Gym and Under The Influence, creator of multiple online programs, and expert health strategist - Jessica Brothers has been described to be a great motivator, passionate in her work, driven in her discipline to succeed, and teaches you how to as well. At 41 years young, she lives strong, confident and in her best health, despite her complications with an Autoimmune disease. She speaks about her expertise, her broken past, and the truths she's discovered in science about ourselves. Her story is captivating, full of hard truths and also inspirational. Jessica Brothers is the example that no matter the adversity, we have the power to change it all in an instant.

The Obvious Truth

Bu Jessica Brothers

It wasn't always like this. I didn't always love life, think positive, control my emotions, or feel grateful, appreciative and truly happy. There was even a time when I wasn't aware of our not-so-secret power. That's actually my favorite part of my story. I wasn't always the vibrant, confident, uplifting woman you'd see and feel if I was standing right in front of you. However, I *was* always smiling—a big-ass smile plastered on my face to fool everyone. It was the mask that demonstrated how good and put together everything was on the outside. Ironically, I was very shy and quiet. You definitely would not have guessed back then who I'd be today. Truth be told, I was completely lost, sad, and angry on the inside. I cried a lot and often spent time by myself.

My first influence of music was my mom's Led Zeppelin and Beatles records. I dressed uniquely—definitely born an artist. I hated wearing jeans and pretty much lived in stretch pants. I In hindsight, I was grooming myself to wear yoga pants as my adult work attire. I played with Barbies, even into my young teens. It's wild to think about now because I don't think I'm much of a girly girl. I also started my first profitable business at twelve years old. Putting all that together, I guess it does make perfect sense that I have grown to be the woman I am today.

Do you have a lucky number? Mine is six. I think it started from one of my earliest, and happiest, memories. It was my birthday. I was six years old, and I was dancing around my mother's car in the driveway of our house. I remember feeling so happy and singing about being six years old. Since that day, the number six has just stuck with me. It is my favorite earliest memory. I have another early memory too—one very contrary to the one I just shared. I was really young, maybe three or four. I remember seeing my mother being abused in our living room at that time. It's foggy, but the memory feels sad. Unfortunately, this would not be my last encounter with abuse.

Before I go much further, please know this is not a sad story. This is a story of success, inspiration, truth and proof that no matter where you are in life (right now, in this very moment) things *can* get better—*way* better than you could even imagine right now. I'm here to share the same awareness I learned that changed it all for me.

It was Easter Sunday, and I was 14 years old. My mother dropped my sister and I off at my grandmother's house, where we spent Easter each year. I got out of the car so proud of the dress I was wearing. I was still in awe that my mom even bought it for me. I mean, it was from Express! You know that trendy-cool adult woman store. I loved it. Like *really* loved it. It was a cute gray midi t-shirt dress with cap sleeves that outlined my tiny, young-girl body. When I say outlined, I mean even the xx small was big on my petite frame.

I stepped into the screened-in porch where my dad, stepmom, grandmother and her husband were sitting. Smiling and feeling happy, the first words out of my stepmother's mouth were, "Don't you look like a little slut." It shut me down. I dropped my head. I felt so ashamed and embarrassed. I don't know what was saddest, the words, the feeling, or the fact that I do not remember a single person even noticing me. Everyone just laughed like it was a joke. I didn't like my dress anymore. My mom never bought me anything from Express again because I wouldn't wear the gray dress, I promised I would wear if she bought it. And I certainly couldn't tell her what happened. She'd call up my stepmom and cuss her out. And I'd end up being more bullied because I told on her.

Another time I was at my dad's house celebrating someone's birthday—which meant there were lots of family members there. I was sitting at the end of the table eating my piece of cake; I loved sugar then. Actually, I still do; I just know better now. I was the last one at the table eating when my stepmom walked in the room and said, "Everyone make sure you watch Jessica after she's done eating so that she doesn't go and puke it up in the bathroom." Apparently, my stepmom thought it was okay to tell everyone I was bulimic. It must have made her feel good, as if to justify whatever failures she was feeling at that time. This is what I've learned: we are mirrors of ourselves in everything we say and do. Meaning, we point out faults in others that we don't like in ourselves. We judge others based on judgements we have about ourselves. Looking back, I realize now that my stepmother had a lot of inner turmoil, and she was taking it out on me. None of it had anything to do with me. It only has to do with the person delivering the emotion, words or actions. We are all responsible for our own actions, and therefore reactions, as well. Nothing truly can affect us without our own consent. Surely life would've been different had I known then what I know now. I bet you can say that too. But the gift is the growth and clarity we receive through the challenges and lessons we face in life. Since I was weak, unaware and shy, I was an easy target for my stepmom to dump all her emotional baggage onto. I could go on for chapters with stories like these, but I want to share one more from those years.

Needless to say, I avoided being in the same room as my stepmom anytime we had family time at my grandmother's house. Sometimes, desperate to be elsewhere, I would go downstairs to the basement where my grandmother's husband had his wood carving shop. He had so many cool hand-carved pieces down there; I could stare at them in awe for hours. I even daydreamed about being able to create some of my own. Unfortunately, being alone down there didn't last for long. Without going into detail, a nasty relative used to come down and purposely start a tickle fight with me until it was no longer tickling, or appropriate. At that time, it seemed like a better option than getting torn apart verbally by my stepmom.

We all have stories from our past. I share some of mine because so many people see me today, as who I am today. They think it was easy for me. They assume that my discipline for eating healthy, working out every day, waking up early, filling my cup first and achieving the things I want to achieve like the bad-ass woman I am is *easy* for me to do. And that's because they didn't see all the days and years before it. They just see me today, the result of the shit I walked through, grinning and bearing. No one's story is better or worse than anyone else's. We all have lived through the contrast varying emotions. What's important is how we react to it all. That's the part that compounds into the result which creates our now and tomorrows.

At twenty-one years old, I found myself standing barefoot on a blue mat inside a dojo on my first day of Martial Arts training. This was where I had landed without realizing it was going to lead me to the biggest turning point of my life. I showed up to release the anger and aggression I was harboring; honestly, I was hoping I could beat some people up. You may laugh at that. But after years of silence, verbal abuse, emotional abuse, and sexual abuse (which led to allowing physical abuse and self-abuse into my life) I needed an outlet. I couldn't hold it in anymore. The last year of drugs and alcohol almost every day couldn't numb the pain anymore. So here I was, in a white Ghi, barefoot, and looking for a fight. However, don't let my tough exterior fool you; I was sad too. Truly, deeply sad. And trust me when I say, I had *no idea* what I was about to get myself into.

After the first day of being kicked and punched and thrown to the ground, I almost quit. Instead, I turned it into a new challenge for myself. That challenge lasted for almost three years—one blackbelt and over a year of kickboxing competitions later. I lived in that dojo, literally practicing for hours on the mats. When mat time was over, I'd go downstairs to the old gym. I'd get my work out on and practice my favorite form of cardio—kickboxing. Apparently, I was a natural. I was just fooling around one day when a coach saw me and wanted to train me. I was all in! That was what led me to the day I realized something powerful.

It was the end of a competition fight. I won but didn't feel the same after this win. I felt guilty and disgusted with myself. I showed up to that fight in an extremely hurt and angered mood. I knew how to pocket and release that energy during competition. This particular fight, I felt a wave of something ugly run through me and went too far. I won the fight… but I lost the war inside myself. With all Martial Arts had taught me about discipline (and the lessons I learned about strength, focus and proper attention) sitting with such an ugly piece of myself felt so powerful. And that, *THAT* was it! The light bulb went on, the clouds cleared. "IT *FELT* SO POWERFUL!" These words echoed in my head. This realization echoed back to tell me, "I am a powerful being...There is so much power behind this anger... and the actions that this anger causes... what if... what if I could use that power with a different emotion... an emotion that makes me feel good?" To say this now seems obvious. But it was a moment I'll never forget. It led to me realizing that I need to be aware of my words, emotions, and reactions and need to always see the light in every situation. The sun is always up and shining, even when it's cloudy. And for the first time, my smile could match the work I was embarking on internally. My real me, my truth, was (in that moment) finally starting to unfold.

It definitely was not all rainbows and butterflies though. Like I said earlier, just because I make it look easy now, doesn't mean it always has been. And just because the word POWERFUL echoed in my head during a pivotal turning point in my life, doesn't mean I'm talking about my favorite part yet. You know. That thing I said earlier about some not-so-secret power of ours. We'll get there.

I took this whole new perspective toward life to a serious level. I saw more opportunities. My journey led me to travel and live in and out of the country. I experienced things that taught me so many lessons—an education that is not taught in any college. I learned to embrace real life challenges and wins. Because *that's* our power. It's our perspective. It's our own choice. This was my journey of self-growth and independence—truly, unapologetically. I stumbled thousands of times, some less gracefully than others. It's a journey for every single one of us—all different and uniquely beautiful. And we can all learn from one another. My journey has led me to writing this chapter and my soon to be released book, producing a podcast, participating in speaking engagements and so much more. All the words I am choosing to put out into the world come from a place of faith that my stories and education will create pivotal, life-changing moments for many. I've seen it. And we all deserve that. We all deserve true happiness in as many moments as we choose.

I realized what I was supposed to do; it's everything I've learned over the past twenty-plus years on this life-journey-experience-thing. I've learned how to truly feel my ultimate best—physically, emotionally, and financially. I'm talking about *really* feeling great, powerful even! I'm talking on-top-of-the-world great. I bet you can tell how excited I get when I speak about these topics.

Answering the question of who I am now is easier than it used to be. I am a strong, confident, relentless, unique, bad ass, who is sometimes softy. I am someone who lives in unwavering health and success, enjoying freedom with my finances and time. It's that not-so-secret power you may or may not be aware of. And looking back on my life-journey, I've traveled from fitness trainer to nutritionist to holistic health strategist to coach to mindset master and have talked for hours on all of it. Living wide-open with awareness and control (as best as can be moment to moment) will lead to some pretty magical things—like suddenly being offered to sell my businesses, deciding to attend a business conference and crossing paths with someone who is teaching me a skill that is currently changing my life into everything I asked for. That unfolding story you'll have to watch in real action on my channels and podcast.

Before I talk about my favorite part of this journey so far, and how I see it happen in real life every day, just know, with an open mind and a gentle shift in perspective, you too can witness it daily. And when you do, it's fun! It took me a while to believe it and not be so skeptical, and then, it took me time to understand and practice it. It's not complicated; humans are. You've heard of it. It's not a secret. However, most of us don't believe or understand it. I surely didn't either until I decided to prove it to myself.

Now we move to a recent part of my story where I chose to take a very difficult road that drove me to a new bottom, only to realize it was the exact choice I needed to jump levels in growth, clarity and in finding truth. I've always loved the science of the body in fitness, nutrition, mindset, sleep, and ultimately health. I definitely have a small obsession with finding truths in those topics. I'm proud to say I have and can help a lot of people with what I've learned. Things we all should be taught. What good are we for anything if we can't show up for ourselves and others as our best. Science helped me discover how the laws of the humanity interact with the laws of the universe. It's funny how many things came to me that led to more answers. What I've found is powerful! It's one hell of a powerful, interconnected truth.

You may have heard it called luck, coincidence, manifestation, miracles, being in the right place at the right time, or even the wrong place at the wrong time. There are many names for it. But the truth is, it's all the same. It's the Law of Attraction—a true law, just like gravity, and it works whether you believe in it or not. It is always in play either for you or against you. Ultimately, it's your choice. The not-so-secret power we hold is the same power used to create worlds—this world. Sadly, it's not in our everyday curriculum. We aren't taught to understand it, how it works or how to use it. Belief is a huge part of it. That is why I even bring God into this—or any religion for that matter. Doesn't matter if it's energy, karma, or *good vibes;* what you believe in is irrelevant. The power is in the belief you hold. If you have a strong, unwavering belief that you know something is true, life proves it to you every time. On a bad day, you ask, "What could go wrong next?" and something always shows up, doesn't it? Or on a good day, you *happen* to get all green lights and someone in line just *happens* to buy your coffee for you. This is simply our human-self attracting more things that match our current emotional state.

The Law of Conservation of Energy states that energy can neither be created nor destroyed, only converted from one form of energy to another. Energy can transform. Changing your mood, or e-motion, is energy in motion. And if we have the power to change our mood or emotion, we have the power to shift and transform our energy in and around us. And this power allows us to do it in an instant. Remember how my pivotal moment taught me to fuel my power differently by choosing happiness instead of anger? I was using the Law of Conservation of Energy without even knowing it. Here's another example: if you were to walk into a funeral service, you would start to feel the sadness from everyone in the room, and your body, emotions and thoughts would all start moving in the direction of sadness. Your energy is being transformed into the frequency of sadness. Conversely, stepping into a room full of laughing people would almost instantly shift your mood and encourage you to start laughing. This will occur by simply being non-resistant to it—letting Law of Conservation naturally occur. Of course, if you are resistant, you end up being the only grumpy person in the comedy club.

I'm merely scratching the surface here. You are either intrigued to know more or are in the same place I was just a short year ago skeptical and thinking this is all fluff. I truly have never felt more light, free, happy, and truly confident that everything will always work out for me. That is, as long as I act in unison with human and universal laws. Otherwise, I'll create a contrast of low-frequency emotion, resulting in more low-frequency thoughts and circumstances. This is the power. This is the truth. This is what my current and future words are filled with. Meet me on my journey with yours.

I truly feel that it's meant for you to be here in this moment, reading these words, and crossing your path with mine. I invite you to expand. Get your questions answered. You can find me, all that I do, and all the places you can follow me at www.jessicabrothers.com. And if you enjoyed the tip of this iceberg, you'll love diving in with me.

My name is Jessica Brothers. And I'm a truly happy soul, creating my best life as my best self because I decided to challenge limiting beliefs and use my God-given universal power without any woo-woo shit, just truths. It is my pleasure to meet you here.

To contact Jessica:

Find out what I'm up to and how to connect with me at www.jessicabrothers.com

You can also email me at jessica@jessicabrothers.com

Afterword

It's finally here! Our new Rich Code Club social media platform has launched! **www.RichCodeCommunity.com**

Kevin Harrington from the TV show Shark Tank and **Jim Britt**, named one of the World's to 20 success coaches and top 50 speakers, along with **over 180 #1 International Best-Selling Authors** have created an exclusive FRE.E social media platform providing how-to content, success strategies, members only live events, podcasts, and interactive connections with top thought leaders and super successful entrepreneurs to help you succeed financially and personally.

I want to give you a personal invitation to join us and START LIVING YOUR LIFE AT LEVEL TEN!

Why join?

- **It's FRE.E**
- Learn from the Best of the Best
- New Content Posted Daily
- Weekly Live Events
- Podcasts and Interviews
- Present Your Business Ideas to Get Feedback from Top Professionals
- Inner-active Free Coaching Sessions
- You'll have access to proven money-making strategies that work!
- This is like a social media platform purely focused on helping you grow. You have all the benefits of a social network including direct messaging and none of the frustrations: no ads, no yelling, no algorithm manipulation.

If you ever wanted to be part of an community that will challenge you to become more than you are and will leave you with enough inspiration to last a lifetime... THIS IS IT!

Join me at The Rich Code Club!
www.RichCodeCommunity.com

Life and business are always a series of transitions... people, places, and things that shape who we are as individuals. Often, you never know that the next catalyst for improving your business and life is around the corner, in the next person you meet, next mentor you hire or the next book you read.

Jim Britt and Kevin Harrington have spent decades influencing individuals and entrepreneurs with strategies to grow their business, developing the right mindset and mental toughness to thrive in today's business environment and to live a better life.

Allow all you have read in this book to create a new you, to reinvent yourself and your business model if required, because every business and life level requires a different you. It is your journey to craft.

Cracking the Rich Code is a series that offers much more than a book. It is a community of like-minded influencers from around the world. A global movement. Each chapter is like opening a surprise gift, that just may contain the one idea that changes everything for you. Watch for future releases and add them to your collection.

The individual and combined works of Jim Britt and Kevin Harrington have filled seminar rooms to maximum capacity and created a worldwide demand. If you get the opportunity to attend one of their live events, jump at the chance. You'll be glad you did.

Be a coauthor: If you are a coach, speaker, consultant of entrepreneur and would like to get the details about becoming a coauthor in the next Cracking the Rich Code book in the series, contact Jim Britt at support@jimbritt.com

STRUGGLING WITH MONEY ISSUES?

Check out Jim's latest program "Cracking the Rich Code" which focuses on the subconscious programs influencing one's financial success, that keeps most living a life of mediocrity. This powerful four-month program is designed to change one's relationship with money and reset your money programming to that of the wealthy. More details at: www.CrackingTheRichCode.com

To Schedule Jim Britt or Kevin Harrington as a featured speaker at your next convention or special event, online or live, email: support@jimbritt.com

Master each moment as they become hours that become days.

Make it a great life!

Your legacy awaits.

STAY IN TOUCH

www.JimBritt.com

www.JimBrittCoaching.com

www.CrackingTheRichCode.com

www.KevinHarrington.tv

https://www.richcode.club/beacoauthor/

For daily strategies and insights from top coaches,

speakers and entrepreneurs, join us at:

THE RICH CODE CLUB---FREE members site.

www.RichCodeCommunity.com